Critical Thinking and Problem Solving

Third Edition

Linda Stevens Hjorth
Teresa Hayes

Houghton Mifflin Company

Boston   New York

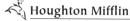 **Houghton Mifflin**
Custom Publishing

222 Berkeley Street • Boston, MA 02116

Address all correspondence and order information to the above address.

Contents

Preface

We implemented a Critical Thinking course at DeVry University several years ago and have been consistently honing the course to meet the needs of an ever-changing student population entering colleges today: students returning to school after having been in the workforce for a while, foreign students who have recently arrived to the U.S.A., high school graduates ready to enter an environment of higher learning, and the list goes on. So how does the course help?

COLL 147 is designed to help our students in a variety of very practical ways. Students will get the hands-on training DeVry is known for in the areas of critical thinking, problem-solving, and collaborative learning. The course is designed so that students will gain exposure to a variety of tools and techniques that will translate not only to their program courses, but also to their workplace environments and "real world" lives as well.

COLL 147 is an essential part of DeVry's commitment to bring to the workforce enlightened individuals who are not only skilled in technical fields but in the essential areas of critical thinking, problem-solving, and oral and written communication that are in such high demand in the workplace today.

Critical Thinking

CHAPTER 1

Linda Stevens Hjorth

OBJECTIVES

CRITICAL THINKING CHECKLIST

By the end of this chapter, you will be able to . . .

1. **Understand what critical thinking is and that it is the foundation for questioning, analyzing, and problem solving.**

2. **Understand that critical thinking often leads to new solutions and new perceptions.**

3. **Become a critical thinker.**

4. **Understand that problem solving is the ability to work out solutions creatively.**

5. **Know and implement steps to problem solving.**

6. **Understand that there are times when failure is okay.**

The purpose of the following checklist is to help you diagnose your ability to think critically.

Check the appropriate answer:

1. Do you usually believe what you read? YES _____ NO _____

2. Do you usually accept as fact what professors or mentors say? YES _____ NO _____

3. When you study, do you often look beyond words for different meanings? YES _____ NO _____

4. Do you ask questions to further your understanding? YES _____ NO _____

5. Do you like to ponder information beyond its superficial meaning? YES _____ NO _____

6. Are you open to new ideas? YES _____ NO _____

7. Do you like to discuss alternative solutions to problems with others? YES _____ NO _____

8. Do you let your mind wander when solving problems? YES _____ NO _____

9. When solving problems, do you sometimes let intuition guide decisions? YES _____ NO _____

10. Do you ask "Why?" or "Is this true?" as you read? YES _____ NO _____

If you are a successful critical thinker, your answers to questions 3–10 were yes, and your answers to questions 1 and 2 were no. Write about your critical thinking skills that still need improvement.

_____

_____

_____

_____

_____

_____

John Broadus wrote the following in *A Treatise on the Preparation and Delivery of Sermons,* published in 1870:

> An educated man is one whose mind is widened out, so that he can take broad views, instead of being narrow-minded; so that he can see the different sides of a question, or at least can know that all questions have different sides. An educated man is one who has the power of patient thinking; who can fasten his mind on a subject, and hold it there while he pleases; who can keep looking at a subject, till he sees into it and sees through it. . . . Again, an educated man is one who has sound judgment, who knows how to reason to right conclusions, and so to argue as to convince others that he is right.

QUICK CHECK

How would you define critical thinking? Provide a specific example that supports your definition.

Broadus felt that individuals need to see different sides of questions, think patiently, look at a subject until it is understood, use sound judgment, and know how to reason until a correct solution is found. In the 1870s, these traits indicated an educated person; today we call people who possess these characteristics critical thinkers. Critical thinking is the ability to dissect information by way of reasoning, questioning, challenging facts, problem solving, and rethinking. These processes allow you to make sense out of confusion, to understand the difference between opinion and fact, and to challenge old thoughts in order to create newer, more effective ones. Critical thinking is a sequential process that plays an important role in such activities as computing mathematical equations, solving roommate conflicts, teaching AIDS prevention to teenagers, or finding one's way around a college campus.

Critical thinking is a process that encourages you to question and wonder before you act or assume; it precedes actions and decisions. College is the perfect place to rekindle your ability to question, wonder, and ask why as you rediscover the child in you. This process enhances the desire to wonder about and question information. Like a child that sees a rock in a yard and cannot leave it unexamined, you should not refuse the inclination to turn over knowledge until it is understood from your perspective. When you were three years old, the word why was a major part of your vocabulary: "Why do fish swim?" "Why does mom have to work

Thinking differently creates powerful results.
University of Wisconsin—Oshkosh.

today?" "Why does a dog wag its tail?" This wonder often fades with age, yet it is this very simple questioning, analyzing, and rethinking that is essential for college success. After you ask a question, do not accept the first answer that comes to mind. Instead, seek alternative answers. Critical thinking involves stretching your thoughts before settling on a definitive answer (see the figure below).

Becoming a Critical Thinker
Think Differently

Why is critical thinking an essential learning tool? Because it forces you to question what you hear, see, or experience. Effective critical thinkers learn to evaluate everything they perceive. Consider the endless barrage of information received daily, ranging from your family's opinions of what you should do with your life, to TV advertisements that lure you to order a pizza, to a biology instructor who tells you that a turkey did not get its name because it comes from Turkey (in fact, it comes from Mexico), but that the bird's name came from the call "turk, turk, turk" (1000 More Questions and Answers, 1989). The processes you use to sort out the family's opinions, the TV's proclamations, and the instructor's remarks on turkeys involve critical thinking.

Question and Challenge Facts

Many educators want students to use critical thinking skills to enhance their knowledge rather than to accept passively all information as fact. If you hear or read something that you disagree with, do not automatically suppress your own opinion and assume that others' opinions are right. Often, differences of opinion provide great insight. Allow your mind to wander, question, analyze, and challenge.

Express and reiterate questions in different ways. If a question is too vague, too trivial, or too difficult, you may miss its purpose. Without purpose, learning and understanding may elude you. If a question seems too overwhelming, break it down into subquestions. Several smaller, more specific questions are easier to analyze than one long, complicated, indirect one. Make sure your questions are clear, concise, significant, and relevant. Trivial questions bring superficial knowledge. Effective questions change perceptions and help new ideas emerge. Never give up searching for answers to tough questions. Through systematic research and analysis, learning increases, and substantial answers can be found (Browne and Keeley, 1994).

Critical thinkers also search for facts supported by data. Their thinking is supported by evidence, proof, statistics, and truth. This is often balanced by using imagination to understand in different ways the material being presented in lectures, labs, and reading. If your instructor claims that farmers can forecast the weather by the behavior of their pigs, would you consider this fact or opinion? In Texas, one farmer correctly forecast eight rainstorms out of ten, while the local meteorologist correctly forecast only one (1000 More Questions and Answers, 1989). On hearing this, what thoughts come to mind that challenge the validity of this information? (For instance, ten pigs is a small sample; has further research been done in this area? What pig behaviors let the farmer know that rain was on its way? Did the farmer condition his pigs to act in weather-predicting ways?) By looking for evidence, questioning research methods, and asking for sources of information, you create a newer, unbiased point of view.

QUICK CHECK

State a fact or theory learned in class. Break it down into two significant subquestions. What did you learn from this process?

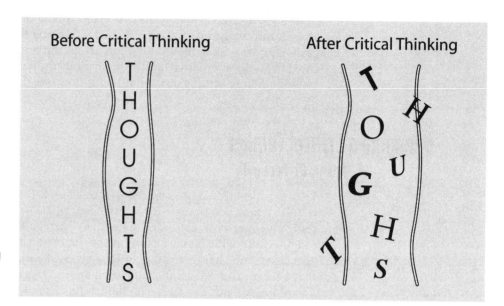

Before Critical Thinking

THOUGHTS

After Critical Thinking

TOGUHTS

The foundation of critical thinking is created by stretching thought into a new form.

Open Your Mind

Seek to understand and learn without bias. By opening your mind to controversy, you learn the value of different thoughts and perceptions. Choose to debate differing viewpoints; disagreements feed new thought. If you listen to someone who is passionate on a topic, you will not be able to stop yourself from learning. Through evaluation of the evidence behind the claims, you will attain new knowledge. Embrace this new information, and allow it to feed your college learning experiences (Beatrice, 1993).

Discuss Issues with Others

Others may discover solutions that have never occurred to you. Involving others in the creative thinking process allows you to consider many ideas and perceptions instead of just your own isolated viewpoint. It is a great way to incorporate the experiences and knowledge of others into your own. Remember that you are the one who must make the final analysis. Never allow others to talk you into a solution with which you feel uncomfortable.

Anticipate Negative and Positive Implications

When using critical thinking to create conclusions or decisions, prevent unexpected consequences by anticipating the results of your thinking process. Critical thinkers realize that for every action there is a reaction, and they attempt to predict what that is before it occurs without being overly pessimistic or blindly optimistic.

Let Your Mind Wander

QUICK CHECK

List two examples where you use objective, nonbiased thinking when studying.

1.

2.

Let your mind wander. By removing the restraints that prevent creative thinking, you can make discoveries that you never imagined. For example, if you censor thoughts that make you feel confused, it will be difficult to take the next step that forces confusion to evolve into understanding. By allowing yourself to entertain a different view, angle, or perception, new, undiscovered thoughts are realized.

Free association and visualization are tools that encourage critical thinking and creative problem solving. Close your eyes and visualize the problem you are facing. Allow all thoughts and associations to flow freely through your mind. Now, open your eyes and write down everything that you thought about and analyze the information. What did you learn about this problem? What did you learn about yourself? Did you find any new solutions to the problem? This creative process works because you are letting ideas happen naturally instead of consciously monitoring each idea that travels through your mind.

Be Intuitive

Trust your gut instincts. Do not let rigid logic get in the way of flexibility and creativity. Logical thinking is important, but sometimes the best critical thinking emerges under the auspices of just "letting it all hang out." Be creative. Do not let rigid logical thinking stunt your imagination or your originality.

You will soon discover that critical thinking is important in everything you do. Creative thinking affects the way you study, manage time and money, read, and solve problems.

Be Aware of Errors in Judgment✳

One major concept that Vincent Ryan Ruggiero presents in his book, Becoming a Critical Thinker, is that critical thinkers need to heighten their awareness of errors in judgment. Ruggiero states, "Errors of judgment occur in the process of sorting out and assessing evidence" (2001). You can probably think of a time or two when you made the wrong choice based on judgment errors. It is the job of the critical thinker to evaluate information effectively, objectively, and efficiently to prevent misunderstanding. One way to prevent judgment errors is to be aware of the most common ones.

Errors of Perception

Errors of perception are not blunders made while examining issues. They are faulty ways of seeing reality, preventing us from being open-minded even before we begin to apply our critical thinking. The following are especially serious.

"Mine is Better" Thinking

As small children we may have said "My mommy is prettier than any other mommy" or "My daddy is bigger and stronger." Perhaps we had similar thoughts about our houses, toys, and finger paintings.

Now that we've gotten older, we probably don't express "mine is better" thinking. Yet we may still indulge in it. Such thinking often occurs in matters that are important to us, such as our race, religion, ethnic group, social class, political party, or philosophy of life.

This habit is not always obvious. In fact, "mine is better" thinking can be quite subtle. We may be quite uninterested in a person until we find out she is Irish, like us. Suddenly we feel a sense of kinship. We may think a person is rather dense until he says something that matches our view. Then we decide he's really quite bright after all.

"Mine is better" thinking is natural and often harmless. Even so, this kind of thinking creates distance between people through a win-lose mentality, which can easily prevent you from learning from others. To prevent this, remember that opening your mind to ideas from other people can broaden your perspective and lead to fresh insights. Give every idea a fair hearing—even an idea that challenges your own.

From Becoming a Critical Thinker, 4/e by Vincent Ryan Ruggiero. Copyright © 2002. Reprinted by permission of Houghton Mifflin Company.

Selective Perception

In one sense, we see selectively most of the time. Let's say you and two friends, a horticulture major and an art major, walk through a shopping mall. You want to buy a pair of shoes; the others are just taking a break from studying. The same reality exists for each of you: stores, potted plants, people passing by. Still, each of you focuses on different things. While you are looking for shoe stores, one friend notices plants. The other studies faces for interesting features.

Later, one of you says, "Hey, did you see the big new store in the mall?" The others say no. Though the store was before all of your eyes, two of you screened it out.

That kind of selective perception is often harmless. Another kind of selective perception takes place when we focus on things that support our current ideas and reject anything that challenges them. Suppose someone thinks that a particular ethnic group is stupid, violent, cheap, or lazy. Then "stupid" behaviors will capture that person's attention. And if his bias is strong enough, he will completely miss intelligent behaviors from members of that group. He'll see only evidence that supports his prejudice.

You can break the habit of selective perception by looking and listening for details you haven't seen before. Also press yourself to balance your perception. If you find yourself focusing on negative details, look for positive ones, and vice versa.

Bias Toward the Majority or the Minority

Bias tends to follow our affections. If we feel more comfortable with the majority on our side, we may choose the majority view. If we identify with the underdog and love the challenge of confronting superior numbers, we may embrace the minority view.

Each of these choices can occur with little or no awareness of our underlying bias. And in each case we put feelings of comfort and personal preference above the evidence. Critical thinking means deciding issues on their merits rather than on the number or the celebrity status of the people on the opposing sides.

Pretending to Know

Some people believe that confessing ignorance makes them look ineffective, so they pretend to know things they really don't. After a while, pretending becomes a habit that hinders critical thinking. Suppose someone says on several occasions, "I've read quite a few books on psychology." Also suppose the truth is different and he's never read a book on the subject. The idea will become so familiar that he might take it for the truth. What's more, he'll begin to confuse his guesses about psychology with real knowledge. Practice staying aware of your statements and remaining alert for pretense. Whenever you find it, acknowledge the truth and resolve not to lie to yourself or others again.

Either/Or Thinking

This error of perception means taking only extreme positions on an issue when other positions are possible. For example, one person thinks that accepting evolution means rejecting the idea of creation. Another person thinks that being Republican means taking a conservative stance on every issue.

Yet it's possible to believe in evolution and creation. You could believe that God created the universe and planned for it to evolve over millions of years. (You could also be a Republican without always taking a conservative stand.)

Either/or thinking hampers critical thinking. This error forces us to take extreme, unreasonable views. To avoid either/or thinking, look for times when there seem to be only two possible views. Ask yourself, "Are these the only possibilities? Could another view be more reasonable—perhaps one that includes elements of both?"

An example is the debate over crime prevention. Some elected officials argue for banning assault weapons and registering handguns. The National Rifle Association argues for getting criminals off the street. You might ask, "Why not take both actions and add others, such as building more prisons, as well?"

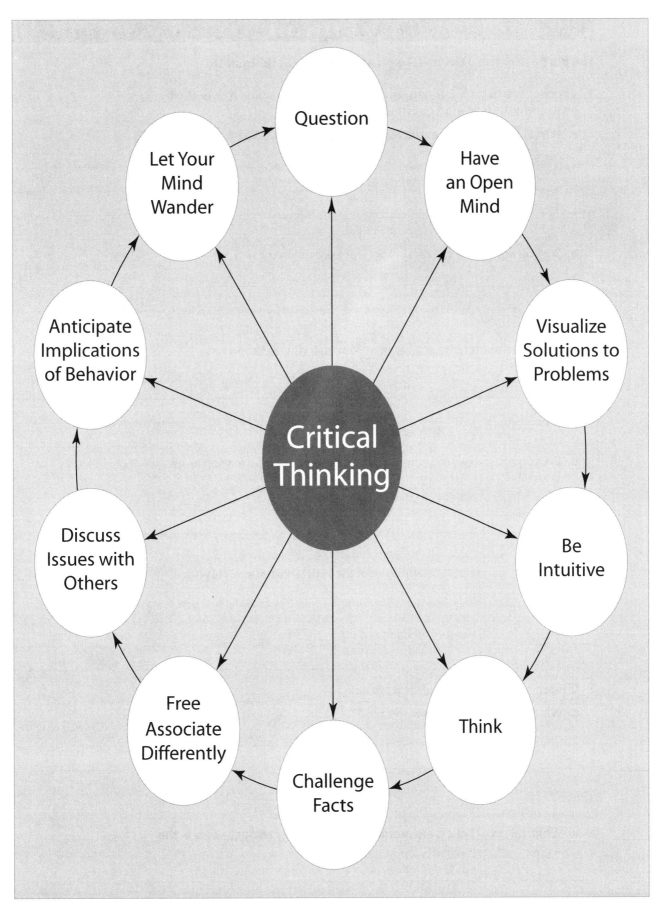

Critical thinking is a continuous process comprising many factors.

EXERCISE

The purpose of this exercise is to practice critical thinking skills.

1. Choose an article from a magazine or journal and examine it critically by answering the following questions:

   a. What is the view presented by the author?

   _____

   _____

   _____

   b. Do you agree with the reasoning process used in the article?

   _____

   _____

   c. If you had written the article, what conclusions would you have developed?

   _____

   _____

   _____

   d. What questions would you use to understand the information more critically?

   _____

   _____

   _____

   e. Provide one concrete example from the article that supports your ideas.

   _____

   _____

   _____

2. Choose a TV show and analyze it critically.

   a. What message is the show sending?

   _____

   _____

   _____

   b. What values or beliefs are promoted by the actors and actresses in the show?

   _____

   _____

   _____

c. How do you feel children or elderly people would react to this show?

_____

_____

_____

d. What questions would you ask to understand the plot more clearly?

_____

_____

_____

e. Provide one concrete example from the show that supports your ideas.

_____

_____

_____

Mastering the fundamentals

Vincent Ryan Ruggiero

What is thinking?

You are staring into space, imagining you are headed for the airport. You picture yourself ready for a month's cruise in the Caribbean, your pockets stuffed with cash. Would this mental process be thinking?

Now imagine you're discussing politics with friends. "It's always the same with politicians," you say. "They're full of promises until they're elected. Then they develop chronic amnesia. I can't see why people get excited over elections." Would you be thinking in this case?

Thinking, as we will define it in this book, is a purposeful mental activity. You control it, not vice versa. For the most part, thinking is a conscious activity. Yet the unconscious mind can continue working on a problem after conscious activity stops—for example, while you sleep.

Given this definition, your ruminations about a Caribbean cruise are not thinking but daydreaming, merely following the drift of your fantasies. On the other hand, your discussion of politics may or may not involve thinking. We can't

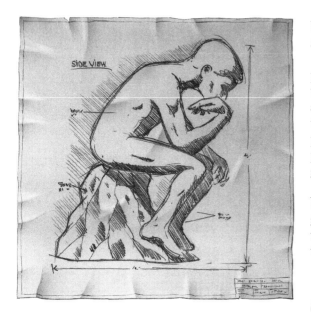

be sure. You might not be thinking at all but just repeating something you'd said or heard before.

Thinking is sometimes regarded as two harmonious processes. One process is the production of ideas (creative thinking), accomplished by *widening* your focus and looking at many possibilities. The key to this process is to resist the temptation to settle for a few familiar ideas. The other process is the evaluation of ideas (critical thinking), accomplished by *narrowing* your focus, sorting out the ideas you've generated, and identifying the almost reasonable ones.

Both processes are natural activities for human beings, but we rarely perform them well without training and diligent practice. This book focuses on evaluating ideas (critical thinking) but also includes some approaches for producing them.

Critical thinking is crucial

Chances are you've received little or no instruction in critical thinking. Your teachers are not to blame for this. In many cases they, and their teachers before them, were denied such training.

Much of our education was built on the idea that thinking can't be taught, or that some subjects teach it automatically. Modern research disproves both ideas. Thinking can be taught—not just to "gifted" students but to all students. No course automatically teaches thinking, though any course can teach it when teachers make thinking skills a direct objective. Then students get regular practice in producing and evaluating ideas. Around the world, schools are exploring ways to make critical thinking a priority.

Success in work depends on thinking skills. It isn't enough for graduates to possess a large body of information in their fields. People who want to succeed must be able to apply what they know to the challenges of their jobs. Employers are looking not for walking encyclopedias but for problem solvers and decision makers.

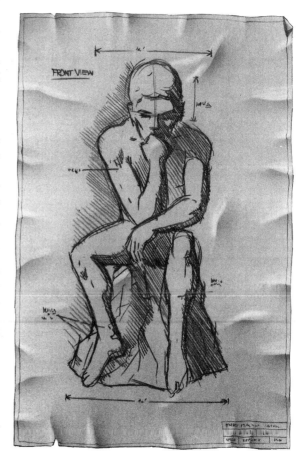

Mental health also depends in large part on skill in thinking. Some authorities believe neuroses stem from shallow, illogical thinking. According to psychologist Albert Ellis, "Man can live the most self-fulfilling, creative, and emotionally satisfying life by intelligently organizing and disciplining his thinking."

Unfortunately, shallow and illogical thinking is common. For example, the drug or alcohol abuser may say, "I'm not addicted—I can quit any time I want." The skeletal anorexic may tell herself, "I'm too fat." Even highly educated people may reason, "My sexual partners are nice people, so I needn't fear catching a sexually transmitted disease."

Illogical thinking plays a big part in abusive behavior. A parent who makes a child cry by screaming at her may reason that hitting the child will make her stop crying. A Miami woman was charged with dousing her husband with rubbing alcohol and setting him on fire because he had been acting crazy and refusing to work. She reasoned that by setting him on fire she'd get him into the hospital for some help. A father kept his 18-year-old daughter chained in the basement because he was afraid she would become a prostitute.

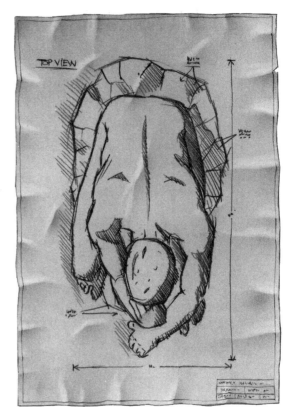

Occasionally we read in the news about an attempted bank robbery that failed. Surely even slow-witted felons realize that banks have cameras and that getaway cars can usually be identified. Also, every police agency, including the FBI, is involved in bank robbery investigations. Yet the robbers somehow manage to reach the conclusion that they will not be caught.

Even when poor thinking is not tragic, it can be embarrassing. Consider the man who loaned money to his friend, a car dealer. After trying unsuccessfully to collect the money, he reasoned: "I'll take a car from his lot and hold it as collateral. Then he'll have to pay me to get his car back." Proud of his plan, he carried it out . . . and quickly found himself in jail on a charge of grand theft auto. Although the charge was dismissed, his humiliation lingered.

Much unpleasantness and disappointment can be avoided by testing ideas for reasonableness before accepting and acting on them. Such testing isn't just for special occasions. It is appropriate whenever someone makes a claim that is open to question. Many such assertions are made daily in every field of study and work.

Testing ideas is so fundamental to critical thinking that this book includes lots of practice in it. When the ideas are unfamiliar, you will probably be quite willing to examine them critically.

The ideas you will be reluctant to examine critically are likely to be ones you are familiar with, particularly the ideas that are widely accepted in our culture. You will assume that other people tested them. Meanwhile, everyone else may be making the same assumption.

Thus, the more widely held the view, the more it is likely to need critical examination.

Be clear about truth

"There's no such thing as objective truth that's the same for all people regardless of their beliefs."

"Truth is subjective and personal."

"Everyone creates his or her own truth."

Statements like these are quite common today. And they do not mean merely that when we believe something to be true, we act as if it were true. (That would be perfectly reasonable.) Instead, they mean that believing something is so *actually makes it so.*

This idea directly opposes the view of truth that has been generally accepted since ancient times. Here is that traditional view:

> Truth is objective reality, the actual state of affairs about things. It is unaffected by people's knowledge or ignorance of it, or by their affirmation or denial. No amount of fantasizing or pretending can alter it.

According to this traditional idea, if a drunk falls into an empty swimming pool, his landing won't be any softer if he believes it is full. If someone accidentally drinks deadly poison believing it is medicine, it won't be any kinder to his body.

These two situations suggest that the traditional view is much more sensible than the popular view that everybody creates his or her own truth. But let's test some more situations to be sure.

When you go to your physician with a health problem, do you want him to *create* the reality of your condition or *discover* it?

Is the Internal Revenue Service likely to accept your subjective, personal truth about your income and deductions, or will they demand the impersonal, objective truth?

If a political officeholder were accused of lying and responded, "No big deal—one person's lie is another person's truth," would you consider that answer reasonable?

Would justice be served if the wording of the standard courtroom oath were changed from, "I swear to tell *the* truth, *the* whole truth, and nothing but *the* truth" to "I swear to tell *my personal* truth . . ."?

Suppose that you got all the test questions correct but received a failing grade anyway and protested to your instructor. Would you be satisfied if she explained, "Your truth was that you deserved to pass. But my truth was the opposite"?

In all these situations, as in the swimming pool and deadly medicine cases, it is ridiculous to speak of *his* truth, *her* truth, *my* truth, *your* truth. All that matters is *the* truth.

Given the popularity of the false notion that truth is personal and subjective, you may have to remind yourself now and then that truth is impersonal and objective. It is something we discover rather than create.

Here is a simple habit that can help you avoid confusion: Use the word *truth* more carefully, reserving it for what is actually so. If an idea is open to question, call it a "belief," "theory," or "contention," not a "truth."

EXERCISE 1

Apply what you learned in this section to the following situations.

Situation   *In the early seventeenth century, virtually everyone agreed that the sun revolved around the earth. Galileo shocked his contemporaries by arguing that the reverse was true. Would it be reasonable to say that Galileo created a subjective truth, valid for him but not necessarily for others? Explain.*

_____

_____

_____

_____

_____

_____

_____

_____

Situation   *Contemporary admirers of Hitler deny the existence of Nazi concentration camps and a Nazi plan to commit genocide against the Jews. Should that view be considered historically legitimate—that is, true for those who wish to believe it? Why or why not?*

_____

_____

_____

_____

_____

_____

_____

_____

Situation   *Throughout this century, a famous painting entitled The Man with the Golden Helmet was believed to be the work of the Dutch master Rembrandt. Some years ago it was proved to have been painted by someone else. Some people would say that the truth about this painting changed. Do you agree? Explain.*

_____

_____

_____

_____

_____

_____

_____

_____

EXERCISE 2

Examine each of the following cases in light of what you've learned about truth in this section. State your view and explain why you hold it.

Maude smokes a pack of cigarettes a day and drinks alcohol immoderately. Will the belief that she can create her own truth help her change these habits?

_____

_____

_____

_____

_____

_____

Ira is a journalist. Will the belief that he can create his own truth make him more or less likely to value accuracy in his reporting?

_____

_____

_____

_____

_____

_____

Bruce is prejudiced toward minorities and women. Which of the following beliefs would be more helpful in overcoming his prejudice: the belief that truth is subjective and created; or the belief that truth is objective and discovered? Explain your reasoning.

_____

_____

_____

_____

_____

EXERCISE 3

Imagine you are writing to a friend. Explain what you learned about truth in this section. Use your own words and make your examples different from the ones included here.

_____

_____

_____

_____

_____
_____
_____
_____
_____
_____
_____
_____
_____
_____
_____
_____
_____
_____
_____
_____

Be alert for contradictions

Contradictions are statements that express the opposite of something stated previously. The reason we should remain alert for contradictions is that they signal errors in thinking and provide a starting point for finding those errors.

The principle of contradiction is as follows:

An idea cannot be both true and false at the same time in the same way.

A few examples will serve to demonstrate that this principle is valid.

Statement: My roommate borrowed my sweater without permission.

Comment: If this statement were both true and false at the same time in the same way, it would mean that you simultaneously *gave* your permission and *didn't give* your permission. That is an impossibility. You must either have given your approval or not given it. This example confirms the principle of contradiction.

Statement: During World War II the Nazis killed millions of Jews in concentration camps.

Comment: Either the Nazis did this horrible deed or they didn't. Since there is no way they did it *and* didn't do it, this example also supports the principle of contradiction.

Statement: Capital punishment is a deterrent to crime.

Comment: Let's assume for the sake of discussion that capital punishment was once a deterrent to crime but no longer is. In other words, that this statement was true at one time but is false today. Does this situation challenge the principle of contradiction? No. The principle specifies that a statement cannot be both true and false *at the same time* in the same way.

Statement: Edgar is richer than Clem.

Comment: If Edgar has more money than Clem, but Clem surpasses him in moral character, then the statement would be both true and false but not *in the same way.* It would be true in one sense and false in another. (To be a contradiction, it would have to say Edgar has more money than Clem *and* does not have more money than Clem.) Thus, this example also confirms the principle of contradiction.

A note of caution: The principle of contradiction does not apply to the many *near*-contradictions that occur in everyday discussion.

Let's suppose that Luke says, "Sally got the highest mark on the mid-term exam" and Freda responds, "No, she didn't—Hank did."

That looks like a contradiction, but is it? No. *Sally did vs. Sally didn't* is a contradiction. *Sally did vs. Hank did* is merely a near-contradiction.

The distinction is important because in an actual contradiction one side must be right and the other wrong. In a near-contradiction, *both* sides may be wrong. In the case at hand, the highest mark on the mid-term exam may be neither Sally's nor Hank's but *Bertha's*.

EXERCISE 4

Classify each of the following dialogues as (a) an actual contradiction or (b) a near-contradiction. Briefly explain each choice.

Mavis: *Big-time college sports are corrupt.*
Cora: *You're absolutely wrong, Mavis.*

Karen: *There are very few real heroes today.*
Hanna: *I think there are more today than there have ever been.*

Brad: *Look at that new Lincoln across the street.*
Clara: *That isn't a Lincoln—it's a Mercury.*

Recognize opinions

Opinions are beliefs or conclusions about reality. Unlike facts, they are open to question and analysis by critical thinking. Before evaluating opinions, distinguish them from facts.

Sometimes it's easy to separate facts from opinions. "Babe Ruth was a famous baseball player" is clearly a fact. "Smoking should be banned in public places" is clearly an opinion. Yet many other statements are more difficult to classify.

Statement: The 2000 Summer Olympic games were held in Tokyo.

Comment: This statement has the form of a fact. Yet it is not factual. The 2000 Summer Olympic games were held in Sydney, Australia.

Statement: Camel's hair brushes are made of Siberian squirrel fur.

Comment: The statement appears ridiculous, yet it is factual.

Statement: Stalin's oppression of the Russian people was more brutal than Hitler's oppression of the German people.

Comment: This statement is an opinion, but it is so well supported by historical evidence that many would consider it a fact. (Stalin killed more of his own people than did Hitler. He also took away more freedoms for a longer period than did Hitler.)

Statement: Eyewitness testimony is generally unreliable.

Comment: This statement is an opinion. To those unfamiliar with the research on eyewitness testimony it may seem untrue. Yet research confirms it.

Being able to recognize opinions will help you decide when an idea calls for support and what kind of support is appropriate. This knowledge can help you develop your own ideas and evaluate ideas from others.

Following are some basic guidelines:

1. If what you state is generally understood to be factual, no support is needed.

    Example: Both John and Robert Kennedy were assassinated.

    Example: The cost of a college education is significantly higher today than it was twenty years ago.

    Comment: Both statements are common knowledge.

2. If what you state is not common knowledge or can't be easily verified, then briefly note the source of the information.

    Example: The gray reef shark uses unusual body language to signal that it feels threatened.

    Comment: This fact is not well known, at least among laypeople, so cite the source. (It is Bill Curtsinger, "Close Encounters with the Gray Reef Shark," *National Geographic,* January, 1995, 45–67.)

3. If the statement is an opinion—a view others might disagree with—then answer any questions others might ask.

Example: More Americans are victimized by chronic laziness than by workaholism.

Comment: However reasonable this statement may seem, some people will undoubtedly disagree. Even those who agree may ask, "Why does the author think this? What cases or examples support this view? Is statistical evidence available? Statements by authorities? What line of reasoning led the author to this conclusion?" Unless these questions are satisfactorily answered, critical readers might not be persuaded.

4. If it is not clear whether a statement is a fact or an opinion, then treat the statement as an opinion.

Remember another important point about opinion. As used in critical thinking, opinion refers only to matters of judgment, not to matters of taste or personal preference. The ancient Roman saying *De gustibus non disputandum est* still holds true today. Loosely translated, this saying means "There's no way to argue profitably or think critically about matters of taste."

Do you favor the now-fashionable slender figure or the older ideal of plumpness? Do you find long or short hair more appealing? Do you wear formfitting athletic shorts or the long, baggy kind now standard in basketball? Do you regard the Lincoln Town Car as beautiful or ugly? Do you enjoy sitcoms more than soap operas? All these are matters of personal preference or taste. They can't be supported by facts but only by assertion—"That's my view because that's my view."

As long as you express matters of taste as such, you need not defend them, even if others find your tastes odd. If you express matters of taste as if they were matters of judgment, then you might be in the awkward position of defending what is difficult or impossible to defend. One solution is to say:

"I prefer slenderness to plumpness."
"I prefer long hair."
"I prefer formfitting athletic pants to long, baggy ones."
"I prefer the look of the Lincoln Town Car to that of any other car."
"I enjoy watching sitcoms more than soap operas."

Make statements like these instead of stating that one thing is superior to another.

EXERCISE 5

Indicate whether each of the following statements is

a)   clearly a fact.
b)   possibly a fact, but not clear without documentation.
c)   an opinion.
d)   a personal preference expressed as a personal preference.
e)   a personal preference incorrectly expressed as an opinion.

Remember, it is sometimes difficult to separate facts and opinions. There may be room for disagreement over some answers. Be prepared to explain your choices.

_____1.   I find blue-eyed redheads appealing.

_____2.   The Chevrolet Camaro is the most stylish car on the market.

_____ 3. All religions share the same fundamental truths.

_____ 4. Darwin's theory of evolution continues to be controversial.

_____ 5. Pornography is an insult to women.

_____ 6. Black people are the victims of crime more often than white people.

_____ 7. Prostitution should be legalized.

_____ 8. People who need organ transplants greatly outnumber organ donors.

_____ 9. The publicity given to suicides leads to most "copycat" suicide attempts.

_____ 10. Comic books are as instructive about life as novels are.

_____ 11. Most students who drop out of school lack the intelligence to succeed.

_____ 12. Surgical procedures have been performed on fetuses while they were still in the uterus.

Case 1

Analyzing Different Accounts of the Assassination of Malcolm X

Let's examine a situation in which a number of different people had somewhat different perceptions about an event they were describing. The work of Malcolm X came to a tragic end in February 1965 with his assassination at a meeting in Harlem. The following are five different accounts of what took place on that day. As you read through the various accounts, pay particular attention to the different perceptions each one presents of this event. After you have finished reading the accounts, analyze some of the differences in these perceptions by answering the questions that follow.

Five Accounts of the Assassination of Malcolm X

The New York Times (February 22, 1965)

Malcolm X, the 39-year-old leader of a militant Black Nationalist movement, was shot to death yesterday afternoon at a rally of his followers in a ballroom in Washington Heights. The bearded Negro extremist had said only a few words of greeting when a fusillade rang out. The bullets knocked him over backwards.

A 22-year-old Negro, Thomas Hagan, was charged with the killing. The police rescued him from the ballroom crowd after he had been shot and beaten.

Pandemonium broke out among the 400 Negroes in the Audubon Ballroom at 160th Street and Broadway. As men, women and children ducked under tables and flattened themselves on the floor, more shots were fired. The police said seven bullets struck Malcolm. Three other Negroes were shot. Witnesses reported that as many as 30 shots had been fired. About two hours later the police said the shooting had apparently been a result of a feud between followers of Malcolm and members of the extremist group he broke with last year, the Black Muslims. . . .

Life (March 5, 1965)

His life oozing out through a half dozen or more gunshot wounds in his chest, Malcolm X, once the shrillest voice of black supremacy, lay dying on the stage of a Manhattan auditorium. Moments before, he had stepped up to the lectern and 400 of the faithful had settled down expectantly to hear the sort of speech for which he was famous—flaying the hated white man. Then a scuffle broke out in the hall and Malcolm's bodyguards bolted from his side to break it up—only to discover that they had been faked out. At least two men with pistols rose from the audience and pumped bullets into the speaker, while a third cut loose at close range with both barrels of a sawed-off shotgun. In the confusion the pistol man got away. The shotgunner lunged through the crowd and out the door, but not before the guards came to their wits and shot him in the leg. Outside he was swiftly overtaken by other supporters of Malcolm and very likely would have been stomped to death if the police hadn't saved him. Most shocking of all to the residents of Harlem was the fact that Malcolm had been killed not by "whitey" but by members of his own race.

The *New York Post* (February 22, 1965)

They came early to the Audubon Ballroom, perhaps drawn by the expectation that Malcolm X would name the men who firebombed his home last Sunday. . . . I sat at the left in the 12th row and, as we waited, the man next to me spoke of Malcolm and his followers: "Malcolm is our only hope. You can depend on him to tell it like it is and to give Whitey hell.". . .

There was a prolonged ovation as Malcolm walked to the rostrum. Malcolm looked up and said, "A salaam aleikum (Peace be unto you)," and the audience replied, "We aleikum salaam (And unto you, peace)."

Bespectacled and dapper in a dark suit, sandy hair glinting in the light, Malcolm said: "Brothers and sisters . . ." He was interrupted by two men in the center of the ballroom, who rose and, arguing with each other, moved forward. Then there was a scuffle at the back of the room. I heard Malcolm X say his last words: "Now, brothers, break it up," he said softly. "Be cool, be calm."

Then all hell broke loose. There was a muffled sound of shots and Malcolm, blood on his face and chest, fell limply back over the chairs behind him. The two men who had approached him ran to the exit on my side of the room, shooting wildly behind them as they ran. I heard people screaming, "Don't let them kill him." "Kill those bastards." At an exit I saw some of Malcolm's men beating with all their strength on two men. I saw a half dozen of Malcolm's followers bending over his inert body on the stage. Their clothes were stained with their leader's blood.

Four policemen took the stretcher and carried Malcolm through the crowd and some of the women came out of their shock and one said: "I hope he doesn't die, but I don't think he's going to make it."

Associated Press (February 22, 1965)

A week after being bombed out of his Queens home, Black Nationalist leader Malcolm X was shot to death shortly after 3 (P.M.) yesterday at a Washington Heights rally of 400 of his devoted followers. Early today, police brass ordered a homicide charge placed against a 22-year-old man they rescued from a savage beating by Malcolm X supporters after the shooting. The suspect, Thomas Hagan, had been shot in the left leg by one of Malcolm's bodyguards as, police said, Hagan and another assassin fled when pandemonium erupted. Two other men were wounded in the wild burst of firing from at least three weapons. The firearms were a .38, a .45 automatic and a sawed-off shotgun. Hagan allegedly shot Malcolm X with the shotgun, a double-barreled sawed-off weapon on which the stock also had been shortened, possibly to facilitate concealment. Cops charged Reuben Frances, of 871 E. 179th St., Bronx, with felonious assault in the shooting of Hagan, and with Sullivan Law violation—possession of the .45. Police recovered the shotgun and the .45.

The *Amsterdam News* (February 27, 1965)

"We interrupt this program to bring you a special newscast. . . ," the announcer said as the Sunday afternoon movie on the TV set was halted temporarily. "Malcolm X was shot four times while addressing a crowd at the Audubon Ballroom on 166th street." "Oh no!" That was my first reaction to the shocking event that followed one week after the slender, articulate leader of the Afro-American Unity was routed from his East Elmhurst home by a bomb explosion. Minutes later we alighted from a cab at the corner of Broadway and 166th St. just a short 15 blocks from where I live on Broadway. About 200 men and women, neatly dressed, were milling around, some with expressions of awe and disbelief. Others were in small clusters talking loudly and with deep emotion in their voices. Mostly they were screaming for vengeance. One woman, small, dressed in a light gray coat and her eyes flaming with indignation, argued with a cop at the St. Nicholas corner of the block. "This is not the end of it. What they were going to do to the statue of Liberty will be small in comparison. We black people are tired of being shoved around." Standing across the street near the memorial park one of Malcolm's close associates commented: "It's a shame." Later he added that "if it's war they want, they'll get it." He would not say whether Elijah Muhammed's followers had anything to do with the assassination. About 3:30 p.m. Malcolm X's wife, Betty, was escorted by three men and a woman from the Columbia Presbyterian Hospital. Tears streamed down her face. She was screaming, "They killed him!" Malcolm X had no last words. . . . The bombing and burning of the No. 7 Mosque early Tuesday morning was the first blow by those who are seeking revenge for the cold-blooded murder of a man who at 39 might have grown to the stature of respectable leadership.

Questions for Analysis

1. What details of the events has each writer *selected* to focus on?

2. How has each writer *organized* the details that have been selected? Remember that most news organizations present what they consider the most important information first and the least important information last.

3. How does each writer *interpret* Malcolm X, his followers, the gunmen, and the significance of the assassination?

4. How has each author used *language* to express his/her perspective and to influence the thinking of the reader?

Thinking Critically About Ethical Choices

Lynn McCutcheon

"The ultimate measure of a man is not where be stands in moments of comfort and convenience, but where be stands at times of challenge and controversy."
Martin Luther King, Jr.

"There is never a right way to do the wrong thing."
Anonymous

1. Why a Chapter about Ethics in a Critical Thinking Textbook?

One answer to the question about ethics in a text about critical thinking is that it is a topic of great importance. As Paul and Elder (2001, p. 256) put it, "behavior has consequences." The fact is that many of the things we do have an impact, for better or for worse, on the lives of others. If I steal money from you, you will have less money to spend on your education, or your safety, or the well-being of your family. If someone aims a gun at you and pulls the trigger they may deprive you of the opportunity to live a full and productive life. More than any other creature on the planet we humans have the capacity to put ourselves in the shoes of others and imagine how they might feel in response to our actions. The sad part is that we so often fail to use this capacity. At the very least we all need to pause and reflect on the fairness of our actions—especially those that are likely to affect others. Are we about to do something that might have a permanently damaging effect on someone else?

A second reason is that employers have become increasingly concerned about the moral values of the people they hire. Many successful companies have a clear vision of the kind of people they need to remain successful. Of course they want people who are able to perform the jobs they have been hired to do. But many of them are also concerned about the integrity and moral character of their employees. The fact that over 2.5 million integrity tests are given annually is testimony to this fact (Murphy & Davidshofer, 1994). No one wants an employee who lies and steals from the company or other employees. No company needs someone who fails to respect the rights of others, regardless of their race, sex, or religious values. Ironically, the leaders of some large companies fail to act ethically themselves (witness Enron and WorldCom, whose leaders in time of crisis acted to protect their own selfish interests rather than the interests of the thousands of people who worked for the company). While this seems like hypocrisy, it could be argued that if more attention had been paid to screening employees, then the leaders of Enron and WorldCom who are responsible for their unethical behaviors would never have risen to power or even been hired in the first place.

Arguably the most important reason for the inclusion of an ethics chapter is the relevance of rational or critical thinking to ethical problems. This does not mean that critical thinking skills will always solve the toughest of ethical dilemmas, but it might help in distinguishing an ethical problem from a legal or religious issue. Perhaps you will at least discover that "knowing right from wrong" is no simple matter.

2. Introductory Thoughts about Ethics and Moral Reasoning

Ethics is about the moral standards by which our actions can be judged to be right or wrong—the rules of conduct that govern our behavior (Hall, 2002). Moral reasoning is undertaken for the purpose of determining what is right or wrong (Andolina, 2002).

The form of moral reasoning is the same as the form for other types of arguments; namely, two (or more) premises are followed by a logical conclusion.

> Lying is always wrong.
> Robert told a lie.
> Therefore, he committed a wrongful act.

Sounds promising, doesn't it? It would appear as though ethics can provide the magic bullet that will solve all of the problems that stem from unethical behavior. All we need to do is use our moral reasoning power to develop some moral arguments, then follow the conclusions in our everyday lives. Unfortunately, things are not that simple. There are at least two reasons why.

First, we humans are selfish creatures who want to maximize our own pleasure. This is combined with a talent for cleverly disguising our selfishness, not only from others, but also ourselves. In other words, we humans are capable of devising elaborate excuses for our unethical behavior—excuses that sometimes fool others. Furthermore, we manage to fool ourselves into thinking that we are behaving morally when we are not.

The mental gymnastics we perform to convince ourselves that we are doing the "right thing" are useful. They protect us from having to confront the brutal truth about our own selfish behavior. They allow us to continue feeling good about ourselves instead of constantly "beating ourselves up" over our bad behavior. But these mental back flips and somersaults come with a price tag attached. That price is our continuing tendency to act badly—to behave unethically all the while we are feeling righteous.

"But I only took a little bit." "Everybody else was doing it." "He started it." "It was my drug habit that forced me to steal." We have all heard these excuses many times, and we have probably used some of them ourselves. If you believe that stealing is always wrong, then it really doesn't matter whether you stole a lot or a little. If an act is morally wrong in your view, then it matters not whether you acted alone or with the support of many others.

The second reason why moral reasoning will never eliminate ethically questionable behaviors is found in a basic rule of logic. That rule is: "premises are not necessarily true." Consider the following example:

> All humans are created equal.
> Danielle is a human.
> Therefore, Danielle is created equal.

The premises do lead to the conclusion, so the logic in this argument is fine. You probably believe that the premises are true, don't you? In our society we are taught that all humans are equal (at least in theory) with respect to the law, and Danielle is a popular name for female humans, so there is reason to believe that Danielle is a human. But suppose I told you that the term "equal" was to be applied to the ability to run the 100-meter dash, and that Danielle is actually the name of my daughter's hamster? The logic remains the same, but the conclusion is false because both premises are untrue.

All A are B.
Danielle is an A.
Therefore, Danielle is a B.

Let's revisit the first premise of the first argument, "lying is always wrong." Is that premise true? Is lying always wrong, regardless of the circumstances? Many philosophers (especially some of those who follow the Golden Consequence ethic) argue that there are times when it is better to lie than to tell the truth. "Your hair looks lovely today, Mrs. Jones." "Your son died a hero, Mr. Anderson." The truth is that Mrs. Jones' hair looks like a rat's nest, and Corporal Anderson lost control of his military vehicle because he was "high" on drugs. Some would argue that it serves no worthwhile purpose to get Mrs. Jones upset about something as trivial as the way her hair looks. Many of those same people would argue that the Andersons need a little consolation in their time of sorrow. Does it not make them feet a little better to think that their son died while defending his country in battle?

The rule that "premises are not necessarily always true" applies to any argument, but, as we shall see, the validity of premises is often hotly debated in ethical arguments. When we examine the Five Golden Approaches we will see that some of the greatest moral philosophers have sharply disagreed with each other about the truthfulness of several moral arguments.

3. Ethics, Laws and Religious Values

Perhaps it has occurred to you that "ethics" is really nothing more than another name for laws or religious values. This is not exactly true. Consider this list of ethical principles approved back in 1948 by the General Assembly of the United Nations. It was signed by representatives of every nation.

Universal Declaration of Human Rights
(abridged version; Paul & Elder, 2001)

All humans are born free with equal rights and dignity.
All humans have the right to life, freedom, and safety.
Slavery is unethical.
Torture and cruelty are unethical.
Everyone has the right to an education.
Everyone has the right to a standard of living that is adequate
  for the provision of health and well-being.
All are entitled to equal protection of the law.
Discrimination based on race, sex, language, religion,
  politics, national origin, property or status is unethical.

Please note how brief this list of ethical considerations is. There is no mention of lying for the purpose of taking advantage of someone or of deceptive business practices. Note also that it raises questions about the interpretation of these ethical principles. For example, at what point does punishment become unnecessarily cruel? How much education is one entitled to? How does one determine an adequate standard of living? Suppose you had the power to change this list. What, if anything, would you add to or subtract from this list?

_____

_____

In spite of the fact that all nations signed this Declaration, violations are common. Until recently, Afghan women were denied an education; slavery still exists in some parts of the world, and in the United States protection under the law is based partly on how much money you have.

It is true that ethical reasoning is the foundation for many laws. The fact that murder is illegal in most societies almost certainly stems from the ethical standard that it is wrong to take the life of another human being. In similar fashion laws against stealing evolved from the ethic that it is wrong to take property that clearly belongs to someone else. But not all laws stem from ethical rules. Some laws are nothing more than social customs that were important enough to some group that they felt the need to make these customs part of the law.

For example, in 1706 the state of New York passed a law making it clear that baptizing slaves into Christianity was not an act that obligated slave-owners to set their slaves free (Binder & Reimers, 1992). Today we can view this act as unethical and self-serving. Many of New York's slave-owners considered themselves good Christians who wished to promote their religious views, but not to the point that they would suffer personal economic losses. Passing this law allowed them to feel like they were doing the right thing (promoting their religious views) without really doing the right thing (freeing their slaves). This sort of moral hypocrisy was probably not uncommon 300 years ago. If anything, it may be even more common today. Recent laboratory studies showed that when people were given a choice between behaving ethically or merely *appearing* to behave ethically, many of them made the latter choice (Batson, Thompson, & Chen, 2002). Sadly, it appears as though many people care less about *doing* the right thing than creating the *impression* that they are behaving ethically.

The nineteenth century laws that clearly favored the husband over the wife strike us as clearly unethical today (see Binder & Reimers, p. 259). However, they reflected the conventional societal customs and wisdom of that time period, namely that women were basically inferior to men.

It also should be pointed out that laws are written not by ethical philosophers, but by politicians. To a certain extent the latter are motivated by the need for power and the desire to preserve their own self interest. It is a safe bet that the various legislative bodies that passed laws that discriminated against women were dominated by men. A vote for such legislation 150 years ago was a "no-brainer." It would certainly be approved by the voters (all of whom were males), and it would work in your favor if you were married.

Just as ethics are *sometimes* the basis for laws, ethics are also *sometimes* reflected in religious values. The ethic that it is wrong to murder someone is reflected in one of the Ten Commandments of the Christian faith, "Thou shall not kill." On the other hand, consider "Thou shall not covet thy neighbors' possessions," another of the Ten Commandments. This means that if you merely *want* to own something that is owned by someone else, you are in violation of a major religious value. But are you being unethical? Is it unethical to *want* something nice that your neighbor happens to own? Assuming that you do not act unfairly to obtain that article, the wish to own something of value is not unethical. The mere wish for something belonging to the person next door does not bring harm to that person. In fact, this desire is so common that it is reflected in the saying, "Keeping up with the Joneses."

Many of the laws designed to regulate sexual behaviors between consenting adults reflect society's religious or personal values rather than ethical considerations. How one has sex with other consenting adults, in what positions, and how often, are issues that are troubling to some religious people. In some instances they have successfully persuaded legislative bodies to enact laws prohibiting certain kinds of sexual conduct that they find distasteful or repulsive. However, sexual behavior between consenting adults is not unethical because it brings no harm (unless one partner has a venereal disease or is HIV positive); it does not interfere with any of the basic rights found in the Declaration of Human Rights.

The debate over the words "under God," found in the Pledge of Allegiance, provides another example of the difference between ethics and religious values. If you are a religious person you may believe that it is "wrong" to remove these two words from the Pledge, but it is "wrong" only from the standpoint of your personal views on religion. From an ethical standpoint, it does not matter whether the words are included or excluded, because it has no bearing on the basic rights of human beings. However the debate is resolved no one will be imprisoned, tortured, or deprived of an education as a direct result.

Mormons believe that it is acceptable for a man to have more than one wife, most other religious groups do not. Catholics pay a great deal of attention to saints, but Protestants do not. Muslims regard Mecca as a holy city, but other religious faiths do not. Jews observe several rituals and holy days that are not observed by other Christians. These differences are very important to many followers of these major religions, but they are not ethical issues. Again, the reason is that they have no direct bearing on the fundamental rights of human beings.

4. Five Golden Approaches

The five golden approaches represent reasonable ways of thinking about what is right and what is wrong (Hall, 2002). They are not the only approaches to thinking about ethics, but perhaps they are the most common. Undoubtedly, you will prefer one over the others. That's okay, but remember that other reasonable people will make other choices.

One) *The Golden Purse*   The basic idea behind the Golden Purse approach is that those who have the most money or power should make the ethical decisions; others should follow. Centuries ago European kings told their subjects that they ruled by Divine right. In other words, it was God's will that they make the rules. Most of their subjects believed this, and endured much personal hardship in order to obey the king's rules. When one king was replaced by another this often meant that the old moral code (or at least portions thereof) was replaced by a new one, all in the name of Divine right. Had critical thinking been more prevalent back then, perhaps many people would have noticed that the codes of conduct seemed to favor the king and his pals at the expense of the common people. The kings got richer, the poor remained poor. Critical thinkers might also have wondered how moral codes could fluctuate from one king to another when all kings were supposedly receiving divine inspiration from the same unchanging God.

Royalty generally lack the power to make codes of moral conduct today, but the Golden Purse concept has not completely disappeared. It lives on, as reflected in statements like "It's their money, they ought to be able to do what they want with it," or "It is fine to have as many children as you want, as long as you can afford to take care of them." The idea that rich and powerful people should be the ones who set the standards of conduct, has been incorporated under the name "authoritarianism" by psychologists. Authoritarianism is a complex idea with several dimensions to it, but one of those dimensions is the willingness to defer to those who have positions of power and authority. According to psychologists like Bob Altermeyer (1999), there is still a large minority of persons whose attitudes reveal a willingness to be guided by the views of authority figures.

The strength of the Golden Purse approach is that it allows you to avoid having to think about ethical issues. Just do as you are told. The weakness of such an ethical approach is that you are at the mercy of the ethical values of those who wield the Golden Purse. Thus, what is right and wrong can change depending on who is currently in charge. Additionally, if you subscribe to the idea that "power corrupts people," then it may not be wise to have ethical standards being prescribed by the rich and the powerful. Should the wealthy be allowed to have eight children at a time when overpopulation is straining the resources of our planet? Remember that behavior has consequences, even if those consequences are barely noticeable in the short run.

Two) *The Golden Mean*   The mean is the arithmetic average of a set of scores. Most of the time the mean falls very close to the middle of those scores. The Golden Mean, an idea traceable all the way back to the teachings of the Greek philosopher, Aristotle, holds that the best ethical position to take on any issue is the one that falls midway between the extremes (Hall, 2002). For example, justice could be regarded as the midpoint between extremely harsh punishment and no accountability at all. Courage could be seen as falling halfway between cowardice and foolhardy, reckless abandon. The Golden Mean approach is one that emphasizes compromise and moderation. Hall (2002) points out that among major religions Confucianism teaches its followers to seek the middle path; such a pathway can be found only by taking into account all of the rational arguments for and against each ethical issue.

The strong point of this approach is the willingness to consider every argument for and against any ethical decision. There are times when taking a middle position does seem to be appropriate. If George Custer had not been so reckless he would not have lost his own life and the lives of the 300 men under his command at the Battle of the Little Big Horn. If George Meade had not been so cautious in the aftermath of Gettysburg he might have won a decisive battle against the Confederates.

Critics can argue that some ethical issues should not or cannot be compromised. Consider the company that advertises that its steel-belted radial tires are the best and safest that money can buy. Any plan to reduce the performance quality of that tire in order to save money should be rejected; compromising with the quality of the tire would be an unethical practice given that the company is on record as promising the best.

The Golden Mean is an ethic that permits a large amount of individual judgment in making decisions about right and wrong—too much individual judgment, according to its critics. Exactly what is "courage," and "cowardice," and "recklessness," and precisely where is the midpoint between the latter two? Although "courage" may be midway between "cowardice" and "recklessness," these terms are so vague that they provide us very little real guidance when faced with real choices to make about issues of right and wrong.

Three) *The Golden Law*   In some ways the Golden Law could be viewed as the perfect antidote to the vagueness of the Golden Mean and the fluctuation in what is right and wrong that is an inevitable consequence of the Golden Purse ethic. The Golden Law is a set of ethical decisions that is viewed as universal; in other words, the same rules always apply to everyone all the time with no exceptions. When faced with an ethical issue people who believe in this approach should ask themselves: "Would it be right if my choice became a universal law?" What is important is not the result of any ethical choice, but the principle underlying it.

The Golden Law stems from the teaching of philosopher Emmanuel Kant, who believed that it is not only possible, but desirable for all human beings to agree on the same set of moral rules—no exceptions, no "what ifs." What are these rules, which he called categorical imperatives? Thou shalt not lie, murder, or steal. Help others who are in need, be grateful to those who have helped you. Kant's categorical imperatives are the same as some of the Ten Commandments. Both were meant to be obeyed without question and without exception.

The idea of a single set of moral laws that applies to everyone sounds fair and just. Certainly the world would be less confusing if we could all agree on what is right and wrong. However, this has proved to be a daunting task. We can't seem to agree on what is right and wrong within our own society. Imagine the difficulty trying to convince people from every cultural background to agree on a single code of ethics. The previously mentioned Universal Declaration of Human Rights is an attempt to do just that, but its language is somewhat vague, and Paul and Elder (2001) note that many nations, including our own, routinely violate this ethical code when it is in their best interest to do so.

Because there is a shortage of young women in China, Vietnamese women are enslaved and brought to China as prostitutes, or, if they are "lucky," they are sold to young men who are looking for wives. The United States imposed an embargo on Iraq, the result of which was much suffering for innocent Iraqi citizens—many of them children who were not yet born when the first Gulf War took place.

A second problem with having a universal code of ethics (assuming we could reach a real agreement on the nature of that code) of the sort advocated by the Golden Law is the "no exceptions" provision. If we humans were really serious about murder, we would all refuse to take part in wars, which are periods when the sanctions against murder are modified. If we all had to tell the truth and nothing but the truth, all the time, imagine how uncomfortable we would feel. "Mrs. Jones, no matter how you get your hair done, you still look ugly." "Sorry, boss, but your idea is the worst one I have heard today, and the fourth worst one I have heard in my entire life." Imagine a life in which we were all morally obligated to help everyone all the time. We would be late most of the time because we stopped on the way to work to help a stranger. We would be obligated to put ourselves in harm's way to help people who might try to harm us.

Of course, in an ideal world no one would try to harm anyone else because that would be unethical. However, human nature being what it is, it is difficult to imagine such a world. Consequently, most of us, including those who claim to follow the Ten Commandments, make exceptions to many of those ethical laws when we need to justify our unethical behavior.

Four) *The Golden Consequence*   The Golden Law ignores the consequences of an act in order to find a set of laws upon which we can all agree. But it is perilous and foolhardy to ignore the consequences of our actions, even if we are trying our best to follow the Golden Law. You might not want to endure the wrath of Mrs. Jones (even if her hair is ugly) and your boss can make your working life miserable (even if his idea was a poor one). If the Golden Law troubles you, perhaps you might want to become a follower of the Golden Consequence ethic. The phrase "the greatest good for the greatest number" provides a concise description of the Golden Consequence. The term "utilitarianism" has been applied to this ethic. The philosophers Jeremy Bentham and John Stuart Mill developed versions of utilitarianism that differ slightly from each other. Bentham's version has no rules or laws; Mills' version does have laws, which he advocates following to the extent possible (Wall, 2001). Followers of this ethic carefully weigh the anticipated consequences of their ethical actions. The best choice is the decision that provides the best possible outcomes for the largest number of people.

It is assumed that no human is any better than any other, so the choice is reduced to a matter of numbers. In theory, a decision that helps 40 people wins out over one that helps only 39. Because every situation is different, and followers of the Golden Consequence must carefully consider every situation, the term "situational ethics" has been used to describe what I am calling the Golden Consequence.

Because it is the "spirit of the law" and not the "letter of the law" that is important to followers of the Golden Consequence, it follows that behaviors that are normally unacceptable are sometimes permissible, if they lead to positive consequences. Telling Mrs. Jones that her hair looks nice will make her feel good; telling her the truth in this situation serves no worthwhile purpose. Making someone angry for no good reason does not seem like either a wise or a kind thing to do. In fact, almost any kind of repulsive act could be deemed ethical if it produces a desirable consequence. If a friend was in a great deal of pain from an incurable disease, she begged you to kill her, and there was no chance of being held legally accountable, would you do it? If you believed in the Golden Consequence you might—murdering your friend would put an end to her suffering (a good consequence) without causing you to land in jail (a negative consequence).

The Golden Consequence, in either Bentham's or Mill's version, is appealing to anyone who is smart and socially skilled enough to weigh the consequences of ethical choices. Even so, the very best and brightest minds are limited in their capacity to predict the consequences of ethical choices. Maybe killing your friend who is suffering a great deal really is the best thing you can do for your friend, but isn't there at least the remote possibility that the pain will spontaneously disappear tomorrow? Isn't there a possibility that some new medicine will cure your friend's disease or at least reduce the pain? We do not have the luxury of the wisdom of hindsight to guide us while we are making a tough ethical choice. Thus, according to Hall (2002), decisions based on the Golden Consequence tend to be focused on short-term consequences, which are somewhat easier to predict than long-term ones.

Five) *The Golden Rule*   Does it bother you that the Golden Consequence forces you to make ethical judgments without the wisdom of hindsight to guide you? If the thought of making a bad ethical judgment (even with the best of intentions) bothers you, then maybe the Golden Rule will appeal to you. As you probably already know, the Golden Rule states that you should do unto others as you would have them do unto you.

One of the interesting facets of the Golden Rule is its widespread popularity and acceptance, For example, Hall (2002) points out that many of the world's major religions include the Golden Rule in one form or another. Hinduism teaches that you should "do naught unto others which would cause you pain if done to you." Buddhists say "Hurt not others in ways that you yourself would find hurtful." Followers of Islam subscribe to the viewpoint that "No one is a believer until he desires for his brother that which he desires for himself." Christians point to Matthew's admonition that "All things whatsoever ye would that men should do to you, do ye even so to them." If so many of the world's major religions subscribe to the Golden Rule, why is it that there is so much conflict, and why does it often fall along religious lines? Give this some thought, then look at one possible answer provided at the end of this chapter. Stumped? Here's a hint. Look near the beginning of the chapter.

The Golden Rule rests on the assumption that we all want what is best for ourselves. From the study of psychology we know that some persons hate themselves; consequently they do things that are self-destructive. Individuals with personality disorders or severe depression sometimes cut themselves or do other things that bring them grief in the long run (Retzlaff, 1995). Thankfully, these kinds of people represent a small minority of the adult population, so the assumption works pretty well most of the time.

It seems obvious that we would not want others to lie to us (at least about important matters), steal from us, or attempt to harm us in any way, so the Golden Rule obligates us to refrain from doing these things to others. The rule does occasionally pose problems for its followers, however. Suppose you see someone steal something. Should you turn him in? You would not want that person to turn you in if you were the one caught stealing, so you decide not to say anything. But reasonable people could argue that your obligation is to the victim, not the perpetrator. If someone witnessed a theft of your property you would want that person to come forward and report what he saw.

Another factor to keep in mind when practicing the Golden Rule is that it involves an exchange of kindness in the abstract sense, as opposed to a strictly literal sense. For example, suppose that you love ice cream and your neighbor hates it. Does this mean you should buy her ice cream, even though she detests it? No, but you can buy her a chocolate cake if that's what she likes. It is the abstract idea of exchanging welcomed gifts that is important, not the gifts themselves. Hall (2002) says that the *idea* of exchanging something of worth is especially important to keep in mind when interacting with persons from a culture different from our own. The particular objects and values that we treasure may differ from one culture to the next, so if we are given a gift we like from such a person, we would do well to respond with one that is likely to be appreciated by that person, even though it may not be something we would desire for ourselves. In other words, we should find culturally appropriate ways to show respect to others, even if those ways seem awkward to us.

Okay, you have now been exposed to five of the most common ethical approaches. How accurately can you distinguish them from each other? Take this little self-quiz and see. The answers can be found at the back of this chapter.

Golden Approaches Self-quiz

One) This approach emphasizes the greatest good for the largest number of people:

A. Rule   B. Purse   C. Consequence   D. none of these

Two) The approach that focuses on the ethical views of the person who has a great deal of money and/or political power:

A. Purse   B. Consequence   C. Law   D. Rule

Three) The approach that obligates you to treat others the way you wish to be treated:

A. Purse   B. Rule   C. Mean   D. none of these

Four) An approach to ethics that stresses moderation—taking the middle position:

A. Rule   B. Consequence   C. Purse   D. Mean

Five) The inability to accurately predict the outcome of ethical decisions has been identified as a weakness of the _____ approach.

A. Consequences   B. Law   C. Mean   D. none of these

Six) The approach that attempts to identify a single set of moral rules that apply to everyone:

A. Purse   B. Law   C. Mean   D. Rule

Seven) The concept of "compromise" is most likely to be associated with:

A. Law   B. Purse   C. Mean   D. Consequences

Eight) Which of these approaches is most likely to find murder acceptable?

A. Law   B. Consequences   C. Mean   D. none of these

What are Your Ethical Values?

All five of the Golden approaches have some strengths and some weaknesses. As you read about each you probably decided that you liked some approaches better than others. If so, that's fine. Perhaps there were others that you did not like at all. If so, that's fine, too. I would like you to give some thought to each of these approaches, and reflect on the reasons why some approaches appealed more to you than others did.

There are several different ways to think about how you view ethical issues. One that overlaps a little bit with the Golden approaches can be explored by taking the *Ethics Analysis Quiz* which follows:

Ethics Analysis Quiz

Instructions: There are several general statements listed below. Each is a commonly held opinion and there are no right or wrong answers. You will probably disagree with some items and agree with others. I am interested in the extent to which you agree or disagree with each item. Please read each statement carefully. Then indicate the extent to which you agree or disagree by placing in front of the statement the number corresponding to your feelings, where:

1 = Completely disagree	4 = Slightly disagree	7 = Moderately agree
2 = Largely disagree	5 = Neither agree or disagree	8 = Largely agree
3 = Moderately disagree	6 = Slightly agree	9 = Completely agree

_____ 1. I should make sure that my actions never intentionally hurt anyone even in the least.

_____ 2. Asking other people to take risks should not be tolerated, regardless of how small the risks might be.

_____ 3. The existence of potential harm to others is always wrong, regardless of the benefits to be gained.

_____ 4. I should never psychologically or physically hurt another person.

_____ 5. I should not do anything that might in any way threaten the dignity and welfare of another person.

_____ 6. If an action of mine could hurt an innocent person, then I should not do it.

_____ 7. Deciding whether or not to do something by balancing the positive outcomes versus the negative outcomes of the act is immoral.

_____ 8. The most important concern in any society should be the dignity and welfare of its citizens.

_____ 9. It is never necessary for anyone to sacrifice the welfare of others.

_____10. A moral action is one which clearly matches the ideals of the most "perfect" action.

_____11. There is no ethical principle so important that it should be a part of any code of ethics.

_____12. Behaviors that are ethical in one situation and society may not be in another.

_____13. Moral standards are individualistic; what I consider to be moral might be judged immoral by others.

_____14. It is impossible to compare the "rightness" of different types of moral viewpoints.

_____15. What is moral or immoral is up to the individual.

_____16. Moral rules are *personal* rules: they are not to be used to make judgments about others.

_____17. Ethical issues are so complicated that people should be permitted to develop their own individual codes.

_____18. Making a rigid ethical position into a law could lead to worse human relations.

_____19. Rules concerning lying can *not* be made; whether a lie is permissible or not permissible depends completely on the situation.

_____20. The circumstances under which a lie is told determine if it is moral or immoral.

Let's score the EAQ, then we will turn our attention to what your scores mean. Add your scores for items one through ten, then divide by the number "10." This can easily be accomplished by moving the decimal point one place to the left. For example, a score of 48 becomes a mean score of 4.8. Now repeat the process for items 11 through 20. The cutoff score for items one through ten is 6.57. Any score above that means that you are a high scorer, an Idealist. Idealists tend to believe that the rights of individual human beings should *never* be sacrificed for the greater good of humanity. Not surprisingly, they tend to be persons who are caring (Forsyth, Nye, & Kelley, 1988). Scores below 6.57 mean you are a low scorer, a Pragmatist. The cutoff score for items 11 through 20 is 6.12. Scores above that number mean that you are a high scorer, a Situationalist. Situationalists tend to believe that you should look carefully at the details of the situation you are in before deciding what is the right or wrong thing to do; scores below that number indicate that you are a low scorer, a Principled person. If your scores are very close to the cutoff points this means either that you do not feel very strongly about these dimensions, or that you have not completely made up your mind, or that your views are similar to the average person. If you would like to know more about the psychometric properties of the EAQ see "More About the EAQ" at the end of this chapter. The combination of either Idealist or Pragmatist multiplied times the combination of either Situationalist or Principled person yields four different groups with differing ethical viewpoints. The following is a description of the four types:

Situational/Idealist   A Situational Idealist is one who scores above the cutoff points on both scales. Situationalists tend to reject the idea of universal moral rules (rules that apply the same way to everyone) in favor of an analysis of each act in each situation. The people in this group are idealistic in the sense that they believe that one should *never* sacrifice the rights or the dignity of one person, even if it might lead to some greater good for humans in general. For them, the possibility of harm to a single person outweighs the potential benefits of using human "guinea pigs."

Situational/Pragmatist   A Situational Pragmatist is someone who scores above the cutoff point on Situationism and below the cutoff on Idealism. In other words, this type of person rejects the idea of a universal set of moral rules (as does the Situationalist/Idealist). They believe that it is occasionally necessary to subject some humans to harm or risk of harm if the possibility of helping others exists. They might be more inclined to look with favor on a study in which prisoners are forced to try a new type of medicine (especially if they felt the risks were small) in the hope that it might be useful to others. This group would be more likely than the other three to approve of the Golden Consequences approach.

Principled/Idealist   A Principled Idealist scores high on the Idealism scale and low on the Situationism scale. This group believes that there are moral rules that apply to everyone. Furthermore, one of these rules is that *all* humans without exception should be treated with the utmost respect. This group would probably be least likely to sanction a study in which prisoners were forced to try a new medicine. They would also be most likely to endorse the Golden Law. Remember that the Golden Law approach argues for a set of universal moral laws.

Principled/Pragmatist   Principled Pragmatists score below the cutoff on both scales. Low scores on this quiz are not necessarily bad. They simply describe people who generally endorse the Golden Law, without endorsing any particular law that requires us to refrain from sacrificing the rights of some humans for the potential good of others.

To further our understanding of ethical thinking in relation to the EAQ, let us examine an ethical dilemma relating to the topic of loyalty. An ethical dilemma poses two ideas about right and wrong against each other—ideas that have been deeply embedded in our society. The dilemma forces us to choose. In so doing we can learn which moral rule is more important, at least to us. Alternatively, for the situationalist, it forces a choice based on an evaluation of the situation within which the choice is to be made.

Loyalty Scenario
(written by Sandra Vance)

Jennifer and I became friends the moment we met the first day of school when we entered first grade. She had just moved from Chicago to the small southeastern Ohio town we proudly called home. Although she was a stranger to the community, she and her family quickly became one of us. All through our school years Jennifer and I were inseparable. We traded clothes, stories and secrets. Although we had many friends, we were like sisters. We had a story that we were fraternal twins that had been separated at birth and raised by different families.

When Jennifer and I were seniors in high school, Jennifer became quite ill; she seemed to be anemic—always catching a cold or the flu. Her parents took her to several specialists, but no one has been able to find the cause, let alone a cure for her illness. She has missed many days of school and her graduation is in jeopardy.

Some time ago when I took some homework assignments to her, Jennifer confided in me that she had an eating disorder, but she told me that she was getting it under control and would soon be okay. She made me promise not to tell her parents. However, Jennifer's health is deteriorating rapidly; I know that some young women have died from this type of illness. I feel this is very serious and not under her control; however, I made a promise. What would you do if you were me?

A. I would tell her parents.

B. I would keep my promise.

Situational Idealist   This group rejects the very *idea* of universal rules. Sometimes this rejection stems from the realization that different cultures learn different ideas about right and wrong (although that is not applicable in this situation). The Situational Idealist will carefully weigh all the pertinent information at hand. "What is the subjective probability that Jennifer will survive without help?" "What is the likelihood that she will seek professional help on her own?" "How much do I care about Jennifer?" "What is the likelihood that our friendship will survive if I tell her parents?" "What is the best possible decision I can make in the best interest of Jennifer?" The Situational Idealist is not going to lose any sleep over the thought of telling a lie, but as an idealist a concern about the welfare of this particular human being will probably result in telling the parents, especially if Jennifer's medical situation worsens.

Situational Pragmatist   This group also takes a dim view of specific moral rules, Therefore, little sleep will be lost worrying about the moral principles involved. Appraisals of any ethical action will begin with the personal values of the individual making the decision. The same situational questions seen above will likely guide the thinking of the Situational Pragmatist.

Principled Idealist   If you are a principled idealist there are universal moral rules that always apply to everyone, regardless of circumstances. Furthermore, there are no exceptions. If one accepts as a moral principle that "Thou shall not lie," then the consequences of lying are irrelevant, and you must honor your promise, even if Jennifer dies. If you also accept the principle that "Thou shall not allow someone to die when you can help" (and an idealist probably would), then you have a real dilemma. As a Principled Idealist you will agonize over which of these two moral rules is more important and decide accordingly.

Principled Pragmatist   Principled Pragmatists agree with Principled Idealists that there are moral rules to which everyone should adhere. The idea of breaking a moral law will bother the Principled Pragmatist. However, the pragmatist allows for a few exceptions. When should we make these exceptions? Perhaps when some greater good can be achieved by bending the rules. Is there a greater good to be achieved by telling a lie—one which will ultimately bring some shame and loss of dignity to Jennifer in the short run, but increase her chances of long-term survival?

Here is another scenario. Look this one over carefully and decide what you would do if you were Mattie.

Courage Scenario (Mattie's Dilemma)
(written by Sandra Vance)

Mattie had lived in the housing projects since she was a small child. In the early years she had enjoyed her home, felt responsible for her neighborhood, and felt a bond with her friends and neighbors. However, that was then and this is now. Things have changed. Too much violence, too many drugs, too much fear, too much isolation—most days she felt she was a prisoner in her own home, sitting behind window bars and doors with deadlock bolts. She was afraid to venture out unless absolutely necessary—such as today when she had to go to the grocery store.

Yes, she could walk well enough with her cane, but it was such an effort and she was so slow. She had joined the "Neighborhood Watch" and always had her whistle, but really what good could she do? Perhaps her friend Martha was right, "It's better just to mind your own business and to take care of yourself." "Don't get involved," that was Martha's motto. But it was so sad; was this truly what life was about?

As Mattie hurried around the corner, passing the alley and just about to enter the door of her building, she heard the unmistakable sounds of a fight. What caught her attention was the painful cry of a hurt child. Fear told her to hurry on, but compassion told her to look. As she ventured into the dark alley she could see two larger boys beating and kicking a small child lying on the ground trying to protect his body. Mattie froze, not knowing what to do . . . what could she do . . . an old woman with a cane? Wait—I have my whistle and I have my cane, a weapon of sorts. At least I can stop the beating and attract some attention. "What would happen to me if I get involved? Do I save my own life or do I try to save the life of this child?"

Mattie does not have much time to think about what she should do, but you do have time. Mattie knows that if she goes into her building the child might get badly injured or even die. It would take a few minutes for her to get to a phone. Even if she called the police right away, she knew that their reluctance to enter her neighborhood would result in a long delay before the small child got help. He could be dead by the time they arrived. What would you do?

A. I would blow my whistle right away.

B. I would quickly get into my house.

How might a Situational Idealist reason about this dilemma?

_____

_____

How might a Situational Pragmatist reason about this dilemma?

_____

_____

How might a Principled Idealist reason about this dilemma?

_____

_____

How might a Principled Pragmatist reason about this dilemma?

_____

_____

For some feedback about your answers see "Mattie's Dilemma" at the end of this chapter.

Thinking Activity

A Simple Ethical Problem?

Almost one out of four persons on this planet lives under conditions of extreme poverty. By "extreme poverty" I mean that these people lack the means to meet the most basic needs for shelter and food. For millions of infants this means that they get less protein than is needed to permit adequate brain development. For 180 million children under the age of five it means suffering from malnutrition (Singer, 1993). Many of us have seen pictures of children with sunken cheeks and legs so slender that they appear to be little more than just sticks.

Experts say that there is currently a combination of food and technology sufficient to feed the entire world. If all the rich nations of the world were willing to do their part, the hunger problem could be virtually eliminated. The rich countries produce a large amount of surplus food, which could be shipped to areas most in need. Wealthy nations also have a large amount of agricultural expertise that could be shared with the farmers in poor countries, the result of which would be big increases in agricultural self-sufficiency (Singer, 1993).

While the cost of developing and maintaining such a program would be high, it is believed to be a bearable one. With the cooperation of our wealthy neighbors we Americans could save millions of lives annually at an individual cost that is quite small. There is some question as to whether we would even notice the difference in our wallets (Singer, 1993).

This seems like an ethical "no-brainer," doesn't it? Do we not have a moral obligation to help those who will suffer and die if we do not intervene? Are we not constantly reminded of this duty through magazine ads and TV commercials for charitable organizations? That obligation seems all the more compelling when we consider that we can accomplish this noble goal without altering our own wealthy lifestyles.

But is this issue really as simple as it appears? If we think critically about the long-term consequences of giving away food we begin to realize that the issue is not so one-sided. As selfish and uncaring as this seems, a strong argument can be made for withholding food from these starving nations. Many of these same countries are doubling their populations at a rate that is much faster than that of the rich countries. If we feed their undernourished people today that will indirectly allow them to produce more children. Those children will grow up to produce even more children, and so on, until even the rich countries will not be able to meet the food demand. Put differently, we can allow a large number of people to die now, maybe 50 million, or we can feed them and their children for roughly the next 20 years. At that point we will no longer be able to afford to keep feeding them, so 100 million will die later. These numbers are very rough estimates. No one can accurately predict what those numbers will actually be; the point is that the amount of suffering and dying will be much greater in the future (Hardin, 1974)

Some kind-hearted people with good intentions have used the familiar proverb: "Give a man a fish and he will eat for a day, teach him how to fish and he will eat for the rest of his days." Following this philosophy makes some sense. Teaching people how to raise food more efficiently has led to increased crop production and more food for people who badly needed it. Unfortunately, the people who might have otherwise perished survived and created more people, thus negating the technological advances (Hardin, 1974).

I would not want to be the leader of a wealthy nation who must look the leader of a poor nation in the eye and say: "Sorry, we are not going to donate food. However, we will help you find humane ways to reduce your population." Although refusing to donate food seems cruel, it is morally defensible. Although our own population is growing much more slowly, if we want bright futures for our grandchildren we will eventually be faced with the same problem ourselves.

Who do you think will find it easier to refuse food to starving nations, a follower of the Golden Consequence, or a follower of the Golden Rule? Why?

_____

_____

_____

If the rich nations tell the poor nations to reduce their populations that might strike some people as arrogant. How do you think a follower of the Golden Purse would respond to that criticism?

_____

_____

_____

The Six Pillars of Character

A pillar is a large post, typically very strong, capable of supporting a great deal of weight. If you would like to become the sort of person who others think of when the term "good character" is mentioned, then you need to build character on the support provided by what some refer to as the six pillars of character (Reece &

Brandt, 2000). Have you slipped up in the past and failed to use one or more of these pillars? If so, there is no time like the present to get back on track.

Trustworthiness—Be the kind of person that everyone can trust. If someone confides in you, earn their respect by not telling the secret to anyone else. You can decide whether you want to strictly adhere to the Golden Law, but at least be honest about the things that matter. Never ask anyone to do something that is dishonest.

Respect—Be respectful of the rights of others. Do not make fun of others, or belittle them because they are not as *talented* as you. Respect everyone, regardless of religion, race, work status, sex or sexual preference.

A few years ago I had a student who was habitually late for class when he bothered to show up at all. He had difficulty controlling his urge to spontaneously comment on everything going on in class, sometimes using profanity and making demeaning comments about women while doing so. After several outbursts of this sort, I warned him not to do this again. He was a bright fellow with a tremendous capacity for grasping complex ideas quickly. He earned a good grade in my class and eventually I no longer saw him at the university where I was teaching. Assuming that he continued on the same pathway, he probably graduated with a high grade point average and had little trouble landing a job. However, his arrogance and general lack of respect for others has either landed him in trouble or will eventually catch up with him. The point is that you can learn to become a very competent, technically proficient person, but if you can't learn to respect others they will simply not want to work with you.

Responsibility—Think about the consequences that your actions may have on others. If you say you are going to meet your study group in the library at one o'clock, be there on time! You have a responsibility to yourself to attend all of your classes. It's like the Nike commercials say—just do it!

Fairness—Treat everyone fairly. It may take awhile, but if you do, eventually the word will get around that you are someone who can be counted on to make important decisions that will win the respect of your co-workers. Part of fairness involves the willingness to be open-minded. This doesn't mean you must like everyone or every thing you come in contact with. It does mean that you should extend the same spirit of tolerance toward those who are different from you that you would extend to your family and friends.

Caring—Show kindness, compassion, and sensitivity toward others. Try to put yourself in the shoes of others, so to speak. Do your utmost to understand the world as others see it. If you can do this I think you will find it easier to care about the welfare of others.

Citizenship—Being a good citizen means showing respect for the rules and laws. In recent times "citizenship" has come to refer to one's relationship to the corporate community as well as one's country. Respect the legitimate rights of those who have the task of enforcing the laws. Participate in the affairs that are a part of your company's "culture." Promote the welfare of your organization by serving as a model for appropriate behavior in the workplace.

If you build your adult life on these six pillars will everyone love you and will you become rich and famous? Probably not! Realistically there will always be those who disagree with you, or dislike you for reasons beyond your control. Eventually, however, you will earn a reputation for being a good person; most of the people around you will come to appreciate you for your integrity, and that may be more important than becoming rich and famous.

Corporate Values and Ethical Decisions

You may be preparing for a career in business or industry. Big businesses often face very important ethical problems. The decisions made by top-level executives in these corporations may have powerful repercussions for low-level employees as well as the general public. At the time I was writing this chapter a corporate giant,

Enron, was going bankrupt. I understand that this happened as the indirect result of the decision made by company leaders to lie about the profits the corporation was making. When the truth was revealed, investors lost faith. Worse yet, thousands of innocent employees lost their jobs and financial benefits. To add insult to their injury these same people could do little but watch while some top executives, who probably saw what was going to happen, protected their assets and bailed out with millions of dollars of company money (Kadlec, 2002).

One might ask: "How could such terrible things happen?" "How could corporate officials ruin the companies they are supposed to be leading?" "How could employees who know that their companies are producing products that are inferior and dangerous keep quiet about it?" "Is the American workforce morally bankrupt?"

It may seem as though no one pays attention to business ethics anymore, but at least one study (Mudrack & Mason, 1995) suggests how something like the Enron and Worldcom financial disasters could have occurred even though company officials actually believed they were behaving ethically. Consider the following scenario:

Slee-zee Motorcycles

You work for the Slee-zee Motorcycle Manufacturing Company. Lately you have been losing a lot of business to Harley-Davidson. One way to regain some of the losses is to reduce costs by using a tire made of low-quality materials that has a tendency to blow at high speeds, with the potential for disastrous consequences. You are an expert on tire performance, you have seen the results of the tests on this tire and you have told the top bosses in the company that the tire is unsafe. However, the tire costs about half what you have been paying for the tires you are currently using. Slee-zee employs 2,000 people, many of whom would have great difficulty finding work if the company folded. Slee-zee's financial status is very shaky, and desperate measures are needed to allow the company to compete. There are no other easy financial solutions to Slee-zee's problems, but if the inferior tire is used it is only a matter of time before some motorcyclist is killed or badly injured. Do you raise a fuss about this, insisting that the company continue to use top-quality tires, or do you say nothing and hope that no one is able to prove in court that Slee-zee was legally responsible for any injuries?

As outsiders, this dilemma is an ethical "no-brainer." It is clearly *unethical* to make a decision that will certainly result in death and serious injury to innocent persons. However, from time to time we hear about companies that do make highly unethical decisions. Consider the cigarette companies, who for many years claimed that their products were not harmful, in spite of an ever-growing body of research suggesting otherwise. Consider the story of Erin Brockovich, whose efforts showed that a large company was disposing of hazardous chemicals by putting them in an area where they would surely get into a town's water supply. Consider auto manufacturers who have allowed vehicles they knew to be unsafe to roll through their assembly lines. How do people who are responsible for making these unethical decisions sleep at night? How might they maintain the viewpoint that they are actually doing something ethical, when most of us would strongly disagree?

Go back and look at the five golden approaches again. In particular, read the description of the Golden Consequence. Then see if you can apply it to the dilemma faced by the tire expert who works for Slee-zee. How might the expert decide that it is ethical for the company to put inferior tires on their ~~cles?~~ One possible answer to this question can be found at the end of this the heading "Slee-zee Motorcycles."

Whistleblowing

One of the options available to the tire expert at Slee-zee Motorcycles is to "blow the whistle." A whistleblower is one who reports organizational wrongdoing to the public or to public officials (McCutcheon, 2000; Reece & Brandt, 2002).

Twenty-five years ago it would have been very difficult to take such a course of action. More recently, however, legislation protecting the whistleblower from reprisals has made it easier for people to report unethical corporate behavior. The legislation even offers financial incentives for those whose actions are judged to be especially worthwhile. Some people would argue that it has become *too* easy to become a whistleblower, in part because financial incentives for doing so can be quite tempting.

Here are some things to think about if you ever consider becoming a whistle-blower. Understand that your action will probably be met with responses ranging from disapproval to open hostility. Some employers have gone so far as to unfairly discredit whistleblowers (McCutcheon, 2000). Don't expect people to like you if they lose their jobs after you blow the whistle. Make sure you give fair warning. The tire expert at Slee-zee made sure that the top executives knew the results of the testing. She or he should also wait until they actually start using the inferior tires to report it. It is not fair to report someone just because they are *thinking* about doing something unethical. Make sure your own motives are pure. Are you blowing the whistle just because you are angry at someone in the organization that you dislike? Or, did this person do something that was clearly unethical, according to your well thought-out ethical viewpoint?

In the wake of legislation passed in the early Nineties designed to curb sexual harassment in the workplace there were many complaints filed. Some were justified because the offense was clearly sexual harassment by any reasonable standard. However, the legislation offered a very vague and liberal interpretation of sexual harassment. As a result, some "victims" reported sexual harassment cases that were actually nothing more than disagreements between employees who did not get along. Employers, confused by the legislation and worried about the possibility of lawsuits if they failed to take action, fired some people who had not really been guilty of sexual harassment. The word got out that the new legislation could be used as a weapon, and some people used it unfairly.

Jeffrey Wigand was the chief researcher for one of the major tobacco companies, and the real-life hero of the movie, *The Insider*. Wigand "went public" with the knowledge that his company had misled consumers about nicotine. Nicotine, as you probably know, is a potentially dangerous drug found in the cigarettes smoked by millions.

The bottom line is this: If you are going to accuse someone in your organization of behaving unethically, make sure your own behavior is completely ethical. Make sure the conduct you are reporting really is unethical, and that the failure to report that conduct could have severe and devastating consequences for innocent people.

Team Building and Ethical Behavior

Team building can be defined as an attempt to improve the effectiveness of a group of people who work together (Clark, 1994). The specific goals of team building are to promote better communication, to become more open, to encourage cooperation, to become more trusting, and to teach mutual concern among group members. In addition, teams are expected, in time, to become more creative, committed to the group, team-centered, responsible, and move from a state of confusion about their roles in the group to a state of clarity about their roles.

Clark (1994) has noted that it is virtually impossible for any one group to achieve all of these goals; instead it is typical to find work teams that vary in quality from moderately effective to largely ineffective. In almost every work team there are two or more individuals who do not agree on much of anything. Furthermore, many teams are led by managers who earned their positions through competitiveness, manipulation, and secrecy—behaviors that are at odds with some of the goals of team building. The result is that you should approach organizational teamwork with realistic expectations. Be cautiously optimistic. Even if a work team does not fully meet all its goals it still may be able to accomplish something worthwhile.

If you are preparing for a job in business or industry you may become part of a work team. Some experts on American business practices claim that the use of work teams is on the rise (Dumaine, 1993; Goodall, 1990), and that work teams are occasionally responsible for notable successes. For example, a team at a Johnson Wax plant figured out how to make the operation run more efficiently, increasing productivity by 30 percent (Dumaine, 1993). If you view teamwork from a positive yet realistic perspective, your willingness to help the team meet its goals may be a good influence on other members of your team.

Because ethical issues are both important and complex, these issues are often explored within the team setting (Reece & Brandt, 2000). Sometimes the discussions focus on the company ethics code and how to apply it to everyday problems. Sometimes the team discusses difficult ethical decisions.

At the Martin Marietta Corporation a training leader presents ethical dilemmas to teams of players. Each team also gets a list containing several possible responses to the dilemma. Each team discusses these responses, then selects what it believes is the best (most ethical) one. Points are assigned to each answer. Presumably the number of points assigned to each decision is based on a combination of ethical criteria and company policy. As a result, the training exercise can be fun (at least for the winners), while providing an opportunity for each team to learn to work together (Reece & Brandt, 2000).

I don't have any points to award for your decision, but you might want to form a group, read the Corporate Courage Scenario that follows, then debate the merits of your choice with the other members of your group. Did everyone in your group agree with your choice? Did anyone bring up a point that you did not consider when you made your choice? Did you change your mind as a result of the debate? If so, why?

Corporate Courage Scenario
(written by Sandra Vance)

A financial manager of a moderate size company analyzed and recommended a new proposal that involved some expensive changes for the company, but changes that would ultimately be very lucrative, with substantial profits within two to three years. The changes were implemented based on his analysis and recommendation.

Recently, while working on another project, he discovered some additional and pertinent information that would have changed his analysis of the previous proposal and his recommendation. Rather than making a profit within a short period of time, the company could actually lose considerable revenue in this venture; it could even bankrupt the business.

Because the material and information was not included in the proposal package that had been submitted to the financial manager, theoretically he is not at fault; however, in the final analysis, he is responsible. As the financial executive it is his responsibility to see that situations such as this do not happen.

He realizes that he has two options. He could go to the CEO explaining the situation, in which case he could be fired, or he could be asked to remain to help in correcting the situation—in either case he would be humiliated. Or, he could say nothing, begin looking for another position, and leave before anyone in the company realizes that his analysis was incorrect. What would you do?

A. I would tell the CEO and try to save the company if asked. _____

B. I would find another job and get out while I could. _____

The Irony of Integrity Testing

An integrity test is a paper-and-pencil quiz designed to determine which job applicants are most likely to steal, become violent, use drugs, and stay home from work (Gregory, 1996; Murphy & Davidshofer, 1994). Generally speaking, there are two varieties.

The first kind, called overt or clear purpose tests, derive their name from the fact that it is clear from the nature of the items (such as "Do you approve of taking company property home without asking permission?") that the tests' purpose is to screen persons who are likely to exhibit unethical behavior in the workplace. One problem with clear purpose integrity tests is that their purpose is all too clear to those who have something to hide. In other words, it is easy to give false answers without being detected (Gregory, 1996).

The second type, personality-based or veiled purpose tests, derive their name from the fact that some personality test items have been found to correlate with undesirable workplace behaviors. Here's how it works.

Large numbers of job applicants are given several brief personality tests at the time they are hired. A careful record of their integrity-related job performance (absenteeism, incidents of violence, drug use, etc.) is kept over an extended period of time. Attempts are made to correlate personality test scores with each of several disruptive workplace behaviors. Most of the test scores are unrelated, but employers are interested in the few that are related. These latter tests can be used to predict which persons are likely to engage in unethical and disruptive behaviors. For example, in one study personality measures of adjustment and achievement correlated -.43 and -.35 with delinquent workplace behaviors, and a measure of dependability correlated -.28 with substance abuse (Hough, Eaton, Dunnette, Kamp, & McCloy, 1990). In other words, those whose scores indicated healthy adjustment and higher achievement were less likely to get into trouble, and dependable persons were less likely to use illegal drugs. Scores on personality-based integrity tests are probably harder to fake because the connection between personality items and unethical work behaviors is less clear.

There is considerable irony surrounding the use of integrity tests. Their purpose is to predict unethical behavior, but some experts argue that the ways in which these tests are used and marketed are unethical (Gregory, 1996; Murphy & Davidshofer, 1994). There seem to be three areas of concern.

The first ethical concern pits the rights of employers to hire the best employees versus the privacy rights of job applicants. No employer wants to hire people who will create problems in the workplace. Any tool that will reduce problems of that sort is welcome. On the other hand, some applicants are offended by the questions, especially those on the clear purpose tests.

A second concern is that of informed consent. Some test publishers recommend that employers tell job applicants little or nothing about the test or the purpose for which it is being used. However, an ethical code for psychologists who give and score tests makes it clear that they are expected to reveal a great deal of information about the tests and their purpose before they are administered (Lowman, 1989).

Finally, there is an ethical issue about the marketing of integrity tests. Some of the publishers make claims that have been labeled as "a disgrace," and "fraudulent"

(Murphy & Davidshofer, 1994, p. 372). The publishers describe their tests in glowing terms that imply something close to perfection. The truth is that integrity tests are more useful as screening devices than nothing at all, but they often result in some mistakes. In other words, some basically honest people fail, and some dishonest troublemakers pass. As an example, recall the -.28 correlation between the measure of dependability and substance abuse. If that number had been .00 it would have no usefulness as a predictor; if that number had been -1.00 it would have perfect predictive power, always correctly identifying those who would make trouble by using drugs in the workplace. The fact that -.28 is closer to .00 than it is to -1.00 tells you that it is far less than perfect (but still useful) as a predictor of substance abuse. Thus the irony is that if you are looking for unethical business practices you can easily find them in the marketing of tests that are designed to measure the tendency to engage in unethical business practices.

Answers to Questions Raised Earlier in the Chapter

Why is There so Much Conflict Even though Major Religions Subscribe to the Golden Rule?

There may be several possible answers to this question. One answer suggested by some comments found in the beginning of the chapter is that we humans are basically selfish creatures. Combined with our intelligence and our ability to hide our true feelings and motives from ourselves and others, we can seemingly do almost anything and convince ourselves that we are doing what is right. Thus, it would not matter if everyone believed in the Golden Rule. There would still be conflict because we could do things that hurt other nations, all the while convincing ourselves that we are behaving morally.

Answers to the Golden Approaches Self-quiz

The correct answer to number one is "C." The Golden Consequence is concerned with the greatest good (positive consequence) for the largest number of people. Number two is "A." The Golden Purse ethic states that those with money and power can make the moral rules. Three is "B." It is the Golden Rule to treat others the way you would like to be treated. Four is "D." The Golden Mean emphasizes the consideration of all sides before choosing an ethical position that falls somewhere near the middle. Five is "A." It is often difficult to predict the consequences of our moral choices. Six is "B." The Golden Law approach attempts to derive universal moral laws. Seven is "C." The Golden Mean could be viewed as a compromise between extreme positions. Eight is "B." None of the approaches advocate murder on a routine basis, but followers of the Golden Consequence argue that under rare circumstances it might produce the best positive outcome for others.

More About the Ethics Analysis Quiz (EAQ)

This description of the Ethics Analysis Quiz is meant primarily for those who have an interest in the psychometric qualities of the Quiz. You can skip over this section if you like. The EAQ relies heavily on the pioneering work of Donelson Forsyth (1980), whose Ethics Position Questionnaire (EPQ) is the conceptual basis for the EAQ. I began by writing items that were similar to each of his; generally speaking mine are shorter and use simpler language. The two scales were given concurrently to 53 undergraduates at a university in Orlando. All but one of the EAQ items correlated at the .01 significance level with their counterparts on his Questionnaire. The internal reliabilities (as measured by Cronbach's alpha) for the Idealist and Situationalist scales of the EAQ were .89 and .81, respectively. Item-to-total correlations ranged from .45 to .77 for the former and .27 to .62 for the latter scale. There was a correlation of .50 between scores on the two scales, meaning that those who scored "high" on one scale tended to score "high" on the other. The EPQ has been shown to have a reasonable amount of validity (Forsyth, 1980; Forsyth, Nye, & Kelley, 1988; Forsyth & Pope, 1984). Since the EPQ and the EAQ are strongly related, this suggests that the EAQ is also a valid instrument for the purpose of measuring the philosophical views about ethics that the instrument was designed to measure.

Mattie's Dilemma

Keep in mind that there are no definitive answers to Mattie's dilemma. Arguments can be raised for direct intervention as well as for minding her own business. However, those with different ethical viewpoints might look at the dilemma a bit differently.

If Mattie had been a Situational Idealist she would try to analyze the scene as quickly and as accurately as possible. The Situational part of this type of person asks questions like: How much danger exists here? Is there any chance that these boys are merely playing "rough?" Will blowing my whistle really do any good? The Idealist part makes it difficult for Mattie to sacrifice the welfare of this one child. If Mattie was a Situational Pragmatist she would still try to analyze the scene to find some ethical guidelines. As a Pragmatist, however, she might be inclined to say that some injustice is inevitable, and that intervention on her part would likely bring her pain and suffering. But would it prevent the child further harm?

If Mattie had been a Principled Idealist she would have already decided that there are universal rules about bringing harm to others, especially those who cannot defend themselves. In our society most people would consider the beating to be a "wrongful" act. Since Mattie is also an Idealist she would find it hard to ignore an injustice, even if it involved just one victim. If Mattie had been a Principled Pragmatist she would probably be just as likely as the Principled Idealist to view the beating as "wrongful." However, as a pragmatist she might be resigned to the idea that some suffering cannot be helped. Is "getting involved" likely to produce a positive outcome for either the child or herself? Mattie has only a few seconds to decide.

Slee-zee Motorcycles

How is it possible to use tires that will ultimately cause injuries and deaths and still maintain the belief that you are behaving ethically? There may be more than one possible answer, but consider this one. If you believe in the Golden Consequence ethic you probably think that the guiding principle should be "the greatest good for the greatest number of people." It is easy to remind yourself that 2,000 people (including yourself) will suffer if the company goes out of business, and that such a negative consequence is definite and looming large in the near future. The negative consequence of injuries and deaths is harder to visualize, seems further removed from the present, and, if you are lucky, will only bring harm to a small number of people. If you scored as a pragmatist (rather than an idealist) on the EAQ you may find it easier to accept the idea that sometimes it is necessary to sacrifice the welfare of a few to protect the interests of many.

The study cited earlier in the chapter found that large numbers of relatively "normal" adults were willing to suspend "conventional ethical standards" (the Golden Law or the Golden Rule, perhaps?) when the welfare of the organization is at stake (Mudrack & Mason, 1995, p. 646). On one level it is disconcerting that people are willing to do things that most of us would see as unethical; on another, it is good that company loyalty is still alive.

References

Altemeyer, B. (1999). To thine own self be untrue: Self-awareness in authoritarians. *North American Journal of Psychology, I,* 157–164.

Andolina, M. (2002). *Practical guide to critical thinking.* Albany, NY: Delmar.

Batson, C. D., Thompson, E. R., & Chen, H. (2002). Moral hypocrisy: Addressing some alternatives. *Journal of Personality and Social Psychology,* 83, 330–339.

Binder, F. M., & Reimers, D. M. (Eds). (1992). *The way we lived: Essays and documents in American social history, Vol. I* (2nd ed.). Lexington, MA: D. C. Heath.

Clark, N. (1994). *Team building: A practical guide for trainers.* London: McGraw-Hill.

Dumaine, B. (1993, Feb. 22). The new non-manager managers. *Fortune,* p. 52.

Forsyth, D. R. (1980). A taxonomy of ethical ideologies. *Journal of Personality and Social Psychology, 39,* 175–184.

Forsyth, D. R., Nye, J. L., & Kelley, K. (1988). Idealism, relativism, and the ethic of caring. *The Journal of Psychology, 122,* 243–248.

Forsyth, D. R., & Pope, W. R. (1984). Ethical ideology and judgments of social psychological research. *Journal of Personality and Social Psychology, 46,* 1364–1375.

Goodall, H. L. (1990). *Small group communication in organizations* (2nd ed.). Dubuque, IA: Wm. C. Brown.

Gregory, R. J. (1996). *Psychological testing: History, principles, and applications* (2nd ed.). Boston: Allyn & Bacon.

Hall, B. J. (2002). *Among cultures: The challenge of communication.* Orlando, FL: Harcourt.

Hardin, G. (1974, Sept.). Lifeboat ethics: The case against helping the poor. *Psychology Today,* 38–43; 123–126.

Hough, L. M., Eaton, N., Dunnette, M., Kamp, J., & McCloy, R. (1990). Criterion-related validities of personality constructs and the effect of response distortion on those validities (Monograph). *Journal of Applied Psychology, 75,* 581–595.

Kadlec, D. (2002, July 29). Everyone, back in the labor pool. *Time,* pp. 22–31.

Lowman, R. (1989). *Pre-employment screening for psychopathology: A guide to professional practice.* Sarasota, FL: Professional Resource Exchange.

McCutcheon, L. E. (2000). Is there a "whistleblower" personality? *Psychology: A Journal of Human Behavior.* 37, 2–9.

Mudrack, P. E., & Mason, E. S. (1995). More on the acceptability of workplace behaviors of a dubious ethical nature. *Psychological Reports, 76,* 639–648.

Murphy, K. R., & Davidshofer, C. O. (1994). *Psychological testing: Principles and applications.* Englewood Cliffs, NJ: Prentice-Hall.

Paul, R., & Elder, L. (2001). *Critical thinking: Tools for taking charge of your learning and your life.* Upper Saddle River, NJ: Prentice-Hall.

Reece, B. L., & Brandt, R. (2000). *Human relations: Principles and practices* (4th ed.). Boston: Houghton Mifflin.

Retzlaff, P. D. (1995). *Tactical psychotherapy of the personality disorders.* Boston: Allyn & Bacon.

Singer, P. (1993). *Practical ethics* (2nd ed.). Cambridge, England: Cambridge University Press.

Wall, T. F. (2001). *Thinking critically about philosophical problems.* Belmont, CA: Wadsworth/Thomson Learning.

(The author wishes to acknowledge the constructive feedback obtained from Joy Easton, Sandra Vance, & Shelley Wyatt while preparing this chapter).

Case 2

Ben & Jerry's Homemade: Managing Social Responsibility and Growth[1]

Ben Cohen and Jerry Greenfield opened their first ice cream shop on May 5, 1978, in a converted gas station in Burlington, Vermont, with $12,000 worth of second-hand equipment. Their business credentials consisted of much enthusiasm and a $5 correspondence course in ice-cream making from Pennsylvania State University. Driven by Cohen and Greenfield's 1960s ideals, Ben & Jerry's Homemade, Inc., has grown very successful, achieving an enviable level of brand-name recognition for the firm's internationally distributed frozen dessert products, including ice cream, frozen yogurt, and sorbets. In addition, there are 337 franchise or company-owned "scoop shops" in the United States, United Kingdom, Holland, France, Israel, Spain, and Lebanon.

From the beginning, Cohen and Greenfield incorporated into their business a strong sense of social responsibility—to their employees, the community, and the world at large. Unlike most companies, Ben & Jerry's Homemade has a three-part mission statement—product, economic, and social. According to the company, it "is the belief that all three parts must thrive equally in a manner that commands deep respect for individuals in and outside the company and supports the communities of which they are a part." Although Ben & Jerry's has experienced some trying times, it remains firmly grounded in its original, socially responsible corporate vision.

---

[1] This case was prepared by O.C. Ferrell, John Fraedrich, and Terry Gable for classroom discussion, rather than to illustrate either effective or ineffective handling of an administrative, ethical, or legal decision by management.

The Ben & Jerry Story

Cohen and Greenfield's converted gas station served rich, all-natural ice cream, which quickly became popular with local residents. During the winter months, however, the customers turned to warmer treats, so Cohen and Greenfield had to come up with new ideas to survive their first year. Soon they were packaging their ice cream and hauling it around to local restaurants. Gradually, they began to include grocery stores among their customers and soon gained shelf space in 150 stores across the state. The first franchise store opened in 1981, and by 1985 Ben & Jerry's was selling pints in stores outside of New England.

Ben & Jerry's has always been a bit unorthodox in its business practices, which range from Greenfield's formal executive title of "Big Cheese" to its products. For example, a popular Ben & Jerry's ice cream flavor is Cherry Garcia, named after (now deceased) guitarist Jerry Garcia of the Grateful Dead. Another flavor, Wavy Gravy, was named after the master of ceremonies at Woodstock and, naturally, was packaged in a tie-dyed container. Another perennial favorite is Phish, named in honor of a popular band from Vermont. The company has also employed some unconventional promotional tactics, like the "Cowmobile," a modified mobile home that Cohen and Greenfield drove cross country to distribute free ice cream scoops.

When the company went public in 1984 as Ben & Jerry's Homemade, Inc., Cohen initially limited the sale of the company's stock to Vermont residents. His idea was that if local residents were part owners of the firm, the community would share in the success of the business. In Cohen's words, "What a strange thing we're discovering: As our business supports the community, the community supports us back." A national stock offering did follow two years later, but the company has continued its philosophy of supporting the local community.

Caring Capitalism

When Cohen and Greenfield first went into business together, they wrote their own rules. Their corporate mission statement listed not only the goals of making and selling the finest-quality natural ice cream and operating in such a way as to achieve success for both shareholders and employees, but also the requirement that they initiate "innovative ways to improve the quality of life of a broad community—local, national, and international."

In the early 1990s, Ben & Jerry's was selling more than $100 million worth of ice cream products annually, and Cohen and Greenfield felt they were losing control of their company—its growth, creativity, organization, and values. Greenfield even dropped out of the business for a while. Cohen considered selling the company until a friend pointed out to him that he could make it into whatever he wanted. He then developed the concept of "caring capitalism," which he applies by donating part of the company's profits to worthy causes as well as by finding creative ways to improve the quality of life of the firm's employees and of the local community. Greenfield rejoined the company soon after.

Shortly after Greenfield rejoined, Cohen set up the Ben & Jerry's Foundation, which is dedicated to encouraging social change through the donation of 7.5 percent of the company's yearly pretax profits. Ben & Jerry's social concern can also be seen in some of its products. One of the firm's ventures was the Peace Pop, an ice cream bar on a stick, from which 1 percent of profits were used to build awareness and raise funds for peace. The company purchases rain-forest nuts for its Rainforest Crunch ice cream, thus providing a market for goods from the rain forests that do not require their destruction. Additionally, sales of Rainforest Crunch are funneled back into rain-forest preservation efforts. Ben & Jerry's environmental concern was apparent when it switched to the "Eco-Pint," a more environmentally friendly unbleached paperboard container. Standard papermaking uses chlorine compounds for bleaching, a process that discharges millions of gallons of organochlorine-laced water daily. Chemicals found in this water are considered hazardous to human health. The company also joined in sponsoring the Rosebud Sioux Tribe Wind Turbine Project in South Dakota, the first large-scale American-Indian-owned wind farm. By purchasing credits in the project, the company can neutralize some of the effects of the carbon monoxide generated by the energy used in its facilities.

Cohen and Greenfield extend their social awareness to their own employees. A salary ratio at the firm keeps the salaries of top executives in line with nonmanagerial employees. This helps give all employees a sense that they're working together as a team. And when it seemed that Ben & Jerry's was expanding too quickly (the company went from a hundred and fifty employees to three hundred almost overnight), company executives made a conscious decision to slow growth to ensure that the company's family atmosphere and core values would not be lost. Among the additional benefits employees receive are three pints of ice cream a week, free health-club memberships, and use of a partially subsidized company child care center.

Another of Ben & Jerry's efforts to utilize the "caring capitalism" concept was in advertising techniques. Rather than buy television, radio, or newspaper advertising, Ben & Jerry's promotes things and events of value to the community. It sponsors peace, music, and art festivals around the country—including the Newport Folk Festival, FarmAid, and its own One World, One Heart festivals—and tries to draw attention to the many social causes it undertakes. One such cause is the founders' opposition to the bovine growth hormone (a substance injected into cows to increase milk production), which they fear will drive small dairy farmers out of business. A venture targeted directly to Burlington residents is the Giraffe Project, which recognizes people who have been willing to stick their own necks out and stand tall for what they believe. Local residents and customers of Ben & Jerry's scoop shops nominate the recipients of these Giraffe Commendations.

Auditing Social Performance

As a public corporation operating on a much-publicized socially responsible platform, Ben & Jerry's must answer to many stakeholders not only for its financial performance but also its conduct. Although a relatively small firm with fewer than one thousand employees, Ben & Jerry's was one of the first corporations to formally report on its performance with respect to its social responsibility vision and goals. The company began reporting its auditing results in 1999.

Ben & Jerry's most recent social audit examined the firm's performance in a number of significant areas, including employee, supplier, and consumer relations; workplace safety; franchise and international operations; the natural environment; and philanthropy. For example, in the area of "workplace and employees," Ben & Jerry's audit examined the firm's benefit programs for employees, including its "livable wage" policy, compensation ratios, relations with unions, and gender and racial equity. Another section of the report identified the firm's continuing efforts to improve workplace safety using measures such as lost-time days and accident rates. Ben & Jerry's has long taken a proactive position on environmental issues, so the social audit devoted considerable space to measures of environmental performance, such as use of water, discharge of wastewater, and overall energy conservation.

Ben & Jerry's social audit also reported on its philanthropic efforts, especially with regard to the Ben & Jerry's Foundation. The company donated $1.2 million to its foundation to support various social causes related to children and families, environmental restoration, sustainable agriculture, and peace. The report also identified numerous organizations and programs supported by the foundation's donations, such as the Vermont Dairy Farm Sustainability Project and Grounds for Health, Inc. in the United States and The Children's Society, ChildLine, and the National Missing Person's Helpline in the United Kingdom.

Long-Term Goals Versus Cost Efficiency

David Korten, a former Harvard Business School professor with years of experience in international development and citizen action, has argued that long-term-oriented, socially responsible companies often face challenges in today's fast-paced, often short-sighted, and profit-minded economic system. According to his perspective, the economic system focuses on the current value of a company's stock, rewarding cost efficiency and punishing inefficiency. Thus, firms that can outsource or otherwise shift their costs to other parties are rewarded, whereas socially responsible organizations are often considered inefficient and wasteful. Consequently, the stock price of such firms suffers, and they may be labeled as "in trouble." According to Korten,

> With financial markets demanding maximum short-term gains and corporate raiders standing by to trash any company that isn't externalizing every possible cost, efforts to fix the problem by raising the social consciousness of managers misdefine the problem. There are plenty of socially conscious managers. The problem is a predatory system that makes it difficult for them to survive. . . . They must either compromise their vision or run a great risk of being expelled by the system. . . . Corporate managers live and work in a system that is virtually feeding on the socially responsible.[2]

Ben & Jerry's has certainly faced its share of difficulties while striving to live up to the ideals established by its founders. One of the firm's biggest challenges occurred when the company was acquired by Unilever, an Anglo-Dutch conglomerate, in April 2000 for $326 million. Under the terms of the sale, Ben & Jerry's retained its independent board of directors so it could provide leadership for the company's social mission and brand integrity. The transaction also rewarded shareholders for their investments; protected Ben & Jerry's employees; maintained agreements to purchase from local, socially minded suppliers; and continued to encourage and fund the firm's social mission. The agreement also provided an opportunity for Ben & Jerry's to contribute to Unilever's social practices worldwide. Both co-founders of the company were to continue to be involved.

In November 2000, Yves Couette was named the new CEO of Ben & Jerry's. One of Unilever's leading ice cream professionals, Couette had worked in the United States, Mexico, Indonesia, and the United Kingdom. Vowing to build on Ben & Jerry's achievements, he said, "I am determined to deliver on Ben & Jerry's social mission commitment." However, Ben Cohen expressed dissatisfaction not only with Unilever's choice of Couette but also that a co-CEO had not been named. Threatening to leave the company he cofounded, Cohen declared, "The only way the social mission of Ben & Jerry's and the heart and soul of the company will be maintained is to have a CEO running the company who has a deep understanding of our values-led social business philosophy, who had experience with the company and with how that worked in practice." Cohen also expressed concern that a promised "social audit" of Unilever's operations had not been completed. He was also upset that Unilever would not allow the creation of a $5 million fund bearing Ben & Jerry's name to help new businesses with a social agenda get on their feet.

Unilever countered Cohen's claims by pointing out that Couette had the needed experience. While he was working in Mexico, Unilever had established an ice cream shop, run by a nonprofit organization, to support disabled children. Couette said, "Working in countries like Mexico and Indonesia, I have seen first hand the glaring social problems people face everyday. This has strengthened my belief that business has an important role to play in achieving social progress." Unilever also offered a list of the company's social objectives for 2001, which included helping to build playgrounds and launching a new flavor tied to that effort; lobbying to extend the life of the Northeast Interstate Dairy Compact, which provides more income for farmers; and developing more environmentally friendly packaging.

---

[2] David C. Korten, When Corporations Rule the World (West Hartford, Conn.: Kumarian Press, 1995), pp. 212–214.

As for Cohen's concern about the $5 million fund not carrying the Ben & Jerry name, a Unilever spokesman replied that Unilever wants to protect the Ben & Jerry's brand name and so the fund could be called "Ben's Venture Capital Fund" but not "Ben & Jerry's Venture Capital Fund." The spokesman said, "We understand that Ben's very concerned. He's a founder of the company. He has a huge emotional stake in the company. Our view is, judge us by our actions."

James Heard, who audited Ben & Jerry's social report, also sounded a note of cautious optimism: "There is definitely an irony to a counterculture company such as Ben & Jerry's being acquired by a global behemoth such as Unilever, and many members of the Ben & Jerry's family are acutely aware of the irony. But fears that Ben & Jerry's would abandon its commitment to caring capitalism have so far proved unfounded."

Questions

1. Discuss how the corporate culture at Ben & Jerry's, as described in this case, influences the daily implementation of ethical decisions at the firm.

2. Visit Ben & Jerry's Web site (www.benjerry.com) and find its most recent social audit. Compare the areas covered in this audit to the audit process described in Chapter 9 of your text. In what other ways could Ben & Jerry's demonstrate to stakeholders its commitment to ethical and socially responsible conduct?

3. Like Ben & Jerry's, many small businesses were founded and grew successful on a platform of ethics and social responsibility. However, more than a few of these companies became so successful that they were acquired by larger firms that may or may not respect the principles and values on which they were founded. How can such companies protect their core values as they grow from small firms into large ones and/or are acquired by multinational conglomerates?

Sources: These facts are from Mark Albright, "At Ben & Jerry's, Social Agenda Churns with Ice Cream," *St. Petersburg Times,* Nov. 11, 1995, p. 1E; "Ben & Jerry's 2001 Social Audit," Ben & Jerry's Homemade, May 2002, www.benjerry.com/our_company/about_us/social_mission/social_audits/2001/letter01.cfm; "Ben & Jerry's & Unilever to Join Forces," Ben & Jerry's Homemade, April 12, 2000, http://lib.benjerry. com/pressrel/join-forces.html; "Ben & Jerry's Announces Environmentally-Friendly Packaging Innovation," Ben & Jerry's Homemade, Feb. 22, 1999, http://lib.benjerry.com/pressrel/unbleached.html; "Ben & Jerry's Appoints Yves Couette as Chief Executive Officer," Ben & Jerry's Homemade, Nov. 20, 2000, http://lib.benjerry.com/pressrel/press1120.html; "Clif Bar Forms Wind-Farm Partnership to Offset CO2 Footprint," GreenBiz.com, Mar. 26, 2003, www.greenbiz.com/news/news_third. cfm?NewsID =24244; Simon Goodley, "Ben & Jerry Frosty over Unilever Choice for Key Job," *Electronic Telegraph,* Dec. 4, 2000, www.telegraph.co.uk/; David Gram, "Ben Worried Ben & Jerry's Good Work Is Melting Away After Merger," *Register Citizen,* Dec. 1, 2000, www.zwire.com; David C. Korten, *When Corporations Rule the World* (West Hartford, Conn.: Kumarian Press, 1995), pp. 212–214; Erik Larson, "Forever Young," *Inc.,* July 1988: pp. 50–62; Maxine Lipner, "Ben & Jerry's: Sweet Ethics Evince Social Awareness," *Compass Readings* July 1991, pp. 22–30; Peter Newcomb, "Is Ben & Jerry's BST-free?" *Forbes,* Sept. 25, 1995, p. 98; Hanna Rosin, "The Evil Empire: The Scoop on Ben & Jerry's Crunchy Capitalism," *New Republic,* Sept. 11, 1995, p. 22; Andrew E. Serwer, "Ben & Jerry's Corporate Ogre," *Fortune,* July 10, 1995, p. 30; "TimeLine," Ben & Jerry's Homemade, www.benjerry.com/our_company/about_us/our_history/timeline/index.cfm (accessed Apr. 18, 2003); Blair S. Walker, "Good-Humored Activist Back to the Fray," *USA Today,* Dec. 8, 1992, pp. 1B, 213; and Eric J. Wieffering, "Trouble in Camelot," *Business Ethics* 5 (Jan.-Feb. 1991): 16–19.

Reasoning Critically

CHAPTER 3

John Chaffee

Reasoning is the type of thinking that uses arguments — reasons in support of conclusions — to decide, explain, predict, and persuade. Effective reasoning involves using all of the intellectual skills and critical attitudes we have been developing in this book, and in this chapter we will further explore various dimensions of the reasoning process.

Inductive Reasoning

In this chapter we will examine *inductive reasoning*, an argument form in which one reasons from premises that are known or assumed to be true to a conclusion that is supported by the premises but does not follow logically from them.

> **inductive reasoning** *An argument form in which one reasons from premises that are known or assumed to be true to a conclusion that is supported by the premises but does not necessarily follow from them*

When you reason inductively, your premises provide evidence that makes it more or less probable (but not certain) that the conclusion is true. The following statements are examples of conclusions reached through inductive reasoning.

1. A recent Gallup poll reported that 74 percent of the American public believes that abortion should remain legalized.

2. On the average, a person with a college degree will earn over $1,140,000 more in his or her lifetime than a person with just a high school diploma.

3. In a recent survey twice as many doctors interviewed stated that if they were stranded on a desert island, they would prefer Bayer Aspirin to Extra Strength Tylenol.

4. The outbreak of food poisoning at the end-of-year school party was probably caused by the squid salad.

5. The devastating disease AIDS is caused by a particularly complex virus that may not be curable.

6. The solar system is probably the result of an enormous explosion — a "big bang" — that occurred billions of years ago.

The first three statements are forms of inductive reasoning known as *empirical generalization*, a general statement about an entire group made on the basis of observing some members of the group. The final three statements are examples of *causal reasoning*, a form of inductive reasoning in which it is claimed that an event (or events) is the result of the occurrence of another event (or events). We will be exploring the ways each of these forms of inductive reasoning functions in our lives and in various fields of study.

In addition to examining various ways of reasoning logically and effectively, we will also explore certain forms of reasoning that are not logical and, as a result, are usually not effective. These ways of pseudo-reasoning (false reasoning) are often termed *fallacies:* arguments that are not sound because of various errors in reasoning. Fallacious reasoning is typically used to influence others. It seeks to persuade not on the basis of sound arguments and critical thinking but rather on the basis of emotional and illogical factors.

> ***fallacies*** *Unsound arguments that are often persuasive and appearing to be logical because they usually appeal to our emotions and prejudices, and because they often support conclusions that we want to believe are accurate*

Empirical Generalization

One of the most important tools used by both natural and social scientists is empirical generalization. Have you ever wondered how the major television and radio networks can accurately predict election results hours before the polls close? These predictions are made possible by the power of *empirical generalization*, a first major type of inductive reasoning that is defined as reasoning from a limited sample to a general conclusion based on this sample.

> ***empirical generalization*** *A form of inductive reasoning in which a general statement is made about an entire group (the "target population") based on observing some members of the group (the "sample population")*

Network election predictions, as well as public opinion polls that occur throughout a political campaign, are based on interviews with a select number of people. Ideally, pollsters would interview everyone in the *target population* (in this case, voters), but this, of course, is hardly practical. Instead, they select a relatively small group of individuals from the target population, known as a *sample*, who they have determined will adequately represent the group as a whole. Pollsters believe that they can then generalize the opinions of this smaller group to the target population. And with a few notable exceptions (such as in the 1948 presidential election, when New York governor Thomas Dewey went to bed believing he had been elected president and woke up a loser to Harry Truman, and the 2000 election, when Al Gore was briefly declared the presidential winner over George W. Bush), these results are highly accurate.

There are three key criteria for evaluating inductive arguments:

▶ Is the sample known?

▶ Is the sample sufficient?

▶ Is the sample representative?

Is the Sample Known?

An inductive argument is only as strong as the sample on which it is based. For example, sample populations described in vague and unclear terms — "highly placed sources" or "many young people interviewed," for example — provide a treacherously weak foundation for generalizing to larger populations. In order for an inductive argument to be persuasive, the sample population should be explicitly *known* and clearly identified. Natural and social scientists take great care in selecting the members in the sample groups, and this is an important part of the data that is available to outside investigators who may wish to evaluate and verify the results.

Is the Sample Sufficient?

The second criterion for evaluating inductive reasoning is to consider the *size* of the sample. It should be sufficiently large enough to give an accurate sense of the group as a whole. In the polling example discussed earlier, we would be concerned if only a few registered voters had been interviewed, and the results of these interviews were then generalized to a much larger population. Overall, the larger the sample, the more reliable the inductive conclusions. Natural and social scientists have developed precise guidelines for determining the size of the sample needed to achieve reliable results. For example, poll results are often accompanied by a qualification such as "These results are subject to an error factor of ± 3 percentage points." This means that if the sample reveals that 47 percent of those interviewed prefer candidate X, then we can reliably state that 44 to 50 percent of the target population prefer candidate X. Because a sample is usually a small portion of the target population, we can rarely state that the two match each other exactly — there must always be some room for variation. The exceptions to this are situations in which the target population is completely homogeneous. For example, tasting one cookie from a bag of cookies is usually enough to tell us whether or not the entire bag is stale.

Is the Sample Representative?

The third crucial element in effective inductive reasoning is the *representativeness* of the sample. If we are to generalize with confidence from the sample to the target population, then we have to be sure the sample is similar to the larger group from which it is drawn in all relevant aspects. For instance, in the polling example the sample population should reflect the same percentage of men and women, of Democrats and Republicans, of young and old, and so on, as the target population. It is obvious that many characteristics, such as hair color, favorite food, and shoe size, are not relevant to the comparison. The better the sample reflects the target population in terms of *relevant* qualities, the better the accuracy of the generalizations. However, when the sample is *not* representative of the target population — for example, if the election pollsters interviewed only females between the ages of thirty and thirty-five — then the sample is termed *biased*, and any generalizations about the target population will be highly suspect.

How do we ensure that the sample is representative of the target population? One important device is *random selection*, a selection strategy in which every member of the target population has an equal chance of being included in the sample.

For example, the various techniques used to select winning lottery tickets are supposed to be random — each ticket is supposed to have an equal chance of winning. In complex cases of inductive reasoning — such as polling — random selection is often combined with the confirmation that all of the important categories in the population are adequately represented. For example, an election pollster would want to be certain that all significant geographical areas are included and then would randomly select individuals from within those areas to compose the sample.

Understanding the principles of empirical generalization is of crucial importance to effective thinking because we are continually challenged to construct and evaluate this form of inductive argument in our lives.

Thinking Activity 3.1
Evaluating Inductive Arguments

Review the following examples of inductive arguments. For each argument, evaluate the quality of the thinking by answering the following questions:

1.   Is the sample known?

2.   Is the sample sufficient?

3.   Is the sample representative?

4.   Do you believe the conclusions are likely to be accurate? Why or why not?

Link Between Pornography and Antisocial Behavior?   In a study of a possible relationship between pornography and antisocial behavior, questionnaires went out to 7,500 psychiatrists and psychoanalysts whose listing in the directory of the American Psychological Association indicated clinical experience. Over 3,400 of these professionals responded. The result: 7.4 percent of the psychiatrists and psychologists had cases in which they were convinced that pornography was a causal factor in antisocial behavior; an additional 9.4 percent were suspicious; 3.2 percent did not commit themselves; and 80 percent said they had no cases in which a causal connection was suspected.

To Sleep, Perchance to Die?   A survey by the Sleep Disorder Clinic of the VA hospital in La Jolla, California (involving more than one million people), revealed that people who sleep more than ten hours a night have a death rate 80 percent higher than those who sleep only seven or eight hours. Men who sleep less than four hours a night have a death rate 180 percent higher, and women with less [than four hours] sleep have a rate 40 percent higher. This might be taken as indicating that too much or too little sleep causes death.

"U.S. Wastes Food Worth Millions"   Americans in the economic middle waste more food than their rich and poor counterparts, according to a study published Saturday. Carried out in Tucson, Arizona, by University of Arizona students under the direction of Dr. William L. Rathje, the study analyzed 600 bags of garbage each week for three years from lower-, middle-, and upper-income neighborhoods. They found that city residents throw out around 10 percent of the food they took home — about 9,500 tons of food each year. The figure amounts to $9 to $11 million worth of food. Most of the waste occurred in middle-class neighborhoods. Both the poor and the wealthy were significantly more frugal.

One in Four British Couples Regret Marriage   One in four British married couples regret the day they tied the knot, a national poll conducted for *Reader's Digest* magazine showed. Middle-aged couples were five times more likely to dream of having a dog rather than fantasize about having an affair. Forty-four percent of women surveyed admitted having a secret they would never tell their husband, against 39 percent of men. Some 22 percent of men under 45 wanted their wives to be more affectionate, and 40 percent wanted to spend more time with their wives. "Men want to talk more — we'd always thought it was women," the editor-in-chief of *Reader's Digest* said. "The state of marriage in Britain in 2002 is puzzling and contradictory," he added.

Young People's Moral Compass   A recent survey of 5,012 students from fourth grade through high school yields important insights about how young people make moral decisions. Asked how they would decide what to do if "unsure of what was right or wrong in a particular situation," these were the responses and how they were described by the researchers:

▶ 23 percent said they would "do what was best for everyone involved," an orientation the researchers labeled "civic humanist."

▶ 20 percent would "follow the advice of an authority, such as a parent, teacher, or youth leader" — "conventionalist."

▶ 18 percent of respondents said they would do what would make them "happy" — "expressivist."

▶ 16 percent would "do what God or Scriptures" say "is right" — "theistic."

▶ 10 percent would "do what would improve their own situations" — "utilitarian."

▶ 9 percent did not know, and 3 percent wrote that they would follow their "conscience."

When young people were asked their beliefs about anything from lying, stealing, and using drugs to abortion or reasons for choosing a job, these rudimentary ethical systems or "moral compasses" turned out to be more important than the background factors that social scientists habitually favor in their search for explanations, like economic status, sex, race, and even religious practice.

Thinking Activity 3.2
Designing a Poll

Select an issue that you would like to poll a group of people about — for example, the population of your school or your neighborhood. Describe in specific terms how you would go about constructing a sample both large and representative enough for you to generalize the results to the target population accurately.

Fallacies of False Generalization

Although generalizing and interpreting are useful in forming concepts, they also can give rise to fallacious ways of thinking, including the following:

▶ Hasty generalization

▶ Sweeping generalization

▶ False dilemma

Hasty Generalization

Consider the following examples of reasoning. Do you think that the arguments are sound? Why or why not?

> My boyfriends have never shown any real concern for my feelings. My conclusion is that men are insensitive, selfish, and emotionally superficial.

> My mother always gets upset over insignificant things. This leads me to believe that women are very emotional.

In both of these cases, a general conclusion has been reached that is based on a very small sample. As a result, the reasons provide very weak support for the conclusions that are being developed. It just does not make good sense to generalize from a few individuals to all men or all women. The conclusions are *hasty* because the samples are not large enough and/or not representative enough to provide adequate justification for the generalization.

Of course, many generalizations are more warranted than the two given here because the conclusion is based on a sample that is larger and more representative of the group as a whole. For example:

> I have done a lot of research in a variety of automotive publications on the relationship between the size of cars and the gas mileage they get. In general, I think it makes sense to conclude that large cars tend to get fewer miles per gallon than smaller cars.

In this case, the conclusion is generalized from a larger and more representative sample than those in the preceding two arguments. As a result, the reason for the last argument provides much stronger support for the conclusion.

Sweeping Generalization

Whereas the fallacy of hasty generalization deals with errors in the process of generalizing, the fallacy of *sweeping generalization* focuses on difficulties in the process of interpreting. Consider the following examples of reasoning. Do you think that the arguments are sound? Why or why not?

> Vigorous exercise contributes to overall good health. Therefore, vigorous exercise should be practiced by recent heart attack victims, people who are out of shape, and women who are about to give birth.

> People should be allowed to make their own decisions, providing that their actions do not harm other people. Therefore, people who are trying to commit suicide should be left alone to do what they want.

In both of these cases, generalizations that are true in most cases have been deliberately applied to instances that are clearly intended to be exceptions to the generalizations because of special features that the exceptions possess. Of course, the use of sweeping generalizations stimulates us to clarify the generalization, rephrasing it to exclude instances, like those given here, that have special features. For example, the first generalization could be reformulated as "Vigorous exercise contributes to overall good health, *except for* recent heart attack victims, people out of shape, and women who are about to give birth." Sweeping generalizations become dangerous only when they are accepted without critical analysis and reformulation.

Review the following examples of sweeping generalizations, and in each case (a) explain *why* it is a sweeping generalization and (b) reformulate the statement so that it becomes a legitimate generalization.

1. A college education stimulates you to develop as a person and prepares you for many professions. Therefore, all persons should attend college, no matter what career they are interested in.

2. Drugs such as heroin and morphine are addictive and therefore qualify as dangerous drugs. This means that they should never be used, even as painkillers in medical situations.

3. Once criminals have served time for the crimes they have committed, they have paid their debt to society and should be permitted to work at any job they choose.

False Dilemma

The fallacy of the *false dilemma* — also known as the "either/or" fallacy or the "black-or-white" fallacy — occurs when we are asked to choose between two extreme alternatives without being able to consider additional options. For example, we may say, "Either you're for me or against me," meaning that a choice has to be made between these alternatives. Sometimes giving people only two choices on an issue makes sense ("If you decide to swim the English Channel, you'll either make it or you won't"). At other times, however, viewing situations in such extreme terms may be a serious oversimplification — for it would mean viewing a complicated situation in terms that are too simple.

The following statements are examples of false dilemmas. After analyzing the fallacy in each case, suggest different alternatives than those being presented.

> **Example:** *"Everyone in Germany is a National Socialist — the few outside the party are either lunatics or idiots." (Adolf Hitler, quoted by the* New York Times, *April 5, 1938)*

> **Analysis:** *This is an oversimplification. Hitler is saying that if you are not a Nazi, then you are a lunatic or an idiot. By limiting the population to these groups, Hitler was simply ignoring all the people who did not qualify as Nazis, lunatics, or idiots.*

1. America — love it or leave it!

2. She loves me; she loves me not.

3. Live free or die.

4. If you're not part of the solution, then you're part of the problem. (Eldridge Cleaver)

5. If you know about BMW, you either own one or you want to.

Causal Reasoning

A second major type of inductive reasoning is *causal reasoning*, a form in which an event (or events) is claimed to be the result of the occurrence of another event (or events).

> **causal reasoning** *A form of inductive reasoning in which an event (or events) is claimed to be the result of another event (or events)*

As you use your thinking abilities to try to understand the world you live in, you often ask the question "Why did that happen?" For example, if the engine of your car is running roughly, your natural question is "What's wrong?" If you wake up one morning with an upset stomach, you usually ask yourself, "What's the cause?" Or maybe the softball team you belong to has been losing recently. You typically wonder, "What's going on?" In each of these cases you assume that there is some factor (or factors) responsible for what is occurring, some *cause* (or causes) that results in the *effect* (or effects) you are observing (the rough engine, the upset stomach, the losing team).

Causality is one of the basic patterns of thinking we use to organize and make sense of our experience. For instance, imagine how bewildered you would feel if a mechanic looked at your car and told you there was no explanation for the poorly running engine. Or suppose you go to the doctor with an upset stomach, he examines you and then concludes that there is no possible causal explanation for the malady. In each case you would be understandably skeptical of the diagnosis and would probably seek another opinion.

Misidentification of the Cause

In causal situations we are not always certain about what is causing what — in other words, what is the cause and what is the effect. *Misidentifying the cause* is easy to do. For example, which are the causes and which are the effects in the following pairs of items? Why?

▶ Poverty and alcoholism

▶ Headaches and tension

▶ Failure in school and personal problems

▶ Shyness and lack of confidence

▶ Drug dependency and emotional difficulties

Of course, sometimes a third factor is responsible for both of the effects we are examining. For example, the headaches and tension we are experiencing may both be the result of a third element — such as some new medication we are taking. When this occurs, we are said to commit the fallacy of *ignoring a common cause*. There also exists the fallacy of *assuming a common cause* — for example, assuming that both a sore toe and an earache stem from the same cause.

Post Hoc Ergo Propter Hoc

The translation of the Latin phrase *post hoc ergo propter hoc* is "After it, therefore because of it." It refers to those situations in which, because two things occur close together in time, we assume that one caused the other. For example, if your team wins the game each time you wear your favorite shirt, you might be tempted to conclude that the one event (wearing your favorite shirt) has some influence on the other event (winning the game). As a result, you might continue to wear this shirt "for good luck." It is easy to see how this sort of mistaken thinking can lead to all sorts of superstitious beliefs.

Consider the causal conclusion arrived at by Mark Twain's fictional character Huckleberry Finn in the following passage. How would you analyze the conclusion that he comes to?

> I've always reckoned that looking at the new moon over your left shoulder is one of the carelessest and foolishest things a body can do. Old Hank Bunker done it once, and bragged about it; and in less than two years he got drunk and fell off a shot tower and spread himself out so that he was just a kind of layer. . . . But anyway, it all come of looking at the moon that way, like a fool.

Can you identify any of your own superstitious beliefs or practices that might have been the result of *post hoc* thinking?

Slippery Slope

The causal fallacy of *slippery slope* is illustrated in the following advice:

> Don't miss that first deadline, because if you do, it won't be long before you're missing all your deadlines. This will spread to the rest of your life, as you will be late for every appointment. This terminal procrastination will ruin your career, and friends and relatives will abandon you. You will end up a lonely failure who is unable to ever do anything on time.

Slippery slope thinking asserts that one undesirable action will inevitably lead to a worse action, which will necessarily lead to a worse one still, all the way down the "slippery slope" to some terrible disaster at the bottom. Although this progression may indeed happen, there is certainly no causal guarantee that it will. Create slippery slope scenarios for one of the following warnings:

▶ If you get behind on one credit card payment . . .

▶ If you fail that first test . . .

▶ If you eat that first fudge square . . .

Review the causal fallacies just described and then identify and explain the reasoning pitfalls illustrated in the following examples:

▶ The person who won the lottery says that she dreamed the winning numbers. I'm going to start writing down the numbers in my dreams.

▶ Yesterday I forgot to take my vitamins, and I immediately got sick. That mistake won't happen again!

▶ I'm warning you — if you start missing classes, it won't be long before you flunk out of school and ruin your future.

▶ I always take the first seat in the bus. Today I took another seat, and the bus broke down. And you accuse me of being superstitious!

▶ I think the reason I'm not doing well in school is that I'm just not interested. Also, I simply don't have enough time to study.

Many people want us to see the cause and effect relationships that they believe exist, and they often utilize questionable or outright fallacious reasoning. Consider the following examples:

VISUAL THINKING

Slipping and Sliding

▶ The fallacy of slippery slope suggests that one undesirable action will inevitably lead to others, taking you down the "slippery slope" to some unavoidable terrible disaster at the bottom. Can you think of an example in which you have used this kind of thinking ("If you continue to _____, then things will get progressively worse until you ultimately find yourself _____")? What are some strategies for clarifying this sort of fallacious thinking?

▶ Politicians assure us that a vote for them will result in "a chicken in every pot and a car in every garage."

▶ Advertisers tell us that using this detergent will leave our wash "cleaner than clean, whiter than white."

▶ Doctors tell us that eating a balanced diet will result in better health.

▶ Educators tell us that a college degree is worth an average of $1,140,000 additional income over an individual's life.

▶ Scientists inform us that nuclear energy will result in a better life for all.

In an effort to persuade us to adopt a certain point of view, each of these examples makes certain causal claims about how the world operates. As critical thinkers, it is our duty to evaluate these various causal claims in an effort to figure out whether they are sensible ways of organizing the world.

Explain how you might go about evaluating whether each of the following causal claims makes sense:

Example: Taking the right vitamins will improve health.

Evaluation: Review the medical research that examines the effect of taking vitamins on health; speak to a nutritionist; speak to a doctor.

▶ Sweet Smell deodorant will keep you drier all day long.

▶ Allure perfume will cause people to be attracted to you.

▶ Natural childbirth will result in a more fulfilling birth experience.

▶ Aspirin Plus will give you faster, longer-lasting relief from headaches.

▶ Listening to loud music will damage your hearing.

Fallacies of Relevance

Many fallacious arguments appeal for support to factors that have little or nothing to do with the argument being offered. In these cases, false appeals substitute for sound reasoning and a critical examination of the issues. Such appeals, known as *fallacies of relevance*, include the following kinds of fallacious thinking, which are grouped by similarity into "fallacy families":

▶ Appeal to authority

▶ Appeal to tradition

▶ Bandwagon

▶ Appeal to pity

▶ Appeal to fear

▶ Appeal to flattery

▶ Special pleading

▶ Appeal to ignorance

▶ Begging the question

▶ Straw man

▶ Red herring

▶ Appeal to personal attack

▶ Two wrongs make a right

Appeal to Authority

Authorities must have legitimate expertise in the area in which they are advising — like an experienced mechanic diagnosing a problem with your car. People, however, often appeal to authorities who are not qualified to give an expert opinion. Consider the reasoning in the following advertisements. Do you think the arguments are sound? Why or why not?

> Hi. You've probably seen me out on the football field. After a hard day's work crushing halfbacks and sacking quarterbacks, I like to settle down with a cold, smooth Maltz beer.

> SONY. Ask anyone.

> Over 11 million women will read this ad. Only 16 will own the coat.

Each of these arguments is intended to persuade us of the value of a product through appeal to various authorities. In the first case, the authority is a well-known sports figure; in the second, the authority is large numbers of people; and in the third, the authority is a select few, appealing to our desire to be exclusive ("snob appeal"). Unfortunately, none of these authorities offer legitimate expertise about the product. Football players are not beer experts; large numbers of people are often misled; exclusive groups of people are frequently mistaken in their beliefs. To evaluate authorities properly, we have to ask:

▶ What are the professional credentials on which the authorities' expertise is based?

▶ Is their expertise in the area they are commenting on?

Appeal to Tradition

A member of the same fallacy family as appeal to authority, *appeal to tradition* argues that a practice or way of thinking is "better" or "right" simply because it is older, it is traditional, or it has "always been done that way." Although traditional beliefs often express some truth or wisdom — for example, "Good nutrition, exercise, and regular medical check-ups are the foundation of good health" — traditional beliefs are often misguided or outright false. Consider, for example, the belief that "intentional bleeding is a source of good health because it lets loose evil vapors in the body" or traditional practices like Victorian rib-crushing corsets or Chinese footbinding. How do we tell which traditional beliefs or practices have merit? We need to think critically, evaluating the value based on informed reasons and compelling evidence. Critically evaluate the following traditional beliefs:

▶ Spare the rod and spoil the child.

▶ Children should be seen and not heard.

▶ Never take "no" for an answer.

▶ I was always taught that a woman's place was in the home, so pursuing a career is out of the question for me.

▶ Real men don't cry — that's the way I was brought up.

Bandwagon

Joining the illogical appeals to authority and tradition, the fallacy *bandwagon* relies on the uncritical acceptance of others' opinions, in this case because "everyone believes it." People experience this all the time through "peer pressure," when an unpopular view is squelched and modified by the group opinion. For example, you may change your opinion when confronted with the threat of ridicule or rejection from your friends. Or you may modify your point of view at work or in your religious organization in order to conform to the prevailing opinion. In all of these cases your views are being influenced by a desire to "jump on the bandwagon" and avoid getting left by yourself on the side of the road. The bandwagon mentality also extends to media appeals based on views of select groups such as celebrities or public opinion polls. Again, critical thinking is the tool that you have to distinguish an informed belief from a popular but uninformed belief. Critically evaluate the following bandwagon appeals:

▶ I used to think that _____ was my favorite kind of music. But my friends convinced me that only losers enjoy this music. So I've stopped listening to it.

▶ Hollywood celebrities and supermodels agree: Tattoos in unusual places are very cool. That's good enough for me!

▶ In the latest Gallup poll 86 percent of those polled believe that economic recovery will happen in the next six months, so I must be wrong.

Appeal to Pity

Consider the reasoning in the following arguments. Do you think that the arguments are sound? Why or why not?

> I know that I haven't completed my term paper, but I really think that I should be excused. This has been a very difficult semester for me. I caught every kind of flu that came around. In addition, my brother has a drinking problem, and this has been very upsetting to me. Also, my dog died

I admit that my client embezzled money from the company, your honor. However, I would like to bring several facts to your attention. He is a family man, with a wonderful wife and two terrific children. He is an important member of the community. He is active in the church, coaches a little league baseball team, and has worked very hard to be a good person who cares about people. I think that you should take these things into consideration in handing down your sentence.

In each of these *appeal to pity* arguments, the reasons offered to support the conclusions may indeed be true. They are not, however, relevant to the conclusion. Instead of providing evidence that supports the conclusion, the reasons are designed to make us feel sorry for the person involved and therefore agree with the conclusion out of sympathy. Although these appeals are often effective, the arguments are not sound. The probability of a conclusion can be established only by reasons that support and are relevant to the conclusion.

Of course, not every appeal to pity is fallacious. There *are* instances in which pity may be deserved, relevant, and decisive. For example, if you are soliciting a charitable donation, or asking a friend for a favor, an honest and straightforward appeal to pity may be appropriate.

Appeal to Fear

Consider the reasoning in the following arguments. Do you think that the arguments are sound? Why or why not?

I'm afraid I don't think you deserve a raise. After all, there are many people who would be happy to have your job at the salary you are currently receiving. I would be happy to interview some of these people if you really think that you are underpaid.

If you continue to disagree with my interpretation of *The Catcher in the Rye*, I'm afraid you won't get a very good grade on your term paper.

In both of these arguments, the conclusions being suggested are supported by an *appeal to fear*, not by reasons that provide evidence for the conclusions. In the first case, the threat is that if you do not forgo your salary demands, your job may be in jeopardy. In the second case, the threat is that if you do not agree with the teacher's interpretation, you will fail the course. In neither instance are the real issues — Is a salary increase deserved? Is the student's interpretation legitimate? — being discussed. People who appeal to fear to support their conclusions are interested only in prevailing, regardless of which position might be more justified.

Appeal to Flattery

Flattery joins the emotions of pity and fear as a popular source of fallacious reasoning. This kind of "apple polishing" is designed to influence the thinking of others by appealing to their vanity as a substitute for providing relevant evidence to support your point of view. Of course, flattery is often a harmless lubricant for social relationships, and it can also be used in conjunction with compelling reasoning. But *appeal to flattery* enters the territory of fallacy when it is the main or sole support of your claim, such as "This is absolutely the best course I've ever taken. And I'm really hoping for an A to serve as an emblem of your excellent teaching." Think critically about the following examples:

▶ You have a great sense of humor, boss, and I'm particularly fond of your racial and homosexual jokes. They crack me up! And while we're talking, I'd like to remind you how much I'm hoping for the opportunity to work with you if I receive the promotion that you're planning to give to one of us.

▶ You are a beautiful human being, inside and out. Why don't you stay the night?

▶ You are *so* smart. I wish I had a brain like yours. Can you give me any hints about the chemistry test you took today? I'm taking it tomorrow.

Special Pleading

This fallacy occurs when someone makes themselves a special exception, *without sound justification,* to the reasonable application of standards, principles, or expectations. For example, consider the following exchange:

> "Hey, hon, could you get me a beer? I'm pooped from work today."
> "Well, I'm exhausted from working all day, too! Why don't you get it yourself?"
> "I need you to get it because I'm really thirsty."

We view the world through our own lenses, and these lenses tend to see the world as tilted toward our interests. That's why *special pleading* is such a popular fallacy: We're used to treating our circumstances as unique and deserving of special consideration when compared to the circumstances of others. Of course, other people tend to see things from a very different perspective. Critically evaluate the following examples.

▶ I know that the deadline for the paper was announced several weeks ago and that you made clear there would be no exceptions, but I'm asking you to make an exception because I experienced some very bad breaks.

▶ I really don't like it when you check out other men and comment on their physiques. I know that I do that toward other women, but it's a "guy thing."

▶ Yes, I would like to play basketball with you guys, but I want to warn you: As a woman, I don't like getting bumped around, so keep your distance.

▶ I probably shouldn't have used funds from the treasury for my own personal use, but after all I *am* the president of the organization.

Appeal to Ignorance

Consider the reasoning in the following arguments. Do you think that the arguments are sound? Why or why not?

> You say that you don't believe in God. But can you prove that He doesn't exist? If not, then you have to accept the conclusion that He does in fact exist.

> Greco Tires are the best. No others have been proved better.

> With me, abortion is not a problem of religion. It's a problem of the Constitution. I believe that until and unless someone can establish that the unborn child is not a living human being, then that child is already protected by the Constitution, which guarantees life, liberty, and the pursuit of happiness to all of us.

When the *appeal to ignorance* argument form is used, the person offering the conclusion is asking his or her opponent to *disprove* the conclusion. If the opponent is unable to do so, then the conclusion is asserted to be true. This argument form is not valid because it is the job of the person proposing the argument to prove the

VISUAL THINKING

Fallacies in Action

▶ **What fallacies do you think are being put forward by the two debaters in this illustration? How persuasive have you found those techniques to be in your own life, from your perspectives as both a speaker and a listener?**

conclusion. Simply because an opponent cannot *disprove* the conclusion offers no evidence that the conclusion is in fact justified. In the first example, for instance, the fact that someone cannot prove that God does not exist provides no persuasive reason for believing that He does.

Begging the Question

This fallacy is also known as circular reasoning because the premises of the argument assume or include the claim that the conclusion is true. For example:

"How do I know that I can trust you?"

"Just ask Adrian; she'll tell you."

"How do I know that I can trust Adrian?"

"Don't worry; I'll vouch for her."

Begging the question is often found in self-contained systems of belief, such as politics or religion. For example:

"My religion worships the one true God."

"How can you be so sure?"

"Because our Holy Book says so."

"Why should I believe this Holy Book?"

"Because it was written by the one true God."

In other words, the problem with this sort of reasoning is that instead of providing relevant evidence in support of a conclusion, it simply "goes in a circle" by assuming the truth of what it is supposedly proving. Critically evaluate the following examples:

▶ Smoking marijuana has got to be illegal. Otherwise, it wouldn't be against the law.

▶ Of course, I'm telling you the truth. Otherwise, I'd be lying.

Straw Man

This fallacy is best understood by visualizing its name: You attack someone's point of view by creating an exaggerated *straw man* version of the position, and then you knock down the straw man you just created. For example, consider the following exchange:

"I'm opposed to the missile defense shield because I think it's a waste of money."

"So you want to undermine the security of our nation and leave the country defenseless. Are you serious?"

The best way to combat this fallacy is to point out that the straw man does not reflect an accurate representation of your position. For instance:

"On the contrary, I'm very concerned about national security. The money that would be spent on a nearly useless defense shield can be used to combat terrorist threats, a much more credible threat than a missile attack. Take your straw man somewhere else!"

How would you respond to the following arguments?

▶ You're saying that the budget for our university has to be reduced by 15 percent to meet state guidelines. That means reducing the size of the faculty and student population by 15 percent, and that's crazy.

▶ "I think we should work at keeping the apartment clean; it's a mess."

"So you're suggesting that we discontinue our lives and become full-time maids so that we can live in a pristine, spotless, antiseptic apartment. That's no way to live!"

Red Herring

Also known as "smoke screen" and "wild goose chase," the *red herring* fallacy is committed by introducing an irrelevant topic in order to divert attention from the original issue being discussed. So, for example:

> I'm definitely in favor of the death penalty. After all, overpopulation is a big problem in our world today.

Although this is certainly a novel approach to addressing the problem of overpopulation, it's not really relevant to the issue of capital punishment. Critically evaluate the following examples:

▶ I think all references to sex should be eliminated from films and music. Premarital sex and out-of-wedlock childbirths are creating moral decay in our society.

▶ I really don't believe that grade inflation is a significant problem in higher education. Everybody wants to be liked, and teachers are just trying to get students to like them.

Appeal to Personal Attack

Consider the reasoning in the following arguments. Do you think that the arguments are valid? Why or why not?

> Your opinion on this issue is false. It's impossible to believe anything you say.

> How can you have an intelligent opinion about abortion? You're not a woman, so this is a decision that you'll never have to make.

Appeal to personal attack has been one of the most frequently used fallacies through the ages. Its effectiveness results from ignoring the issues of the argument and focusing instead on the personal qualities of the person making the argument. By trying to discredit the other person, this argument form tries to discredit the argument — no matter what reasons are offered. This fallacy is also referred to as the "*ad hominem*" argument, which means "to the man" rather than to the issue, and "*poisoning the well*," because we are trying to ensure that any water drawn from our opponent's well will be treated as undrinkable.

The effort to discredit can take two forms, as illustrated in the preceding examples. The fallacy can be *abusive* in the sense that we are directly attacking the credibility of our opponent (as in the first example). The fallacy can be *circumstantial* in the sense that we are claiming that the person's circumstances, not character, render his or her opinion so biased or uninformed that it cannot be treated seriously (as in the second example). Other examples of the circumstantial form of the fallacy would include disregarding the views on nuclear plant safety given by an owner of one of the plants or ignoring the views of a company comparing a product it manufactures with competing products.

Two Wrongs Make a Right

This fallacy attempts to justify a morally questionable action by arguing that it is a response to another wrong action, either real or imagined, in fact, that *two wrongs make a right*. For example, someone undercharged at a store might justify keeping the extra money by reasoning that "I've probably been overcharged many times in the past, and this simply equals things out." Or he or she might even speculate, "I am likely to be overcharged in the future, so I'm keeping this in anticipation of being cheated." This is a fallacious way of thinking because each action is independent and must be evaluated on its own merits. If you're overcharged and knowingly keep the money, that's stealing. If the store knowingly overcharges you, that's stealing as well. If the store inadvertently overcharges you, that's a mistake. Or as expressed in a common saying, "Two wrongs *don't* make a right." Critically evaluate the following examples:

▶ Terrorists are justified in killing innocent people because they and their people have been the victims of political repression and discriminatory policies.

▶ Capital punishment is wrong because killing murderers is just as bad as the killings they committed.

Thinking Activity 3.3
Identifying Fallacies

Locate (or develop) an example of each of the following kinds of false appeals. For each example, explain why you think that the appeal is not warranted.

1. Appeal to authority

2. Appeal to pity

3. Appeal to fear

4. Appeal to ignorance

5. Appeal to personal attack

The Critical Thinker's Guide to Reasoning

This book has provided you with the opportunity to explore and develop many of your critical thinking and reasoning abilities. As you have seen, these abilities are complex and difficult to master. The process of becoming an accomplished critical thinker and effective reasoner is a challenging quest that requires ongoing practice and reflection. This section will present a critical thinking/reasoning model that will help you pull together the important themes of this book into an integrated perspective. This model is illustrated on page 71. In order to become familiar with the model, you will be thinking through an important issue that confronts every human being: Are people capable of choosing freely?

What Is My Initial Point of View?

Reasoning always begins with a point of view. As a critical thinker, it is important for you to take thoughtful positions and express your views with confidence. Using this statement as a starting point, respond as specifically as you can:

▶ *I believe (or don't believe) that people can choose freely because . . .*

Here is a sample response:

I believe that people are capable of choosing freely because when I am faced with choosing among a number of possibilities, I really have the feeling that it is up to me to make the choice that I want to.

How Can I Define My Point of View More Clearly?

After you state your initial point of view, the next step is to define the issues more clearly and specifically. As you have seen, the language that we use has multiple levels of meaning, and it is often not clear precisely what meaning(s) people are expressing. To avoid misunderstandings and sharpen your own thinking, it is essential that you clarify the key concepts as early as possible. In this case the central concept is "choosing freely." Respond by beginning with the following statement:

▶ *From my point of view, the concept of "choosing freely" means . . .*

Here is a sample response:

> *From my point of view, the concept of "choosing freely" means that when you are faced with a number of alternatives, you are able to make your selection based solely on what you decide, not on force applied by other influences.*

What Is an Example of My Point of View?

Once your point of view is clarified, it's useful to provide an example that illustrates your meaning. The process of forming and defining concepts involves the process of generalizing (identifying general qualities) and the process of interpreting (locating specific examples). Respond to the issue we have been considering by beginning with the following statement:

▶ *An example of a free choice I made (or was unable to make) is . . .*

Here is a sample response:

> *An example of a free choice I made was deciding what area to major in. There are a number of career directions I could have chosen to go with, but I chose my major entirely on my own, without being forced by other influences.*

What Is the Origin of My Point of View?

To fully understand and critically evaluate your point of view, it's important to review its history. How did this point of view develop? Have you always held this view, or did it develop over time? This sort of analysis will help you understand how your perceiving lenses regarding this issue were formed. Respond to the issue of free choice by beginning with the following statement:

▶ *I formed my belief regarding free choice . . .*

Here is a sample response:

> *I formed my belief regarding free choice when I was in high school. I used to believe that everything happened because it had to, because it was determined. Then when I was in high school, I got involved with the "wrong crowd" and developed some bad habits. I stopped doing schoolwork and even stopped attending most classes. I was on the brink of failing when I suddenly came to my senses and said to myself, "This isn't what I want for my life." Through sheer willpower, I turned everything around. I changed my friends, improved my habits, and ultimately graduated with flying colors. From that time on I knew that I had the power of free choice and that it was up to me to make the right choices.*

What Are My Assumptions?

Assumptions are beliefs, often unstated, that underlie your point of view. Many disputes occur and remain unresolved because the people involved do not recognize or express their assumptions. For example, in the very emotional debate over abortion, when people who are opposed to abortion call their opponents "murderers," they are assuming the fetus, at *any* stage of development from the fertilized egg onward, is a "human life," since murder refers to the taking of a human life. When people in favor of abortion call their opponents "moral fascists," they are assuming that antiabortionists are merely interested in imposing their narrow moral views on others.

Thus, it's important for all parties to identify clearly the assumptions that form the foundation of their points of view. They may still end up disagreeing, but at least they will know what they are arguing about. Thinking about the issue that we have been exploring, respond by beginning with the following statement:

▶ *When I say that I believe (or don't believe) in free choice, I am assuming . . .*

Here is a sample response:

> *When I say that I believe in free choice, I am assuming that people are often presented with different alternatives to choose from, and I am also assuming that they are able to select freely any of these alternatives independent of any influences.*

What Are the Reasons, Evidence, and Arguments That Support My Point of View?

Everybody has opinions. What distinguishes informed opinions from uninformed opinions is the quality of the reasons, evidence, and arguments that support the opinions. Respond to the issue of free choice by beginning with the following statement:

▶ *There are a variety of reasons, evidence, and arguments that support my belief (or disbelief) in free choice. First . . . Second . . . Third . . .*

Here is a sample response:

> *There are a variety of reasons, evidence, and arguments that support my belief in free choice. First, I have a very strong and convincing personal intuition when I am making choices that my choices are free. Second, freedom is tied to responsibility. If people make free choices, then they are responsible for the consequences of their choices. Since we often hold people responsible, that means that we believe that their choices are free. Third, if people are not free, and all of their choices are determined by external forces, then life would have little purpose and there would be no point in trying to improve ourselves. But we do believe that life has purpose and we do try to improve ourselves, suggesting that we also believe that our choices are free.*

What Are Other Points of View on This Issue?

One of the hallmarks of critical thinkers is that they strive to view situations from perspectives other than their own, to "think empathically" within other viewpoints, particularly those of people who disagree with their own. If we stay entrenched in our own narrow ways of viewing the world, the development of our minds will be severely limited. This is the only way to achieve a deep and full understanding of life's complexities. In working to understand other points of view, we need to identify the reasons, evidence, and arguments that have brought people to these conclusions. Respond to the issue we have been analyzing by beginning with the following statement:

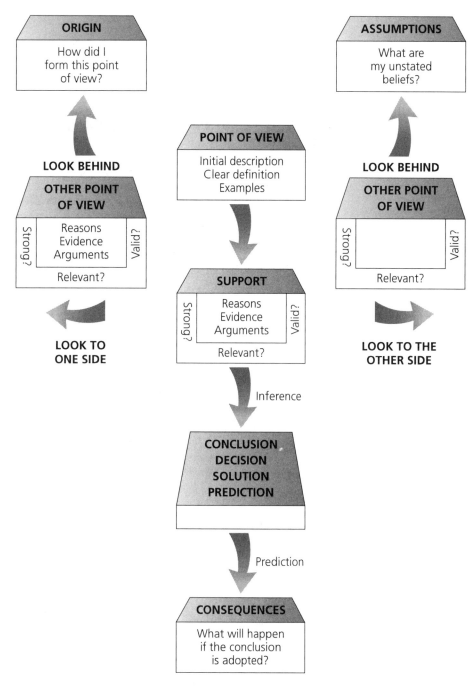

A modified version of a schema originally devised by Ralph H. Johnson; design and layout by J. A. Blair

▶ *A second point of view on this issue might be . . . A third point of view on this issue might be . . .*

Here is a sample response:

> *A second point of view on this issue might be that many of our choices are conditioned by experiences that we have had in ways that we are not even aware of. For example, you might choose a career because of someone you admire or because of the expectations of others, although you may be unaware of these influences on your decision. Or you might choose to date someone because he or she reminds you of someone from*

your past, although you believe you are making a totally free decision. A third point of view on this issue might be that our choices are influenced by people around us, although we may not be fully aware of it. For example, we may go along with a group decision of our friends, mistakenly thinking that we are making an independent choice.

What Is My Conclusion, Decision, Solution, or Prediction?

The ultimate purpose of reasoning is to reach an informed and successful conclusion, decision, solution, or prediction. With respect to the sample issue we have been considering — determining whether we can make free choices — the goal is to achieve a thoughtful conclusion. This is a complex process of analysis and synthesis in which we consider all points of view; evaluate the supporting reasons, evidence, and arguments; and then construct our most informed conclusion. Respond to our sample issue by using the following statement as a starting point:

▶ *After examining different points of view and critically evaluating the reasons, evidence, and arguments that support the various perspectives, my conclusion about free choice is . . .*

Here is a sample response:

> *After examining different points of view and critically evaluating the reasons, evidence, and arguments that support the various perspectives, my conclusion about free choice is that we are capable of making free choices but that our freedom is sometimes limited. For example, many of our actions are conditioned by our past experience, and we are often influenced by other people without being aware of it. In order to make free choices, we need to become aware of these influences and then decide what course of action we want to choose. As long as we are unaware of these influences, they can limit our ability to make free, independent choices.*

What Are the Consequences?

The final step in the reasoning process is to determine the *consequences* of our conclusion, decision, solution, or prediction. The consequences refer to what is likely to happen if our conclusion is adopted. Looking ahead in this fashion is helpful not simply for anticipating the future but also for evaluating the present. Identify the consequences of your conclusion regarding free choice by beginning with the following statement:

▶ *The consequences of believing (or disbelieving) in free choice are . . .*

Here is a sample response:

> *The consequences of believing in free choice are taking increasing personal responsibility and showing people how to increase their freedom. The first consequence is that if people are able to make free choices, then they are responsible for the results of their choices. They can't blame other people, bad luck, or events "beyond their control." They have to accept responsibility. The second consequence is that, although our freedom can be limited by influences of which we are unaware, we can increase our freedom by becoming aware of these influences and then deciding what we want to do. If people are not able to make free choices, then they are not responsible for what they do, nor are they able to increase their freedom. This could lead people to adopt an attitude of resignation and apathy.*

Thinking Activity 3.4
Applying the "Guide to Reasoning"

Identify an important issue in which you are interested, and apply **The Critical Thinker's Guide to Reasoning** to analyze it.

▶ What is my initial point of view?

▶ How can I define my point of view more clearly?

▶ What is an example of my point of view?

▶ What is the origin of my point of view?

▶ What are my assumptions?

▶ What are the reasons, evidence, and arguments that support my point of view?

▶ What are other points of view on this issue?

▶ What is my conclusion, decision, solution, or prediction?

▶ What are the consequences?

Case 3
Critical Thinking and Obedience to Authority

by John Sabini and Maury Silver

In his 1974 book, *Obedience to Authority,* Stanley Milgram reports experiments on destructive obedience. In these experiments the subjects are faced with a dramatic choice, one apparently involving extreme pain and perhaps injury to someone else. When the subject arrives at the laboratory, the experimenter tells him (or her) and another subject—a pleasant, avuncular, middle-aged gentleman (actually an actor)—that the study concerns the effects of punishment on learning. Through a rigged drawing, the lucky subject wins the role of teacher and the experimenter's confederate becomes the "learner."

In the next stage of the experiment, the teacher and learner are taken to an adjacent room; the learner is strapped into a chair and electrodes are attached to his arm. It appears impossible for the learner to escape. While strapped in the chair, the learner diffidently mentions that he has a heart condition. The experimenter replies that while the shocks may be painful, they cause no permanent tissue damage. The teacher is instructed to read to the learner a list of word pairs, to test him on the list, and to administer punishment—an electric shock—whenever the learner errs. The teacher is given a sample shock of 45 volts (the only real shock administered in the course of the experiment). The experimenter instructs the teacher to increase the level of shock one step on the shock generator for each mistake. The generator has thirty switches labeled from 15 to 450 volts. Beneath these voltage readings are labels ranging from "SLIGHT SHOCK" to "DANGER: SEVERE SHOCK," and finally "XX."

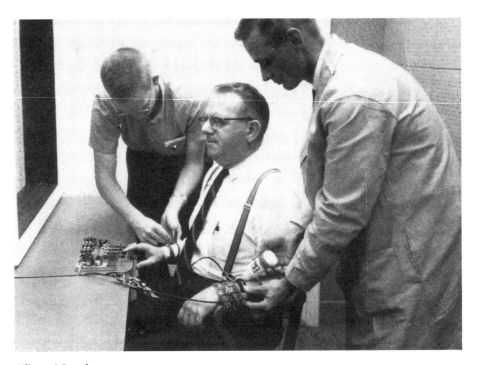

Milgram's Experiment

▶ In this actual photo from Milgram's obedience study, the man being strapped into the chair for the experiment is one of Milgram's research assistants and will receive no shock. What do you think the research assistant thought of the experiment? In his place, would you have been surprised by the findings?

The experiment starts routinely. At the fifth shock level, however, the confederate grunts in annoyance, and by the time the eighth shock level is reached, he shouts that the shocks are becoming painful. Upon reaching the tenth level (150 volts), he cries out, "Experimenter, get me out of here! I won't be in the experiment any more! I refuse to go on!" This response makes plain the intensity of the pain and underscores the learner's right to be released. At the 270-volt level, the learner's response becomes an agonized scream, and at 300 volts the learner refuses to answer further. When the voltage is increased from 300 volts to 330 volts, the confederate shrieks in pain at each shock and gives no answer. From 330 volts on, the learner is heard from no more, and the teacher has no way of knowing whether the learner is still conscious or, for that matter, alive (the teacher also knows that the experimenter cannot tell the condition of the victim since the experimenter is in the same room as the teacher).

Typically the teacher attempts to break off the experiment many times during the session. When he tries to do so, the experimenter instructs him to continue. If he refuses, the experimenter insists, finally telling him, "You must continue. You have no other choice." If the subject still refuses, the experimenter ends the experiment.

We would expect that at most only a small minority of the subjects, a cross section of New Haven residents, would continue to shock beyond the point where the victim screams in pain and demands to be released. We certainly would expect that very, very few people would continue to the point of administering shocks of 450 volts. Indeed, Milgram asked a sample of psychiatrists and a sample of adults with various occupations to predict whether they would obey the orders of the experimenter. All of the people asked claimed that they would disobey at some point. Aware that people would be unwilling to admit that they themselves would obey such an unreasonable and unconscionable order, Milgram asked another sample of middle-class adults to predict how far other people would go in such a procedure.

The average prediction was that perhaps one person in a thousand would continue to the end. The prediction was wrong. In fact, 65 percent (26/40) of the subjects obeyed to the end.

It is clear to people who are not in the experiment what they should do. The question is, *What features of the experimental situation make this clear issue opaque to subjects?* Our aim is to suggest some reasons for such a failure of thinking and action and to suggest ways that people might be trained to avoid such failures— not only in the experiment, of course, but in our practical, moral lives as well. What are some of the sources of the failure?

The experimental conditions involve entrapment, and gradual entrapment affects critical thought. One important feature inducing obedience is the gradual escalation of the shock. Although subjects in the end administered 450-volt shocks, which is clearly beyond the limits of common morality and, indeed, common sense, they began by administering 15-volt shocks, which is neither. Not only did they begin with an innocuous shock, but it increased in innocuous steps of 15 volts. This gradualness clouds clear thinking: we are prepared by our moral training to expect moral problems to present themselves categorically, with good and evil clearly distinguished. But here they were not. By administering the first shock, subjects did two things at once—one salient, the other implicit. They administered a trivial shock, a morally untroublesome act, and they in that same act committed themselves to a policy and procedure which ended in clear evil.

Surely in everyday life, becoming entrapped by gradual increases in commitment is among the most common ways for us to find ourselves engaging in immoral acts, not to mention simple folly. The corrective cannot be, of course, refusing to begin on any path which *might* lead to immorality, but rather to foresee where paths are likely to lead, and to arrange for ourselves points beyond which we will not go. One suspects that had the subjects committed themselves—publicly— to some shock level they would not exceed, they would not have found themselves pushing the 450-volt lever. We cannot expect to lead, or expect our young to lead, lives without walking on slopes: our only hope is to reduce their slipperiness.

Distance makes obedience easier. Another force sustaining obedience was the *distance* between the victim and the subject. Indeed, in one condition of the experiment, subjects were moved physically closer to the victim; in one condition they had to hold his hand on the shock plate (through Mylar insulation to protect the teachers from shock). Here twelve out of forty subjects continued to the end, roughly half the number that did so when the subjects were farther from their victim.

Being closer to the victim did not have its effect by making subjects think more critically or by giving them more information. Rather it intensified their *discomfort* at the victim's pain. Still, being face to face with someone they were hurting probably caused them at least to focus on their victim, which might well be a first step in their taking seriously the pain they were causing him.

Both the experimenter's presence and the objective requirements of the situation influenced decisions to obey authority. The experimenter's *presence* is crucial to the subjects' obedience. In one version of the experiment he issued his commands at a distance, over the phone, and obedience was significantly reduced — to nine out of forty cases. The experimenter, then, exerts powerful *social influence* over the subjects.

One way to think about the experimenter's influence is to suppose that subjects uncritically cede control of their behavior to him. But this is too simple. We suggest that if the experimenter were to have told the subjects, for example, to shine his shoes, every subject would have refused. They would have refused because shining shoes is not a sensible command within the experimental context. Thus, the experimenter's ability to confuse and control subjects follows from his issuing commands which make sense given the ostensible purpose of the experiment; he was a guide, for them, to the experiment's objective requirements.

This interpretation of the experimenter's *role* is reinforced by details of his behavior. For example, his language and demeanor were cold — bureaucratic rather than emotional or personal. The subjects were led to see his commands to them as his dispassionate interpretations of something beyond them all: the requirements of the experiment.

Embarrassment plays a key role in decisions to obey authority. The experimenter entrapped subjects in another way. Subjects could not get out of the experiment without having to explain and justify their abandoning their duty to the experiment and to him. And how were they to do this?

Some subjects attempted to justify their leaving by claiming that they could not bear to go on, but such appeals to "personal reasons" were rebutted by the experimenter's reminding them of their duty to stay. If the subjects could not escape the experiment by such claims, then how could they escape? *They could fully escape his power only by confronting him on moral grounds.* It is worth noting that this is something that virtually none of the hundreds of subjects who took part in one condition or another fully did. Failing to address the experimenter in moral terms, even "disobedient" subjects just passively resisted; they stayed in their seats refusing to continue until the experimenter declared the experiment over. They did *not* do things we might expect them to: leave, tell the experimenter off, release the victim from his seat, and so on. Why did even the disobedient subjects not confront the experimenter?

One reason seems too trivial to mention: confronting the experimenter would be embarrassing. This trivial fact may have much to do with the subjects' obedience. To confront the experimenter directly, on moral grounds, would be to disrupt in a profound way implicit expectations that grounded this particular, and indeed most, social interaction: namely, that the subject and experimenter would behave as competent moral actors. Questioning these expectations is on some accounts, at least, the source of embarrassment….

How can we train individuals to avoid destructive obedience? Our analysis leads to the view that obedience in the Milgram experiment is not primarily a result of a failure of knowledge, or at least knowledge of the crucial issue of what is right or wrong to do in this circumstance. People do not need to be told that torturing an innocent person is something they should not do — even in the context of the experiment. Indeed, when the experimenter turns his back, most subjects are able to apply their moral principles and disobey. The subjects' problem instead is not knowing how to break off, how to make the moral response without social stickiness. If the subjects' defect is not primarily one of thinking correctly, then how is education, even education in critical thinking, to repair the defect? We have three suggestions.

First, we must teach people how to confront authority. We should note as a corollary to this effort that teaching has a wide compass: we teach people how to ride bikes, how to play the piano, how to make a sauce. Some teaching of how to do things we call education: we teach students how to do long division, how to parse sentences, how to solve physics problems. We inculcate these skills in students not by, or not only by, giving them facts or even strategies to remember, but also by giving them certain sorts of experiences, by correcting them when they err, and so on. An analogy would be useful here. Subjects in the Milgram experiment suffered not so much from a failure to remember that as center fielders they should catch fly balls as they did from an inability to do so playing under lights at night, with a great deal of wind, and when there is ambiguity about whether time-out has been called. To improve the players' ability to shag fly balls, in game conditions, we recommend practice rather than lectures, and the closer the circumstances of practice to the conditions of the actual game, the more effective the practice is likely to be.

Good teachers from Socrates on have known that the intellect must be trained; one kind of training is in criticizing authority. We teachers are authorities and hence can provide practice. Of course, we can only do that if we *remain* authorities. Practice at criticizing us if we do not respect our own authority is of little use. We do not have a recipe for being an authority who at the same time encourages criticism, but we do know that is what is important. And sometimes we can tell when we are either not encouraging criticism or when we have ceased being an authority. Both are equally damaging.

Practice with the Milgram situation might help too; it might help for students to "role play" the subjects' plight. If nothing else, doing this might bring home in a forcible way the embarrassment that subjects faced in confronting authority. It might help them develop ways of dealing with this embarrassment. Certainly, it would at least teach them that doing the morally right thing does not always "feel" right, comfortable, natural. There is no evidence about whether such experiences generalize, but perhaps they do.

If they are to confront authority assertively, individuals must also be taught to use social pressure in the service of personal values. Much of current psychology and education sees thought, even critical thought, as something that goes on within individuals. But we know better than this. Whether it be in science, law, or the humanities, scholarship is and must be a public, social process. To train subjects to think critically is to train them to expose their thinking to others, to open *themselves* to criticism, from their peers as well as from authority. We insist on this in scholarship because we know that individual thinking, even the best of it, is prey to distortions of all kinds, from mere ignorance to "bad faith."

Further, the support of others is important in another way. We know that subjects who saw what they took to be two other naive subjects disobey, and thus implicitly criticize the action of continuing, were very likely to do so themselves. A subject's sense that the experimenter had the correct reading was undermined by the counter reading offered by the "other subjects." Public reinforcement of our beliefs can liberate us from illegitimate pressure. The reason for this is twofold.

Agreement with others clarifies the cognitive issue and helps us see the morally or empirically right answer to questions. But it also can have another effect — a nonrational one.

We have claimed that part of the pressure subjects faced in disobeying was produced by having to deal with the embarrassment that might emerge from confrontation. Social support provides a counter-pressure. Had the subjects committed themselves publicly to disobedience before entering the experiment then they could have countered pressures produced by disobedience (during the experiment) by considering the embarrassment of admitting to others (after the experiment) that they had obeyed. Various self-help groups like Alcoholics Anonymous and Weight Watchers teach individuals to manage social pressures to serve good ends.

Social pressures are forces in our lives whether we concede them or not. The rational person, the person who would keep his action in accord with his values, must learn to face or avoid those pressures when they act to degrade his action, but equally important he ought to learn to *employ* the pressure of public commitment, the pressure implicit in making clear to others what he values, in the service of his values.

Students should know about the social pressures that operate on them. They should also learn how to use those pressures to support their own values. One reason we teach people to think critically is so that they may take charge of their own creations. We do not withhold from engineers who would create buildings knowledge about gravity or vectors or stresses. Rather we teach them to enlist this knowledge in their support.

A second area requires our attention. We need to eliminate intellectual illusions fostering nonintellectual obedience. These are illusions about human nature which the Milgram experiment renders transparent. None of these illusions is newly discovered; others have noticed them before. But the Milgram experiment casts them in sharp relief.

The most pernicious of these illusions is the belief, perhaps implicit, that only evil people do evil things and that evil announces itself. This belief, in different guises, bewildered the subjects in several ways.

First, the experimenter looks and acts like the most reasonable and rational of people: a person of authority in an important institution. All of this is, of course, irrelevant to the question of whether his commands are evil, but it does not seem so to subjects. The experimenter had no personally corrupt motive in ordering subjects to continue, for he wanted nothing more of them than to fulfill the requirements of the experiment. So the experimenter was not seen as an evil man, as a man with corrupt desires. He was a man, like Karl Adolf Eichmann, who ordered them to do evil because he saw that evil as something required of him (and of them) by the requirements of the situation they faced together. Because we expect our morality plays to have temptation and illicit desire arrayed against conscience, our ability to criticize morally is subverted when we find evil instructions issued by someone moved by, of all things, duty. [For a fuller discussion of this point, see Hannah Arendt's *Eichmann in Jerusalem* (1965), where the issue is placed in the context of the Holocaust.]

And just as the experimenter escaped the subjects' moral criticism because he was innocent of evil desire, the subjects escaped their own moral criticism because *they too* were free of evil intent: they did not *want* to hurt the victim; they really did not. Further, some subjects, at least, took action to relieve the victim's plight — many protested the experimenter's commands, many tried to give the victim hints about the right answers — thus further dramatizing their purity of heart. And because they acted out of duty rather than desire, the force of their conscience against their own actions was reduced. But, of course, none of this matters in the face of the evil done.

The "good-heartedness" of people, their general moral quality, is something very important to us, something to which we, perhaps rightly, typically pay attention. But if we are to think critically about the morality of our own and others' acts, we must see through this general fact about people to assess the real moral quality of the acts they do or are considering doing.

A second illusion from which the subjects suffered was a confusion about the notion of responsibility. Some subjects asked the experimenter who was responsible for the victim's plight. And the experimenter replied that he was. We, and people asked to predict what they would do in the experiment, see that this is nonsense. We see that the experimenter cannot discharge the subjects' responsibility — no more than the leader of a bank-robbing gang can tell his cohorts, "Don't worry. If we're caught, I'll take full responsibility." We are all conspirators when we participate in planning and executing crimes.

Those in charge have the right to assign *technical* responsibility to others, responsibility for executing parts of a plan, but moral responsibility cannot be given, taken away, or transferred. Still, these words — mere words — on the part of the experimenter eased subjects' "sense of responsibility." So long as the institutions of which we are a part are moral, the need to distinguish technical from moral responsibility need not arise. When those institutions involve wanton torture, we are obliged to think critically about this distinction.

There is a third illusion illustrated in the Milgram experiment. When subjects threatened to disobey, the experimenter kept them in line with prods, the last of which was, "You have no choice; you must go on." Some subjects fell for this, believed that they had no choice. But this is also nonsense. There may be cases in life when we *feel* that we have no choice, but we know we always do. Often feeling we have no choice is really a matter of believing that the cost of moral action is greater than we are willing to bear — in the extreme we may not be willing to offer our lives, and sometimes properly so. Sometimes we use what others have done to support the claim that we have no choice; indeed, some students interpret the levels of obedience in the Milgram experiment as proof that the subjects had no choice. But we all know they did. Even in extreme situations, we have a choice, whether we choose to exercise it or not. The belief that our role, our desires, our past, or the actions of others preclude our acting morally is a convenient but illusory way of distancing ourselves from the evil that surrounds us. It is an illusion from which we should choose to disabuse our students.

Questions for Analysis

1. The authors of this article describe the reasons they believe that the major-ity of subjects in the Stanley Milgram experiment were willing to inflict apparent pain and injury on an innocent person. Explain what you believe were the most significant reasons for this disturbing absence of critical thinking and moral responsibility.

2. The authors argue that the ability to think critically must be developed within a social context, that we must expose our thinking to the criticism of others because "individual thinking, even the best of it, is prey to distortions of all kinds, from mere ignorance to 'bad faith.'" Evaluate this claim, supporting your answer with examples and reasons.

3. The authors contend that in order to act with critical thinking and moral courage, people must be taught to confront authority. Explain how you think people could be taught and encouraged to confront authority in a constructive way.

4. "Even in extreme situations, we have a choice, whether we choose to exercise it or not. The belief that our role, our desires, our past, or the actions of others preclude our acting morally is a convenient but illusory way of distancing ourselves from the evil that surrounds us." Evaluate this claim and give examples and reasons to support your view.

Solving Problems

John Chaffee

Thinking Critically About Problems

Throughout your life, you are continually solving problems, including the many minor problems that you solve each day: negotiating a construction delay on the road, working through an unexpected difficulty at your job, helping an upset child deal with a disappointment. As a student, you are faced with a steady stream of academic assignments, quizzes, exams, and papers. Relatively simple problems like these do not require a systematic or complex analysis. You can solve them with just a little effort and concentration. For example, in order to do well on an exam, you need to *define* the problem (what areas will the exam cover, and what will be the format?), identify and evaluate various *alternatives* (what are possible study approaches?), and then put all these factors together to reach a *solution* (what will be your study plan and schedule?). But the difficult and complicated problems in life require more attention.

The idea of "having a problem" certainly conjures up unpleasant associations for most people, but the truth is that solving problems is an integral and natural part of the process of living. It is the human ability to solve problems that accounts for our successful longevity on this planet. At the same time, it is our *inability* to solve problems that has resulted in senseless wars, unnecessary famine, and irrational persecution. You can undoubtedly discern this same duality in your own life: your most satisfying accomplishments are likely to be the consequence of successful problem-solving, while your greatest disappointments probably resulted at least in part from your failure to solve some crucial problems. For example, think about some of the very difficult problems you have solved through dedication and intelligent action. How did your success make you feel? What were some of the positive results of your success? On the other hand, review some of the significant problems that you were not able to solve. What were some of the negative consequences of your failed efforts? The psychiatrist and author M. Scott Peck sums up the centrality of problems in our lives:

> Problems call forth our courage and our wisdom; indeed, they create our courage and our wisdom. It is only because of problems that we grow mentally and spiritually. When we desire to encourage the growth of the human spirit, we challenge and encourage the human capacity to solve problems, just as in school we deliberately set problems for our children to solve.
>
> Problems are the crucible that forges the strength of our characters. When you are tested by life, forced to overcome adversity and think your way through the most challenging situations—you will emerge a more intelligent, resourceful, and

resilient person. However, if you lead a sheltered existence which insulates you from life's trials, or if you flee from situations at the first sign of trouble—then you will be weak and unable to cope with the eruptions and explosions that are bound to occur in your carefully protected world. Adversity reveals for all to see the person you have become, the character you have created. As the Roman philosopher and poet Lucretius explained, "So it is more useful to watch a man in times of peril, and in adversity to discern what kind of man he is; for then, at last, words of truth are drawn from the depths of his heart, and the mask is torn off, reality remains."

The quality of your life can be traced in large measure to your competency as a problem-solver. The fact that some people are consistently superior problem-solvers is largely due to their ability to approach problems in an informed and organized way. Less competent problem-solvers just muddle through when it comes to confronting adversity, using hit-or-miss strategies that rarely provide the best results. How would you rate yourself as a problem-solver? Do you generally approach difficulties confidently, analyze them clearly, and reach productive solutions? Or do you find that you often get "lost" and confused in such situations, unable to understand the problem clearly and to break out of mental ruts? Of course, you may find that you are very adept at solving problems in one area of your life—such as your job—and miserable at solving problems in other areas, such as your love life or your relationships with your children.

If you are less able to solve complex and challenging problems than you would like to be, don't despair! Becoming an expert problem-solver is not a genetic award; it is, for the most part, a learned skill that you can develop by practicing and applying the principles described in this chapter. You can learn to view problems as *challenges,* opportunities for growth instead of obstacles or burdens. You can become a person who attacks adversity with confidence and enthusiasm. This possibility may seem unlikely to you at this point, but I can assure you that, based on my experience teaching thousands of people for the past twenty years, becoming an expert problem-solver is well within your grasp.

Introduction to Solving Problems

Consider the following problem:

> My best friend is addicted to drugs, but he won't admit it. Jack always liked to drink, but I never thought too much about it. After all, a lot of people like to drink socially, get relaxed, and have a good time. But over the last few years he's started using other drugs as well as alcohol, and it's ruining his life. He's stopped taking classes at the college and will soon lose his job if he doesn't change. Last week I told him that I was really worried about him, but he told me that he has no drug problem and that in any case it really isn't any of my business. I just don't know what to do. I've known Jack since we were in grammar school together and he's a wonderful person. It's as if he's in the grip of some terrible force and I'm powerless to help him.

In working through this problem, the student who wrote this description will have to think carefully and systematically in order to reach a solution. When we think effectively in situations like this, we usually ask ourselves a series of questions, although we may not be aware of the process that our minds are going through.

1. What is the *problem?*
2. What are the *alternatives?*

3. What are the *advantages* and/or *disadvantages* of each alternative?

4. What is the *solution?*

5. How well is the solution *working?*

Let's explore these questions further—and the thinking process that they represent—by applying them to the problem described here. Put yourself in the position of the student whose friend seems to have a serious drug problem.

What Is the Problem?

There are a variety of ways to define the problem facing this student. Describe as specifically as possible what *you* think the problem is.

What Are the Alternatives?

In dealing with this problem, you have a wide variety of possible actions to consider before selecting the best choices. Identify some of the alternatives you might consider.

Successful problem-solvers are able to deal effectively with the many problems that they encounter in daily life.

1. Speak to my friend in a candid and forceful way to convince him that he has a serious problem.

2.

etc.

What Are the Advantages and/or Disadvantages of Each Alternative?

Evaluate the strengths and weaknesses of each of the problems you identified so you can weigh your choices and decide on the best course of action.

1. Speak to my friend in a candid and forceful way to convince him that he has a serious problem.

   Advantage: He may respond to my direct emotional appeal, acknowledge that he has a problem, and seek help.

   Disadvantage: He may react angrily, further alienating me from him and making it more difficult for me to have any influence on him.

2.

   Advantage:

   Disadvantage:

etc.

What Is the Solution?

After evaluating the various alternatives, select what you think is the most effective alternative for solving the problem and describe the sequence of steps you would take to act on the alternative.

How Well Is the Solution Working?

The final step in the process is to review the solution and decide whether it is working well. If it is not, you must be able to modify your solution or perhaps choose an alternate solution that you had disregarded earlier. Describe what results would inform you that the alternative you had selected to pursue was working well or poorly. If you concluded that your alternative was working poorly, describe what your next action would be.

In this situation, trying to figure out the best way to help your friend recognize his problem and seek treatment leads to a series of decisions. This is what the thinking process is all about—trying to make sense of what is going on in our world and acting appropriately in response. When we solve problems effectively, our thinking process exhibits a coherent organization. It follows the general approach we have just explored.

Problem-Solving Method (Basic)

1. What is the *problem?*

2. What are the *alternatives* available to me?

3. What are the *advantages* and/or *disadvantages* of each alternative?

4. What is the *solution?*

5. How well is the solution *working?*

If we can understand the way our minds operate when we are thinking effectively, then we can apply this understanding to improve our thinking in new, challenging situations. In the remainder of this chapter, we will explore a more sophisticated version of this problem-solving approach and will apply it to a variety of complex, difficult problems.

Thinking Activity 4.1

Analyzing a Problem You Solved

1. Describe in specific detail an important problem you have solved recently.

2. Explain how you went about solving the problem. What were the steps, strategies, and approaches you used to understand the problem and make an informed decision?

3. Analyze the organization exhibited by your thinking process by completing the five-step problem-solving method we have been exploring.

4. Share your problem with other members of the class and have them try to analyze and solve it. Then explain the solution you arrived at.

Solving Complex Problems

Imagine yourself in the following situations. What would your next move be, and what are your reasons for it?

Procrastination   I am a procrastinator. Whenever I have something important to do, especially if it's difficult or unpleasant, I tend to put it off. Though this chronic delaying bothers me, I try to suppress my concern and instead work on more trivial things. It doesn't matter how much time I allow for certain responsibilities, I always end up waiting until the last minute to really focus and get things done, or I over-schedule too many things for the time available. I usually meet my deadlines, but not always, and I don't enjoy working under this kind of pressure. In many cases I know that I'm not producing my best work. To make matters worse, the feeling that I'm always behind is causing me to feel really stressed out and is undermining my confidence. I've tried every kind of schedule and technique, but my best intentions simply don't last, and I end up slipping into my old habits. I must learn to get my priorities in order and act on them in an organized way so that I can lead a well-balanced and happier life.

Losing weight   My problem is the unwelcome weight that has attached itself to me. I was always in pretty good physical shape when I was younger, and if I gained a few extra pounds, they were easy to lose if I adjusted my diet slightly or exercised a little more. As I've gotten older, however, it seems easier to add the weight and more difficult to take it off. I'm eating healthier than I ever have before and getting just as much

Solving complex problems requires us to think critically about the problem, analyzing it with a thoughtful, organized approach.

exercise, but the pounds just keep on coming. My clothes are tight, I'm feeling slow and heavy, and my self-esteem is suffering. How can I lose excess poundage?

Smoking   One problem in my life that has remained unsolved for about twelve years is my inability to stop smoking. I know it is dangerous for my health, and I tell my children that they should not smoke. Then they tell me that *I* should stop, and I explain to them that it is very hard to do. I have tried to stop many times without success. The only times I previously was able to stop were during my two pregnancies, because I didn't want to endanger my children's health. But after their births, I went back to smoking, although I realize that second-hand smoke can also pose a health hazard. I want to stop smoking because it's dangerous, but I also enjoy it. Why do I continue, knowing it can only damage me and my children?

Loss of Financial Aid   I'm just about to begin my second year of college, following a very successful first year. To this point, I have financed my education through a combination of savings, financial aid, and a part-time job (sixteen hours per week) at a local store. However, I just received a letter from my college stating that it was reducing my financial aid package by half due to budgetary problems. The letter concludes, "We hope this aid reduction will not prove to be too great an inconvenience." From my perspective, this reduction in aid isn't an inconvenience—it's a disaster! My budget last year was already tight, and with my job, I had barely enough time to study, participate in a few college activities, and have a modest (but essential) social life. To make matters worse, my mother has been ill, a condition which has reduced her income and created financial problems at home. I'm feeling panicked! What in the world am I going to do?

When we first approach a difficult problem, it often seems a confused tangle of information, feelings, alternatives, opinions, considerations, and risks. The problem of the college student just described is a complicated situation that does not seem to offer a single simple solution. Let's imagine ourselves in the student's predicament. Without the benefit of a systematic approach, our thoughts might wander through the tangle of issues like this:

I want to stay in school . . . I'm not going to have enough money. . . . I could work more hours at my job . . . but I might not have enough time to study and get top grades . . . and if all I'm doing is working and studying, what about my social life? . . . and what about mom and the kids? . . . They might need my help. . . . I could drop out of school for a while . . . but if I don't stay in school, what kind of future do I have? . . .

Very often when we are faced with difficult problems like this, we simply do not know where to begin in trying to solve them. Every issue is connected to many others. Frustrated by not knowing where to take the first step, we often give up trying to understand the problem. Instead, we may

1. *Act impulsively* without thought or consideration (e.g., "I'll just quit school").

2. *Do what someone else suggests* without seriously evaluating the suggestion (e.g., "Tell me what I should do—I'm tired of thinking about this").

3. *Do nothing* as we wait for events to make the decision for us (e.g., "I'll just wait and see what happens before doing anything").

None of these approaches is likely to succeed in the long run, and they can gradually reduce our confidence in dealing with complex problems. An alternative to these reactions is to *think critically* about the problem, analyzing it with an organized approach based on the five-step method described earlier.

Problem-Solving Method (Advanced)

1. Step 1: What is the problem?
   a. What do I know about the situation?
   b. What results am I aiming for in this situation?
   c. How can I define the problem?

2. Step 2: What are the alternatives?
   a. What are the boundaries of the problem situation?
   b. What alternatives are possible within these boundaries?

3. Step 3: What are the advantages and/or disadvantages of each alternative?
   a. What are the advantages of each alternative?
   b. What are the disadvantages of each alternative?
   c. What additional information do I need to evaluate each alternative?

4. Step 4: What is the solution?
   a. Which alternative(s) will I pursue?
   b. What steps can I take to act on the alternative(s) chosen?

5. Step 5: How well is the solution working?
   a. What is my evaluation?
   b. What adjustments are necessary?

Although we will be using an organized method for working through difficult problems and arriving at thoughtful conclusions, the fact is that our minds do not always work in such a logical, step-by-step fashion. Effective problem-solvers typically pass through all the steps we will be examining, but they don't always do so in the sequence we will be describing. Instead, the best problem-solvers have an integrated and flexible approach to the process in which they deploy a repertoire of problem-solving strategies as needed. Sometimes exploring the various alternatives helps them go back and redefine the original problem; similarly, seeking to implement the solution can often suggest new alternatives.

The key point is that although the problem-solving steps are presented in a logical sequence here, you are not locked into following these steps in a mechanical and unimaginative way. At the same time, in learning a problem-solving method like this it is generally not wise to skip steps, because each step deals with an important aspect of the problem. As you become more proficient in using the method, you will find that you can apply its concepts and strategies to problem-solving in an increasingly flexible and natural fashion, just as learning the basics of an activity like driving a car gradually gives way to a more organic and integrated performance of the skills involved.

Before applying a method like the one just outlined above to your problem, however, you need to first ready yourself by *accepting* the problem.

Accepting the Problem

To solve a problem, you must first be willing to *accept* the problem by *acknowledging* that the problem exists and *committing* yourself to trying to solve it. Sometimes you may have difficulty recognizing there *is* a problem unless it is pointed out to you. Other times you may actively resist acknowledging a problem, even when it is pointed out to you. The person who confidently states, "I don't really have any problems," sometimes has very serious problems—but is simply unwilling to acknowledge them.

On the other hand, mere acknowledgment is not enough to solve a problem. Once you have identified a problem, you must commit yourself to trying to solve it. Successful problem-solvers are highly motivated and willing to persevere through the many challenges and frustrations of the problem-solving process. How do you find the motivation and commitment that prepare you to enter the problem-solving process? There are no simple answers, but a number of strategies may be useful to you.

1. *List the benefits.* Making a detailed list of the benefits you will derive from successfully dealing with the problem is a good place to begin. Such a process helps you clarify why you might want to tackle the problem, motivates you to get started, and serves as a source of encouragement when you encounter difficulties or lose momentum.

2. *Formalize your acceptance.* When you formalize your acceptance of a problem, you are "going on record," either by preparing a signed declaration or by signing a "contract" with someone else. This formal commitment serves as an explicit statement of your original intentions that you can refer to if your resolve weakens.

3. *Accept responsibility for your life.* Each one of us has the potential to control the direction of our lives, but to do so we must accept our freedom to choose and the responsibility that goes with it. As you saw in the last chapter, critical thinkers actively work to take charge of their lives rather than letting themselves be passively controlled by external forces.

4. *Create a "worst-case" scenario.* Some problems persist because you are able to ignore their possible implications. When you use this strategy, you remind yourself, as graphically as possible, of the potentially disastrous consequences of your actions. For example, using vivid color photographs and research conclusions, you can remind yourself that excessive smoking, drinking, or eating can lead to myriad health problems and social and psychological difficulties as well as an early and untimely demise.

5. *Identify what's holding you back.* If you are having difficulty accepting a problem, it is usually because something is holding you back. For example, you might

be concerned about the amount of time and effort involved, you might be reluctant to confront the underlying issues that the problem represents, you might be worried about finding out unpleasant things about yourself or others, or you might be inhibited by other problems in your life, such as a tendency to procrastinate. Whatever the constraints, using this strategy involves identifying and describing all of the factors that are preventing you from attacking the problem and then addressing these factors one at a time.

Step 1: What Is the Problem?

The first step in solving problems is to determine exactly what the central issues of the problem are. If you do not clearly understand what the problem really is, then your chances of solving it are considerably reduced. You may spend your time trying to solve the wrong problem. For example, consider the different formulations of the following problems. How might these formulations lead you in different directions in trying to solve the problems?

"School is boring." vs. "I feel bored in school."
"I'm a failure." vs. "I just failed an exam."

In each of these cases, a very general conclusion (left column) has been replaced by a more specific characterization of the problem (right column).

The general conclusions ("I'm a failure") do not suggest productive ways of resolving the difficulties. they are too absolute, too all encompassing. On the other hand, the more specific descriptions of the problem situation ("I just failed an exam") *do* permit us to attack the problem with useful strategies. In short, the way you define a problem determines not only *how* you will go about solving it, but also whether you feel that the problem can be solved at all. Correct identification of a problem is essential if you are going to be able to perform a successful analysis and reach an appropriate conclusion. If you misidentify the problem you can find yourself pursuing an unproductive and even destructive course of action.

Let us return to the problem of the college finances we encountered on page 84 and analyze it using our problem-solving method. (*Note:* As you work through this problem-solving approach, apply the steps and strategies to an unsolved problem in your own life. You will have an opportunity to write up your analysis when you complete Thinking Activity 4.2 on page 99.) In order to complete the first major step of this problem-solving approach— "What is the problem?"—you need to address three component questions:

1. What do I know about the situation?

2. What results am I aiming for in this situation?

3. How can I define the problem?

Step 1A: What Do I Know About the Situation?

Solving a problem begins with determining what information you *know* to be the case and what information you *think* might be the case. You need to have a clear idea of the details of your beginning circumstances to explore the problem successfully. Sometimes a situation may appear to be a problem when it really isn't simply because your information isn't accurate. For example, you might be convinced that someone you are attracted to doesn't reciprocate your interest. If this belief is inaccurate, however, then your "problem" doesn't really exist.

You can identify and organize what you know about the problem situation by using *key questions*. There are six types of questions that can be used to explore situations and issues systematically: *fact, interpretation, analysis, synthesis, evaluation,* and *application.* By asking—and trying to answer—questions of fact, you are establishing a sound foundation for the exploration of your problem. Answer the following questions of fact—who, what, where, when, how, why—about the problem described at the beginning of the chapter.

1. *Who* are the people involved in this situation?
   Who will benefit from solving the problem?
   Who can help me solve this problem?

2. *What* are the various parts or dimensions of the problem?
   What are my strengths and resources for solving this problem?
   What additional information do I need to solve this problem?

3. *Where* can I find people or additional information to help me solve the problem?

4. *When* did the problem begin?
   When should the problem be resolved?

5. *How* did the problem develop or come into being?

6. *Why* is solving this problem important to me?
   Why is this problem difficult to solve?

7. *Additional questions:*

Step 1B: What Results Am I Aiming for in This Situation?

This second part of answering the question "What is the problem?" consists of identifying the specific *results* or objectives you are trying to achieve. The results are those goals that will eliminate the problem if you are able to attain them. Whereas the first part of Step 1 oriented you in terms of the history of the problem and the current situation, this part encourages you to look ahead to the future. In this respect, it is similar to the process of establishing and working toward your goals. To identify your results, you need to ask yourself this question: "What are the objectives that, once achieved, will solve this problem?" For instance, one of the results or objectives in the sample problem might be having enough money to pay for college. Describe additional results you might be trying to achieve in this situation.

Step 1C: How Can I Define the Problem?

After exploring what you know about the problem and the results you are aiming to achieve, you need to conclude Step 1 by defining the problem as clearly and specifically as possible. Defining the problem is a crucial task in the entire problem-solving process because this definition will determine the direction of the analysis. To define the problem, you need to identify its central issue(s). Sometimes defining the problem is relatively straightforward, such as : "Trying to find enough time to exercise." Often, however, identifying the central issue of a problem is a much more complex process. For example, the statement "My problem is relating to other people" suggests a complicated situation with many interacting variables that resists simple definition. In fact, you may only begin to develop a clear idea of the problem as you engage in the process of trying to solve it. You might begin by believing that your problem is, say, not having the *ability* to succeed and end by concluding that the problem is really a *fear* of success. As you will see, the same insights apply to nonpersonal problems as well. For example, the problem of high school dropouts might initially be defined in terms of problems in the school system, whereas later formulations may identify drug use or social pressure as the core of the problem.

Viewing a problem from different perspectives helps us define the problem clearly and generate a variety of possible solutions.

Although there are no simple formulas for defining challenging problems, you can pursue several strategies in identifying the central issue most effectively:

1. *View the problem from different perspectives.* Perspective-taking is a key ingredient of thinking critically, and it can help you zero in on many problems as well. For example, when you describe how various individuals might view a given problem—such as the high school dropout rate—the essential ingredients of the problem begin to emerge. In the college finances problem, how would you describe the following perspectives?

   Your perspective:

   The college's perspective:

   Your mother's perspective:

2. *Identify component problems.* Larger problems are often composed of component problems. To define the larger problem, it is often necessary to identify and describe the subproblems that comprise it. For example, poor performance at school might be the result of a number of factors, such as ineffective study habits, inefficient time management, and preoccupation with a personal problem. Defining, and dealing effectively with, the larger problem means defining and dealing with the subproblems first. Identify possible subproblems in the sample problem:

   Subproblem a:

   Subproblem b:

3. ***State the problem clearly and specifically.*** A third defining strategy is to state the problem as clearly and specifically as possible, based on an examination of the results that need to be achieved to solve the problem. This sort of clear and specific description of the problem is an important step in solving it. For if you state the problem in *very general* terms, you won't have a clear idea of how best to proceed in dealing with it. But if you can describe your problem in more *specific terms,* then your description will begin to suggest actions you can take to solve the problem. Examine the differences between the statements of the following problem:

General: "My problem is money."

More specific: "My problem is budgeting my money so that I won't always run out near the end of the month."

Most specific: "My problem is developing the habit and the discipline to budget my money so that I won't always run out near the end of the month."

Review your analysis of the sample problem and then state the problem as clearly and specifically as possible.

Step 2: What are the Alternatives?

Once you have identified your problem clearly and specifically, your next move is to examine each of the possible actions that might help you solve the problem. Before you list the alternatives, however, it makes sense to determine first which actions are possible and which are impossible. You can do this by exploring the *boundaries* of the problem situation.

Step 2A: What Are the Boundaries of the Problem Situation?

Boundaries are the limits in the problem situation that you cannot change. They are a part of the problem, and they must be accepted and dealt with. For example, in the sample situation, the fact that a day has only twenty-four hours must be accepted as part of the problem situation. There is no point in developing alternatives that ignore this fact. At the same time, you must be careful not to identify as boundaries circumstances that can actually be changed. For instance, you might assume that your problem must be solved in your current location without realizing that relocating to another, less expensive college is one of your options. Identify additional boundaries that might be a part of the sample situation and some of the questions you would want to answer regarding the boundary. For example:

Time limitations: How much time do I need for each of my basic activities—work, school, social life, travel, and sleep? What is the best way to budget this time?

Step 2B: What Alternatives Are Possible Within These Boundaries?

After you have established a general idea of the boundaries of the problem situation, you can proceed to identify the possible courses of action that can take place within these boundaries. Of course, identifying all the possible alternatives is not always easy; in fact, it may be part of your problem. Often we do not see a way out of a problem because our thinking is set in certain ruts, fixed in certain perspectives. We may be blind to other approaches, either because we reject them before seriously considering them ("That will never work!") or because they simply do not occur to us. You can use several strategies to overcome these obstacles.

The best approach to solving problems involves generating many different possible alternatives instead of just a few.

1. ***Discuss the problem with other people.*** Discussing possible alternatives with others uses a number of the aspects of critical thinking you explored in Chapter 2. As you saw then, thinking critically involves being open to seeing situations from different viewpoints and discussing your ideas with others in an organized way. Both of these abilities are important in solving problems. As critical thinkers we live—and solve problems—in a community, not simply by ourselves. Other people can often suggest possible alternatives that we haven't thought of, in part because they are outside the situation and thus have a more objective perspective, and in part because they naturally view the world differently than we do, based on their past experiences and their personalities. In addition, discussions are often creative experiences that generate ideas the participants would not have come up with on their own. The dynamics of these interactions often lead to products that are greater than the individual "sum" of those involved.

2. ***Brainstorm ideas.*** Brainstorming, a method introduced by Alex Osborn, builds on the strengths of working with other people to generate ideas and solve problems. In a typical brainstorming session, a group of people work together to generate as many ideas as possible in a specific period of time. As ideas are produced, they are not judged or evaluated, as this tends to inhibit the free flow of ideas and discourages people from making suggestions. Evaluation is deferred until a later stage. People are encouraged to build on the ideas of others since the most creative ideas are often generated through the constructive interplay of various minds.

3. ***Change your location.*** Your perspective on a problem is often tied into the circumstances in which the problem exists. For example, a problem you may be having in school is tied into your daily experiences and habitual reactions to these experiences. Sometimes what you need is a fresh perspective, getting away

from the problem situation so that you can view it with more clarity and in a different light. Using these strategies, as well as your own reflections, identify as many alternatives to help solve the sample problem as you can think of.

Step 3: What Are the Advantages and/or Disadvantages of Each Alternative?

Once you have identified the various alternatives, your next step is to *evaluate* them by using evaluation questions. Each possible course of action has certain advantages in the sense that if you select that alternative, there will be some positive results. At the same time, each of the possible courses of action likely has disadvantages as well in the sense that if you select that alternative, there may be a cost involved or a risk of some negative results. It is important to examine the potential advantages and/or disadvantages in order to determine how helpful each course of action would be in solving the problem.

Step 3A: What Are the Advantages of Each Alternative?

The alternative you listed in Step 2 for the sample problem ("Attend college part-time") might include the follow advantages:

Alternatives:	Advantages:
1. Attend college part time	This would remove some of the immediate time and money pressures I am experiencing while still allowing me to prepare for the future. I would have more time to focus on the courses that I am taking and to work additional hours.

Identify the advantages of each of the alternatives that you listed in Step 2. Be sure that your responses are thoughtful and specific.

Step 3B: What are the Disadvantages of Each Alternative?

You also need to consider the disadvantages of each alternative. The alternative you listed for the sample problem might include the following disadvantages:

Alternatives:	Disadvantages:
1. Attend college part time	It would take me much longer to complete my schooling, thus delaying my progress toward my goals. Also, I might lose motivation and drop out before completing school because the process was taking so long. Being a part-time student might even threaten my eligibility for financial aid.

Now identify the disadvantages of each of the alternatives that you listed. Be sure that your responses are thoughtful and specific.

Step 3C: What Additional Information Do I Need to Evaluate Each Alternative?

The next part of Step 3 consists of determining what you must know (*information needed*) to best evaluate and compare the alternatives. For each alternative there are questions that must be answered if you are to establish which alternatives make sense and which do not. In addition, you need to figure out where best to get this information (*sources*).

One useful way to identify the information you need is to ask yourself the question "*What if* I select this alternative?" For instance, one alternative in the sample problem was "attend college part-time." When you ask yourself the question "*What if* I attend college part-time?" you are tying to predict what will occur if you select this course of action. To make these predictions, you must answer certain questions and find the information to answer them.

▶ How long will it take me to complete my schooling?

▶ How long can I continue in school without losing interest and dropping out?

▶ Will I threaten my eligibility for financial aid if I become a part-time student?

The information—and the sources for it—that must be located for the first alternative in the sample problem might include the following:

Alternative:	*Information Needed and Sources:*
1. Attend college part time	*Information:* How long will it take me to complete my schooling? How long can I continue in school without losing interest and dropping out? Will I threaten my eligibility for financial aid if I become a part-time student?
	Sources: Myself, other part-time students, school counselors, the financial aid office.

Identify the information needed and the sources of this information for each of the alternatives that you identified. Be sure that your responses are thoughtful and specific.

Step 4: What Is the Solution?

The purpose of Steps 1 though 3 is to analyze your problem in a systematic and detailed fashion—to work through the problem in order to become thoroughly familiar with it and the possible solutions to it. After breaking down the problem in this way, the final step should be to try to put the pieces back together—that is, to decide on a thoughtful course of action based on your increased understanding. Even though this sort of problem analysis does not guarantee finding a specific solution to the problem, it should *deepen your understanding* of exactly what the problem is about. And in locating and evaluating your alternatives, it should give you some very good ideas about the general direction you should move in and the immediate steps you should take.

Step 4A: Which Alternative(s) Will I Pursue?

There is no simple formula or recipe to tell you which alternatives to select. As you work through the different courses of action that are possible, you may find that you can immediately rule some out. For example, in the sample problem you may know with certainty that you do not want to attend college part-time (alternative 1) because you will forfeit your remaining financial aid. However, it may not be so simple to select which of the other alternatives you wish to pursue. How do you decide?

The decisions we make usually depend on what we believe to be most important to us. These beliefs regarding what is most important to us are known as *values.* Our values are the starting points of our actions and strongly influence our decisions. For example, if we value staying alive (as most of us do), then we will

Effective problem-solvers develop creative solutions to solve their problems.

make many decisions each day that express this value—eating proper meals, not walking in front of moving traffic, and so on.

Our values helps us *set priorities* in life—that is, decide what aspects of our lives are most important to us. We might decide that for the present going to school is more important than having an active social life. In this case, going to school is a higher priority than having an active social life. Unfortunately, our values are not always consistent with each other—we may have to choose *either* to go to school or to have an active social life. Both activities may be important to us; they are simply not compatible with each other. Very often the *conflicts* between our values constitute the problem. Let's examine some strategies for selecting alternatives that might help us solve the problem.

1. ***Evaluate and compare alternatives.*** Although each alternative may have certain advantages and disadvantages, not all advantages are equally desirable or potentially effective. For example, giving up on college entirely would certainly solve some aspects of the sample problem, but its obvious disadvantage would rule out this solution for most people. Thus it makes sense to try to evaluate and rank the various alternatives based on how effective they are likely to be and how they match up with your value system. A good place to begin is the "Results" stage, Step 1B. Examine each of the alternatives and evaluate how well it will contribute to achieving the results you are aiming for in the situation. You may want to rank the alternatives or develop your own rating system to assess their relative effectiveness.

After evaluating the alternatives in terms of their anticipated *effectiveness,* the next step is to evaluate them in terms of their *desirability,* based on your needs, interests, and value system. Again, you can use either a ranking or a rating system to assess their relative desirability. After completing these two separate evaluations, you can then select the alternative(s) that seem most appropriate. Review the alternatives you identified in the sample problem and then rank or rate them according to their potential effectiveness and desirability, assuming this problem was your own.

2. ***Combine alternatives.*** After reviewing and evaluating the alternatives you generated, you may develop a new alternative that combines the best qualities of several options while avoiding the disadvantages some of them would have if chosen exclusively. In the sample problem, you might combine attending college part-time during the academic year with attending school during the summer session so that progress toward your degree won't be impeded. Examine the alternatives you identified and develop a new option that combines the best elements of several of them.

3. ***Try out each alternative in your imagination.*** Focus on each alternative and try to imagine, as concretely as possible, what it would be like if you actually selected it. Visualize what impact your choice would have on your problem and what the implications would be for your life as a whole. By trying out the alternative in your imagination, you can sometimes avoid unpleasant results or unexpected consequences. As a variation of this strategy, you can sometimes test alternatives on a very limited basis in a practice situation. For example, if you are trying to overcome your fear of speaking in groups, you can practice various speaking techniques with your friends or family until you find an approach you are comfortable with.

After trying out these strategies on the sample problem, select the alternative(s) you think would be most effective and desirable from your standpoint.

Alternative(s):

Step 4B: What Steps Can I Take to Act on the Alternative(s) Chosen?

Once you have decided on the correct alternative(s) to pursue, your next move is to plan the steps you will have to take to put it into action. Planning the specific steps you will take is extremely important. Although thinking carefully about your problem is necessary, it is not enough if you hope to solve the problem. You have to *take action,* and planning specific steps is where you begin. In the sample problem, for example, imagine that one of the alternatives you have selected is "Find additional sources of income that will enable me to work part-time and go to school full-time." The specific steps you would want to take might include the following:

1. Contact the financial aid office at the school to see what other forms of financial aid are available and what you have to do to apply for them.

2. Contact some of the local banks to see what sort of student loans are available.

3. Look for a higher-paying job so that you can earn more money without working additional hours.

4. Discuss the problem with students in similar circumstances in order to generate new ideas.

Identify the steps you would have to take in pursuing the alternative(s) you have identified.

Of course, plans do not implement themselves. Once you know what actions you have to take, you need to commit yourself to taking the necessary steps. This is where many people stumble in the problem-solving process, paralyzed by inertia or fear. Sometimes, to overcome these blocks and inhibitions, you need to reexamine your original acceptance of the problem, perhaps making use of some of the strategies you explored on page 88. Once you get started, the rewards of actively attacking your problem are often enough incentive to keep you focused and motivated.

Step 5: How Well Is the Solution Working?

As you work toward reaching a reasonable and informed conclusion, you should not fall into the trap of thinking that there is only one "right" decision and that all is lost if you do not figure out what it is and carry it out. You should remind yourself that any analysis of a problem situation, no matter how careful and systematic, is ultimately limited. You simply cannot anticipate or predict everything that is going to happen in the future. As a result, every decision you make is provisional in the sense that your ongoing experience will inform you if your decisions are working out or if they need to be changed and modified. This is precisely the attitude of the critical thinker—someone who is *receptive* to new ideas and experiences and *flexible* enough to change or modify beliefs based on new information. Critical thinking is not a compulsion to find the "right" answer or make the "correct" decision; it is an ongoing process of exploration and discovery.

Step 5A: What Is My Evaluation?

In many cases the relative effectiveness of your efforts will be apparent. In other cases it will be helpful to pursue a more systematic evaluation along the lines suggested in the following strategies:

1. ***Compare the results with the goals.*** The essence of evaluation is comparing the results of your efforts with the initial goals you were trying to achieve. For example, the goals of the sample problem are embodied in the results you specified on page 90. Compare the anticipated results of the alternative(s) you selected. To what extent will your choice meet these goals? Are there goals that are not likely to be met by your alternative(s)? Which ones? Could they be addressed by other alternatives? Asking these and other questions will help you clarify the success of your efforts and provide a foundation for future decisions.

2. ***Get other perspectives.*** As you have seen throughout the problem-solving process, getting the opinions of others is a productive strategy at virtually every stage, and this is certainly true for evaluation. Other people can often provide perspectives that are both different and more objective than yours. Naturally, the evaluations of others are not always better or more accurate than your own, but even when they are not, reflecting on these different views usually deepens your understanding of the situation. It is not always easy to receive the evaluations of others, but open-mindedness toward outside opinions is a very valuable attitude to cultivate, for it will stimulate and guide you to produce your best efforts.

   To receive specific, practical feedback from others, you need to ask specific, practical questions that will elicit this information. General questions ("What do you think of this?") typically result in overly general, unhelpful responses ("It sounds okay to me"). Be focused in soliciting feedback, and remember: You do have the right to ask people to be *constructive* in their comments, providing suggestions for improvement rather than flatly expressing what they think is wrong.

Step 5B: What Adjustments Are Necessary?

As a result of your review, you may discover that the alternative you selected is not feasible or is not leading to satisfactory results. For example, in the sample problem, you may find that it is impossible to find additional sources of income so that you can work part-time instead of full-time. In that case, you simply have to go back and review the other alternatives to identify another possible course of action. At other times you may find that the alternative you selected is working out fairly well but still requires some adjustments as you continue to work toward your desired outcomes. In fact, this is a typical situation that you should expect to occur. Even when things initially appear to be working reasonably well, an active thinker continues to ask questions such as "What might I have overlooked?" and "How could I have done this differently?" Of course, asking—and trying to answer—questions like these is even more essential if solutions are hard to come by (as they usually are in real-world problems) and if you are to retain the flexibility and optimism you will need to tackle a new option.

Thinking Activity 4.2

Analyzing an Unsolved Problem

Select a problem from your own life. It should be one that you are currently grappling with and have not yet been able to solve. After selecting the problem you want to work on, strengthen your *acceptance* of the problem by using one or more of the strategies described on page 88 and describing your efforts. Then analyze your problem using the problem-solving method described in this chapter. Discuss your problem with other class members to generate fresh perspectives and unusual alternatives that might not have occurred to you. Using your own paper, write your analysis in outline style, giving specific responses to the questions in each step of the problem-solving method. Although you might not reach a "guaranteed" solution to your problem, you should deepen your understanding of the problem and develop a concrete plan of action that will help you move in the right direction. Implement your plan of action and then monitor the results.

Thinking Activity 4.3

Analyzing College Problems

Analyze the following problems using the problem-solving approach presented in this chapter.

Problem 1: Background Information

The most important unsolved problem that exists for me is my inability to make that crucial decision of what to major in. I want to be secure with respect to both money and happiness when I make a career for myself, and I don't want to make a mistake in choosing a field of study. I want to make this decision before beginning the next semester so that I can start immediately in my career. I've been thinking about managerial studies. However, I often wonder if I have the capacity to make executive decisions when I can't even decide on what I want to do with my life.

Problem 2: Background Information

One of my problems is my difficulty in taking tests. It's not that I don't study. What happens is that when I get the test, I become nervous and my mind goes blank. For example, in my social science class, the teacher told the class on Tuesday that there would be a test on Thursday. That afternoon I went home and began studying for the test. By Thursday I knew most of the material, but when the test was handed out, I got nervous and my mind went blank. For a long time I just stared at the test, and I ended up failing it.

Problem 3: Background Information

One of the serious problems in my life is learning English as a second language. It is not so easy to learn a second language, especially when you live in an environment where only your native language is spoken. When I came to this country three years ago, I could speak almost no English. I have learned a lot, but my lack of fluency is getting in the way of my studies and my social relationships.

Problem 4: Background Information

This is my first year of college, and in general I'm enjoying it a great deal. The one disturbing thing I have encountered is the amount of drinking that students engage in when they socialize. Although I enjoy drinking in moderation, most students drink much more than "in moderation" at parties. they want to "get drunk," "lose control," "get wasted." And the parties aren't just on weekends–they're every night of the week! The problem is that there is a lot of pressure for me to join in the drinking and partying. Most of the people I enjoy being with are joining in, and I don't want to be left out of the social life of the college. But it's impossible to party so much and still keep up to date with my course work. And all that drinking certainly isn't good for me physically. But on the other hand, I don't want to be excluded from the social life, and when I try to explain that I don't enjoy heavy drinking, my friends make me feel immature and a little silly. What should I do?

Looking Critically @ Troubleshooting on the Internet

You're in the middle of fine-tuning a very important term paper, fixing the typos and streamlining the text, when poof!—your computer's mouse disappears from view. *Or* a message flashes on the screen telling you that there is insufficient memory to save your document after you have just spent four hours editing it. *Or* your monitor is turning funny colors and displaying flashing, wiggly lines, making it impossible to read. *Or* you're doing research at a major library via the Internet, and your network connection (usually a modem) cuts you off and won't allow you to redial. What do you do?

Don't panic; all is not lost. Help is on the way! And no, you do not have to cart your equipment to a repair store and pay a zillion dollars for someone to peek at the hard drive's insides or tweak some gadget. Depending upon the situation, you may have the solution right at your fingertips. First and most import, *THINK like a problem-solver **before** you ACT*. Analyze the situation: What exactly is the problem? Which piece of hardware or which software might be causing the difficulty? What are your alternatives for solving the problem? How can you test the various alternatives? If you can find the answers to your problems by yourself, while still at your computer, just think of the time and money you will save and the aggravation you will avoid. You will also be better able to anticipate how to prevent the problem from happening again.

Successful problem-solving–and troubleshooting—always begin with gathering information. Keep your manuals handy and refer to them often. For software questions, check the user's guide that comes with the original package or use the "Help" feature that is often right there on your screen. If your computer is still operable, and you have access to the Internet or an online service, you may be able to find ways to troubleshoot common problems. Many hardware and software manufacturers have established 1–800 help lines or Web sites with customer service departments and FAQ ("Frequently Asked Questions") message boards. Newspapers and magazines that offer computer columns often let you search current and back issues online for articles that may pertain to your dilemma. Sometimes the authors will even answer you via email to help you out of a tough spot. And there are forums, chat groups, live conferences, bulletin or message boards, and newsgroups on the Internet—all being areas where you can correspond or start a round robin of questions and answers to solicit advice from professionals in the field as well as from fellow computer users. Today's new computers often come with preinstalled "utility" programs that can detect problems and offer solutions through steps that you can handle yourself. Or you can purchase programs that act like computer "doctors" to help diagnose and repair problems. Look for and take advantage of these applications to help solve your puzzles.

What about the vanishing mouse? Sometimes you need to reboot your computer (turn it on and off), particularly when you are shifting between DOS-based and Windows-based programs, to refresh the settings. It's something of a mystery why this method works, but it may be the simplest way to fix an annoying glitch that occurs when mixing old programs with newer versions.

In addition, the customary advice for dealing with all electronic equipment that goes on the blink also applies to computers: *check the plugs!* The myriad of wires hooking up the printer, keyboard, monitor, joystick, mouse, hard drive, fax, and modem can become tangled, undone, or loosened just by feather dusting "back there." So before carting the equipment off to the store, securely fasten all the plugs and cords, turn the computer off, count to ten, and then turn it back on.

No, your computer is not aging gracefully when it tells you it's "Out of Memory." Instead, it could be telling you that it's running too many programs at once, and like people who juggle too many tasks at a time, it just may not be able to handle that many tasks at once. So the short-term "fix" is to shut down some of the applications and see if that helps; the long-range plan would be to see if your PC could be upgraded with more RAM (random access memory) or space on your hard drive. In the meantime, try saving your file to a floppy disk (if the file is small enough), *or,* if you're working in a computer lab, find out whether you can save the file on a different part of the network. And, by the way, the folks who run your computer lab and your fellow students are often great sources for help solving problems. You can also try deleting some unnecessary files or moving them elsewhere to make room for the one you need to keep now. And remember, if you are not already backing up the data you want to keep on a regular basis (also known as making emergency copies, often in a compressed format) learn how—and do it regularly.

Browsing the Internet can be fun, but it can also contribute to your computer's memory problems and cause your modem to cut you off. Those colorful Web pages temporarily load into your computer's upper memory and take up a lot of space, so you may find yourself being disconnected from your modem and looking at a blank screen on a regular basis. Of course, being "punted" offline can also mean someone in your house has picked up an extension of your phone line and inadvertently cut you off. Maybe the person is trying to tell you that you're spending too much time online!

Finally, what could be making your monitor freak out? Are you sure you're using the right "driver" (software that is used to run extensions like printers, external CD-ROM drives, and scanners)? First things first: check to ensure that the program running your system is the right one (now, where is that manual?). Before you start pricing new video cards (another internal "organ" of your computer), see if any of these possibilities apply: Your monitor might just be getting tired and old and wearing out from use. The circuit that your computer is plugged into might be shared with your refrigerator so that every time the self-defroster goes on, it creates a power blip that surges through your computer. *Or* perhaps your computer is too close to another current, like a cable TV line. Try moving your computer to another location in your room, plug it into a different socket on a different electrical line, and see if the rainbow effect on your screen happens at specific times or on certain days of the week. If all else fails, hook it up to someone else's computer and see if it misbehaves there as well. If it is still psychedelic, it may be time for a visit to the computer shop.

Begin looking critically at troubleshooting by engaging in the following activity. Create a problem that you think you might be faced with as you use your computer (or perhaps your professor will hand out sample problems). How would you solve the problem? Think before you act: examine the situation you've created and write about both your situation and your solution. First, describe the problem as specifically as possible and identify the resources you can use to solve it. What are your alternatives for solving the problem? What are the advantages and disadvantages of each alternative? What do you think is the best solution? By developing the habit of approaching your computer problems in this way, you'll soon find yourself naturally anticipating and troubleshooting unexpected difficulties you may encounter—in other words, you'll be thinking critically about using your computer.

Solving Nonpersonal Problems

The problems we have analyzed up to this point have been "personal" problems in the sense that they represent individual challenges encountered by us as we live our lives. Problems are not only of a personal nature, however. We also face problems as members of a community, a society, and the world. As with personal problems, we need to approach these kinds of problems in an organized and thoughtful way in order to explore the issues, develop a clear understanding, and decide on an informed plan of action. For example, racism and prejudice directed toward African Americans, Hispanics, Asians, Jews, homosexuals, and other minority groups seems to be on the rise at many college campuses. There has been an increase of overt racial incidents at colleges and universities during the past several years, a particularly disturbing situation given the lofty egalitarian ideals of higher education. Experts from different fields have offered a variety of explanations to account for this behavior. Describe why you believe these racial and ethnic incidents are occurring with increasing frequency.

Making sense of a complex, challenging situation like this is not a simple process. Although the problem solving method we have been using in this chapter is a powerful approach, its successful application depends on having sufficient information about the situation we are trying to solve. As a result, it is often necessary for us to research articles and other sources of information to develop informed opinions about the problem we are investigating.

The famous newspaperman H. L. Mencken once said, "To every complex question there is a simple answer—and it's wrong!" We have seen in this chapter that complex problems do not admit simple solutions, whether they concern personal problems in our lives or larger social problems like racial prejudice or world hunger. We have also seen, however, that by working through these complex problems thoughtfully and systematically, we can achieve a deeper understanding of their many interacting elements, as well as develop strategies for solving them.

Becoming an effective problem-solver does not merely involve applying a problem-solving method in a mechanical fashion any more than becoming a mature critical thinker involves mastering a set of thinking skills. Rather, solving problems, like thinking critically, reflects a total approach to making sense of experience. When we think like problem-solvers, we approach the world in a distinctive way. Instead of avoiding difficult problems, we have the courage to meet them head-on and the determination to work through them. Instead of acting impulsively or relying exclusively on the advice of others, we are able to make sense of complex problems in an organized way and develop practical solutions and initiatives.

A sophisticated problem-solver employs all of the critical-thinking abilities that we have examined so far and those we will explore in the chapters ahead. And while we might agree with H. L. Mencken's evaluation of simple answers to complex questions, we might endorse a rephrased version: "To many complex questions there are complex answers—and these are worth pursuing!"

Thinking Activity 4.4

Analyzing Social Problems

Identify an import local, national, or international problem that needs to be solved. Locate two or more articles that provide background information and analysis of the problem. Using these articles as a resource, analyze the problem using the problem-solving method developed in this chapter.

Thinking Passage

Young Hate

The final section of this chapter consists of an article dealing with a significant social problem in our lives today. "Young Hate," by David Shenk, examines the problem of intolerance on college campuses. This information provides a foundation from which we can construct a thoughtful analysis of this troubling problem and perhaps develop some productive solutions. After reading the article, identify and analyze the problem being discussed by using the problem-solving method developed in this chapter.

Young Hate
by David Shenk

Death to gays. Here is the relevant sequence of events: On Monday night Jerry Mattioli leads a candlelight vigil for lesbian and gay rights. *Gays are trash.* On Tuesday his name is in the school paper and he can hear whispers and feel more, colder stares than usual. On Wednesday morning a walking bridge in the middle of the Michigan State campus is found to be covered with violent epithets warning campus homosexuals to *be afraid, very afraid,* promising to *abolish faggots from existence,* and including messages specifically directed at Mattioli. Beginning Friday morning fifteen of the perpetrators, all known to Mattioli by name and face, are rounded up and quietly disciplined by the university. *Go home faggots.* On Friday afternoon Mattioli is asked by university officials to leave campus for the weekend, for his own safety. He does, and a few hours later receives a phone call from a friend who tells him that his dormitory room has been torched. MSU's second annual "Cross-Cultural Week" is over.

"Everything was ruined," Mattioli says. "What wasn't burned was ruined by smoke and heat and by the water. On Saturday I sat with the fire investigator all day, and we went through the room, literally ash by ash.... The answering machine had melted. The receiver of the telephone on the wall had stretched to about three feet long. That's how intense the heat was."

"Good news!" says Peter Jennings. A recent *Washing Post*/ABC News poll shows that integration is up and racial tension is down in America, as compared with eight years ago. Of course, in any trend there are fluctuations, exceptions. At the University of Massachusetts at Amherst, an estimated two thousand whites chase twenty blacks in a clash after a . . . World Series game, race riots break out in Miami . . . and in Virginia Beach . . . ; and on college campuses across the country, our nation's young elite experience an entire decade's aberration from the poll's findings: incidents of ethnic, religious, and gender-related harassment surge throughout the [decade].

Greatest hits include Randy Bowman, a black student at the University of Texas, having to respectfully decline a request by two young men wearing Ronald Reagan masks and wielding a pistol to exit his eighth-floor dorm room through the window; homemade T-shirts, *Thank God for AIDS* and *Aryan by the Grace of God,* among others, worn proudly on campus; Jewish student centers shot at, stoned, and defaced at Memphis State, University of Kansas, Rutgers *(Six million, why not),* and elsewhere; the black chairperson of United Minorities Council at U Penn getting a dose of hi-tech hate via answering machines: *We're going to lynch you, nigger shit. We are going to lynch you.*

The big picture is less graphic, but just as dreadful: reports of campus harassment have increased as much as 400 percent since 1985. Dropout rates for black students in predominantly white colleges are as much as five times higher than white dropout rates at the same schools and black dropout rates at black schools. The Anti-Defamation League reports a six-fold increase in anti-Semitic episodes on campuses between 1985 and 1988. Meanwhile, Howard J. Ehrlich of the National Institute Against Prejudice and Violence reminds us that "up to 80 percent of harassed students don't report the harassment." Clearly, the barrage of news reports reveals only the tip of a thoroughly sour iceberg.

Colleges have responded to incidents of intolerance—and the subsequent demands of minority rights groups—with the mandatory ethnic culture classes and restrictions on verbal harassment. But what price tranquillity? Libertarian and conservative student groups, faculty, and political advisors lash out over limitations on free speech and the improper embrace of liberal political agendas. "Progressive academic administrations," writes University of Pennsylvanian professor Alan Charles Kors in the *Wall Street Journal,* "are determined to enlighten their morally benighted students and protect the community from political sin."

Kors and kind bristle at the language of compromise being attached to official university policy. The preamble to the University of Michigan's new policy on discriminatory behavior reads, in part, "Because there is tension between freedom of speech, the right of individuals to be free from injury caused by discrimination, and the University's duty to protect the educational process . . . it may be necessary to have varying standards depending on the locus of regulated conduct." The policy tried to "strike a balance" by applying different sets of restrictions to academic centers, open areas, and living quarters, but in so doing, hit a wall. Before the policy could go into effect, it was struck down in a Michigan court as being too vague. At least a dozen schools in the process of formulating their own policies scurried in retreat as buoyant free-speech advocates went on the offensive. Tufts University president Jean Mayer voluntarily dismissed his school's "Freedom of Speech versus Freedom from Harassment" policy after a particularly inventive demonstration by late-night protesters, who used chalk, tape, and poster board to divide the campus into designated free speech, limited speech, and non-free speech zones. "We're not working for a right to offensive speech," says admitted chalker Andrew Zappia, co-editor of the conservative campus paper, *The Primary Source*. "This is about protecting free speech, in general, and allowing the community to set its own standards about what is appropriate. . . .

"The purpose of the Tufts policy was to prosecute people for what the university described as 'gray area'—meaning unintentional—harassment." Zappia gives a hypothetical example: "I'm a Catholic living in a dorm, and I put up a poster in my room [consistent with my faith] saying that homosexuality is bad. If I have a gay roommate or one who doesn't agree with me, he could have me prosecuted, not because I hung it there to offend him, but because it's gray areas harassment. . . . The policy was well intended, but it was dangerously vague. They used words like *stigmatizing, offensive, harassing*—words that are very difficult to define."

Detroit lawyer Walter B. Connolly, Jr., disagrees. He insists that it's quite proper for schools to act to protect the victims of discrimination as long as the restrictions stay out of the classroom. "Defamation, child pornography, fighting words, inappropriate comments on the radio—there are all sorts of areas where the First Amendment isn't the preeminent burning omnipotence in the sky. . . . Whenever you have competing interests of a federal statute [and] the Constitution, you end up balancing."

If you want to see a liberal who follows this issue flinch, whisper into his or her ear the name Shelby Steele. Liberals don't like Steele, an (African American) English professor at California' San Jose State; they try to dismiss him as having no professional experience in the study of racial discrimination. But he's heavily into the subject, and his analyses are both lucid and disturbing. Steele doesn't favor restrictions on speech, largely because they don't deal with what he sees as the problem. "You don't gain very much by trying to legislate the problems away, curtailing everyone's rights in the process," he says. In a forum in which almost everyone roars against a shadowy, usually nameless contingent of racist thugs, Steele deviates, choosing instead to accuse the accusers. He blames not the racists, but the weak-kneed liberal administrators and power-hungry victims' advocates for the mess on campuses today.

"Racial tension on campus is the result more of racial equality than inequality," says Steele. "On campuses today, as throughout society, blacks enjoy equality under the law—a profound social advancement. . . . What has emerged in recent years . . . in a sense as a result of progress . . . is *a politics of difference,* a troubling, volatile politics in which each group justifies itself, its sense of worth and its pursuit of power, through difference alone." On nearly every campus, says Steele, groups representing blacks, Hispanics, Asians, gays, women, Jews, and any combinations therein solicit special resources. Asked for—often demanded, in intense demonstrations—are funds for African-American (Hispanic . . .) cultural centers, separate (face it, segregated) housing, ethnic studies programs, and even individual academic incentives—at Penn State, minority students are given $275 per semester if they ear a C average, twice that if they do better than 2.75.

These entitlements, however, do not just appear *deus ex machina.* Part two of Steele's thesis addresses what he calls the "capitulation" of campus presidents. To avoid feelings of guilt stemming from past discrimination against minority groups, Steele says, "[campus administrators have] tended to go along with whatever blacks put on the table, rather than work with them to assess their real needs. . . . Administrators would never give white students a theme house where they could be 'more comfortable with people of their own kind,' yet more and more universities are doing this for black students." Steel sees white frustration as the inevitable result.

"White students are not invited to the negotiating table from which they see blacks and others walk away with concessions," he says. "The presumption is that they do not deserve to be there, because they are white. So they can only be defensive, and the less mature among them will be aggressive."

Course, some folks see it another way. The students fighting for minority rights aren't wicked political corruptors, but champions of a cause far too long suppressed by the white male hegemony. Responsive administrators are engaged not in capitulation, but in progress. And one shouldn't look for the cause of this mess on any campus, because he doesn't live on one. His address used to be the White House, but then he moved to 666 St. Cloud Road. Ronald Reagan, come on down.

Dr. Manning Marble, University of Colorado: "The shattering assault against the economic, social, and political status of the black American community as a whole [is symbolized by] the Reagan Administration in the 1980s. The Civil Rights Commission was gutted; affirmative action became a 'dead letter'; social welfare, health care, employment training, and educational loans were all severely reduced. This had a disproportionately more negative impact upon black youth."

The "perception is already widespread that the society at large is more permissive toward discriminatory attitudes and behaviors, and less committed to equal opportunity and affirmative action," concluded a 1988 conference at Northern Illinois University. John Wiener, writing in *The Nation,* attacks long-standing institutions of bigotry, asserting, for example, that "racism is endemic to the fraternity subculture," and praises the efforts of some schools to double the number of minority faculty and increase minority fellowships. On behalf of progressives across the land, Wiener writes off Shelby Steele as someone who is content to "blame the victim."

So the machine has melted, the phone has stretched to where it is useless. This is how intense the heat is. Liberals, who largely control the administration, faculty, and students' rights groups of leading academic institutions, have, with virtually no intensive intellectual debate, inculcated schools with their answers to the problem of bigotry. Conservatives, with a long history of insensitivity to minority concerns, have been all but shut out of the debate, and now want back in. Their intensive pursuit of the true nature of bigotry and the proper response to it— working to assess the "real needs" of campuses rather than simply bowing to pressure—deserves to be embraced by all concerned parties, and probably would have been by now but for two small items: (a) Reagan, their fearless leader, clearly *was* insensitive to ethnic/feminist concerns (even Steele agrees with this); and (b) some of the more coherent conservative pundits *still* show a blatant apathy to the problems of bigotry in this country. This has been sufficient ammunition for liberals who are continually looking for an excuse to keep conservatives out of the dialogue. So now we have clashes rather than debates: on how much one can say, on how much one should have to hear. Two negatives: one side wants to crack down on expression, the other on awareness. The machine has melted, and it's going to take some consensus to build a new one. Intellectual provincialism will have to end before young hate ever will.

A Month in the Life of Campus Bigotry

April 1.
Vandals spray-paint "Jewhaters will pay" and other slogans on the office walls of *The Michigan Daily* (University of Michigan) in response to editorials condemning Israel

for policies regarding the Palestinians. Pro-Israeli and pro-Palestinian shanties [are] defaced; one is burned.

U of M: Fliers circulated over the weekend announce "White Pride Month."

Southern Connecticut State University reportedly suspends five fraternity officers after racial brawl.

April 2.
Several gay men of the University of Connecticut are taunted by two students, who yell "faggot" at them.

April 3.
The University of Michigan faculty meet to discuss a proposal to require students to take a course on ethnicity and racism.

April 4.
Students at the University of California at Santa Barbara suspend hunger strike after university agrees to negotiate on demands for minority faculty hiring and the changed status of certain required courses.

April 5.
The NCAA releases results of survey on black student athletes, reporting that 51 percent of black football and basketball players at predominantly white schools express feelings of being different; 51 percent reported feelings of racial isolation; 33 percent report having experienced at least six incidents of individual racial discrimination.

The *New York Times* prints three op-ed pieces by students on the subject of racial tension on campus.

Charges filed against a former student of Penn State of racial harassment of a black woman.

April 6.
University of Michigan: Hundreds of law students wear arm bands, boycott classes to protest lack of women and minority professors.

Michigan State University announces broad plan for increasing the number of minority students, faculty, and staff; the appointment of a senior advisor for minority affairs; and the expansion of multicultural conferences. "It's not our responsibility just to mirror society or respond to mandates," President John DiBioggio tells reporters, "but to set the tone."

April 7.
Wayne State University (Detroit, Michigan) student newspaper runs retraction of cartoon considered offensive following protest earlier in the week.

Controversy develops at the State University of New York at Stony Brook, where a white woman charges a popular black basketball player with rape. Player denies charges. Charges are dismissed. Protests of racism and sexual assault commence.

April 12.
Twelve-day sit-in begins at Wayne State University (Michigan) over conditions for black students on campus.

April 14.
Racial brawl at Arizona State.

April 20.
Demonstrations at several universities across the country (Harvard, Duke, Wayne State, Wooster College, Penn State, etc.) for improvements in black student life.

Separate escort service for blacks started at Penn State out of distrust of the regular service.

April 21.
200-student sit-in ends at Arizona State University when administrators agree to all thirteen demands.

April 24.
Proposed tuition increase at City Universities of New York turns into racial controversy.

April 25.
After eighteen months in office, Robert Collin, Florida Atlantic University's first black dean, reveals he has filed a federal discrimination complaint against the school.

Two leaders of Columbia University's Gay and Lesbian Alliance receive death threat[s]. "Dear Jeff, I will kill you butt fucking faggots. Death to COLA!"

April 26.
A black Smith College (Massachusetts) student finds note slipped under door, ". . . African monkey do you want some bananas? Go back to the jungle. . . ."

"I don't think we should have to constantly relive our ancestors' mistakes," a white student at the University of North Carolina at Greensboro tells a reporter. "I didn't oppress anybody. Blacks are now equal. You don't see any racial problems anymore."

White Student Union is reported to have been formed at Temple University in Philadelphia, "City of Brotherly Love."

April 28.
Note found in Brown University (Rhode Island) dorm. "Once upon a time, Brown was a place where a white man could go to class without having to look at little black faces, or little yellow faces or little brown faces, except when he went to take his meals. Things have been going downhill since the kitchen help moved into the classroom. Keep white supremecy [sic] alive!!! Join the Brown chapter of the KKK today." Note is part of series that began in the middle of the month with "Die Homos." University officials beef up security, hold forum.

April 29.
Controversy reported over proposed ban on verbal harassment at Arizona State.

April 30.
Anti-apartheid shanty at University of Maryland, Baltimore County, is defaced. Signs read "Apartheid now," and "Trump Plaza."

University of California at Berkeley: Resolution is passed requiring an ethnic studies course for all students.

University of Connecticut: Code is revised to provide specific penalties for acts of racial intolerance.

Case 4
The Craig Middle School: Part A*

Objectives

▶ To provide experience in defining a problem and its causes

▶ To analyze the management and implementation of a change

Background

Managing change is an important skill for managers in today's fast-paced world. One aspect of managing change is the ability to define and resolve problems that occur during the implementation phase. This case allows students to develop their skills in defining a problem and its causes. It can also be used in a more general way to examine the management of change.

Problem Solving

There are numerous models that describe the problem-solving process. Most begin with an analysis of the situation, i.e., problem definition. On the surface, it would appear to be simple to analyze a situation and define the problem. Unfortunately, this phase of problem solving is often marked by errors that can have serious consequences.

Problem definition should focus on the visible signs of distress. Problem solvers should ask what is not happening as expected or desired that affects the achievement of the organization's goals. It is important to avoid defining problems that do not directly affect the organization's goals. This will help eliminate defining causes or solutions as problems. For example, while Ms. Carole may indeed be causing teachers to call in sick, defining the problem as her behavior does not describe a problem directly affecting the achievement of the school's goal to educate children. Absenteeism, however, directly affects the education of the children. This problem definition does not preclude Ms. Carole from being examined as a possible cause. It does, however, keep open the possibility that there are other causes.

Consequences of Incorrectly Defining a Problem

One obvious consequence of an error in problem definitions is that the problems causing the greatest loss of effectiveness will not get addressed. When this happens, managers are always putting out fires. They spend most of their time resolving the most pressing issues without understanding why these "fires" are constantly being lit. As a result, a manager may successfully resolve a particular issue but never address the underlying problem that caused the issue to surface. For example, the principal of the

*These case notes were written by Steven B. Wolff and Maida Williams. Used with permission.

Craig Middle School notices the increase in absenteeism. This is a "visible sign of distress" that needs attention. Yet, the problem is often defined as Ms. Carole's aggressive style or the extra work required of teachers. These are possible causes of the absenteeism, not "visible signs of distress," i.e., a definition of the problem. As is seen in part B of the case, these are not causing the bulk of absentee problem. Focusing attention on these issues probably will not significantly lower absenteeism and may lead to another negative consequence of incorrectly defining a problem—creation of a self-fulfilling prophecy.

Many managers are quick to attribute problems to employees. When this happens they may actually create a problem where none previously existed. Ms. Carole is a hard-working teacher who expends much energy for the students. While some teachers said they wish she were less bossy and disruptive, no data suggests that this has become a demotivating factor for them. They may very well recognize the energy Ms. Carole devotes to her work and have high respect for her even though she is deemed to be overzealous at times. If it is assumed that Ms. Carole is the cause of the absenteeism, then not only will the problem not be resolved, but Ms. Carole may become resentful and demotivated. This may result in a loss of energy and an increase in her absentee rate, thus exacerbating the problem that we are trying to solve.

Human Factors Leading to Incorrect Problem Definition

Defining a problem is often hindered by the human tendency to try to fit a current situation into experience. While past experience is certainly useful in understanding many situations, it cannot bring to light an understanding of the unique aspects of a particular problem. People will examine their memory for similar situations and attribute causes or solutions from that problem to the current situation. The result is that problems are often defined in terms of a cause or a solution. For example, instead of defining the problem as an increase in absenteeism, it might be defined as Ms. Carole's aggressiveness (a possible cause), or the need to make participation in the after-school program voluntary (a possible solution). When a problem is defined as a cause or solution, it prevents the exploration of alternative causes or solutions. If the problem is defined as absenteeism, then Ms. Carole might be one possible cause, but adherence to a problem-solving process would require looking for other possible explanations. Alternatively, if the problem is defined as Ms. Carole, the cause of increased absenteeism may never be found.

The Rest of the Problem-Solving Process

Once a problem is defined, it is important to collect data that specifically describes the problem. Often this will help in the next step, which is to define possible causes. In the Craig case, the data has been collected on the absentee rates by grade and by day of the week. Although this should give away the definition of the problem, many students will still avoid defining the problem as absenteeism. It is important to stress that a full understanding of the problem generally requires collection of information.

After defining the problem, possible causes must be considered. There are usually multiple causes to any problem. It is important to consider as many as feasible and avoid jumping to conclusions. Data should be collected to determine how much each cause contributes to the problem if at all. This is the stage at which Part B of the case ends.

The remaining stages of the problem-solving process are to develop, implement, and monitor solutions. When the most probable causes have been determined through careful examination of the data, solutions can then be devised to address them. An implementation plan should be constructed, keeping in mind the various constituencies affected by the solution. This will determine who must be involved in the planning, who must be sold on the idea, and who must be kept informed. When the plan is put into practice, it must be monitored to ensure its effectiveness. Areas where the plan is not working can then be defined as problems, and the process repeated.

Managing Change

Managing change is very similar to the problem-solving process. Once the need for a change is recognized (problem definition), a plan must be devised and implemented (solution implementation). The implementation must be monitored and adjustments made to the plan as necessary; this is the phase of the change process that characterizes the Craig Middle School.

One aspect of managing change that is not addressed in the problem-solving model is resistance. Resistance to change can occur for many reasons; a major reason is a perception that something of value will be lost, such as stability when the outcome of the change is unknown and thus more uncertain; a feeling of competence when the change requires new skills; or economic security when the change may result in lower compensation or new work rules requiring more energy for the same pay.

Each of these possible resistances is potentially present at the Craig Middle School. The teachers will be implementing new programs but cannot know if these will be better than the current methods until they have been tried. Teachers are being asked to teach in new ways. The methods they have been comfortable with may have to change. They are also being asked to invest more time and energy, especially in the after-school program.

Resistance to change may be overcome using a variety of methods. Education concerning the reasons for change can help people realize that it is necessary to do things differently to cope with new environmental demands. People will be less hesitant to change if they understand the need for it. Involving people in the change process can increase understanding and buy-in. We may become invigorated by changes done by us but resist changes done to us. Ms. Smith's effort to involve the teachers in making changes has led to the participation of most teachers in decision making and planning.

It also important to provide support and coaching to those going through a change. If people feel they are being helped to develop new skills and are allowed to make mistakes as they try them out, they generally will be less resistant to change. Ms. Smith has been providing support that is appreciated by the teachers and serves to reduce resistance.

Discussing the Case

The case can be used to discuss the problem-solving process or to analyze change at the Craig Middle School. If you want to focus on problem solving, assign Part A as preparation for an in-class discussion. If you want to focus on change, hand out Part B, and have the students read both parts of the case and answer the questions regarding change at the end of Part B. This can be done as a written assignment or as an in-class discussion.

Problem-Solving Discussion

Using this case to discuss problem solving helps students develop the critical skills of defining a problem and its causes.

The case presents much circumstantial data about problems and their causes at the Craig Middle School. In a real situation, much information must be processed and filtered before a problem can be defined. The additional data presented in this case is intended to simulate this condition and lead the students into making some of the common mistakes that are made in defining a problem.

Students should first focus on defining the problem. If you develop a list of problem definitions on the board, it most likely will have many perspectives. Many will be causes, and others will be solutions. You might get items such as teachers being overworked, Ms. Carole's behavior, the old building, the need to make the after school program voluntary, and teacher absences. Point out that a good problem definition should focus on the visible signs of distress that affect achievement of the organization's goals. Also point out that there may be multiple problems, and these must be prioritized. Ask, "Which problems can we do something about, and of those, which will have the greatest impact on organizational goals?" With this in mind, go through the list of problems generated, and help the students weed out those that are not within the school's control. Ask students to consider the following:

Issue: Teachers being overworked

Response: This only affects the education of students through some behavior. If teachers are calling in sick because they are overwhelmed, then being overworked is a cause of a problem. By defining the problem as teachers being overworked, the focus is shifted from absenteeism, which may have other causes.

Issue: Ms. Carole's behavior

Response: This is also a potential cause of some other behavior that might directly affect student education. See the first discussion. Defining the problem this way may cause other problems such as a decline in Ms. Carole's performance. This is one reason the problem definition is so critical. It is often possible to create more problems than are solved when personnel are incorrectly implicated.

Issue: The old building

Response: It could be argued that the poor condition of the building affects the ability of the teachers to provide a good education. Ask whether this is something that can be addressed at this time. The case states that a renovation is scheduled in two years. The implication is the problem has been recognized and addressed. There is probably nothing that could be done at this time. You might also ask whether this is the highest priority problem at this time. Are there other problems, such as absenteeism, which have a more immediate affect on student education?

Issue: The need to make the after-school program voluntary

Response: This is a solution stated as a problem. Ask the students why this necessary, and the answer is likely to be to lower absenteeism. Point out that the need to make the after-school program voluntary is not a visible sign of distress. It is a solution to another problem. By focusing on the solution, other possible causes of absenteeism may be overlooked.

Issue: Teacher absences

Response: This is a visible sign of distress that affects the education of students. This should be one, if not the only, problem left on the list when you are through examining all the items. If there are other legitimate problems, have the students prioritize them. Absenteeism should be close to the top of the list. The remainder of the case assumes absenteeism is the main issue. For purposes of the case discussion, explain to the students that you would like to focus on absenteeism.

Once the problem has been defined, stress that additional information, such as the data on absences in Part A, should be gathered to help further define the situation.

When sufficient data has been collected about the problem, possible causes can be suggested. Ask students to brainstorm possible causes of absenteeism. After generation of many possible causes, ask them what their next steps would be. These should be to collect data to determine which cause is contributing the most to the problem. Because the reason for the bulk of the absences is purposely not readily apparent, you can emphasize human tendency to jump to conclusions. Students are likely to have missed the major cause altogether. Unless the causes have been researched and properly defined, it is likely that much time and energy will be wasted on solutions that do not address the problem. It is also likely that attacking the wrong causes will create more problems than are solved.

At the end of Part B, students have enough information to know that the major cause of absences is the research being done by the eighth grade teachers. There is not enough data to suggest that resentment is causing the bulk of the problems. The data suggest that even though there is some resentment, the teachers are professionals and hesitate to take sick days.

At this point you should ask the students what their next steps should be. It is important to examine whether the eighth grade teachers account for all the additional absences. While it is likely that they account for the bulk, there may be additional causes that must be examined. Perhaps some teachers are indeed unhappy with the changes. While this is not the major cause of the increase in absences, it may become the highest priority problem after the main cause is found. Students should not assume the problem is solved because they have found the major contributing factor. Doing so may mask additional problems that need attention.

Alternative Problem-Solving Discussion

A powerful way to illustrate that our personal preferences will affect the definition of a problem is to have the class discuss the case in groups. Before the class, have students fill out the "The X-Y Scale" and turn it in with their name on it. Group students according to their scores. You should have a Theory X group, a Theory Y group, and a range of groups in between. Don't tell the students how the groups were formed until the debriefing session.

Ask students to do the following in their groups:

1.   Define the problem at the Craig Middle School.
2.   Describe the causes of the problem.

Give the groups about 30 minutes for discussion. When time is up, have a reporter from each group put their answers on the board on a matrix, with one column for each group and a row for each question.

The usual outcome is that the Theory X group tends to define the problem in terms of people, i.e., Ms. Carole, and the Theory Y group tends to avoid people in the definition of the problem. This provides a powerful example of how people's perspectives affect the way they define problems and causes. Use this to discuss some of the consequences of defining the problem inaccurately. For example, if Ms. Carole is defined as the problem or its cause, it is likely that confronting her will create additional problems.

Although there is usually a clear distinction in the way groups define problems and causes, this is not a foregone conclusion. If there are no major differences, you can congratulate the students on their ability to maintain a balanced perspective in their definition of the problem regardless of their personal inclinations. You can still make the point about perspectives affecting problem definition by referring to our observations that there have been differences among the groups in all but one class where we have used the case in this manner.

Choosing this alternative does not preclude you from holding the discussion as described in the previous section of these notes. It only adds the possibility of additional understanding regarding the influence of personal perspectives in defining a problem.

Managing Change

At the Craig Middle School, teachers have been asked to try new programs and teach in new ways. They have been asked to give up habits, develop new skills, and put in additional effort, the outcomes of which were uncertain.

At this point, the Craig Middle School has gone through the stages of change as described in Greiner's six step model or Lewin's unfreezing, change, and refreezing. Monitoring and reevaluating, the steps that begin the change process again—change being a continuous process—are now taking place.

Over the past two and a half years, Ms. Smith's management style has been helpful in overcoming some of the resistances that are naturally found when an organization goes through the kind of changes that have been brought about at the Craig Middle School. While little change seemed to have come about under the aegis of the previous parade of principals, one wonders just what it is that Mrs. Smith did right.

To begin, Ms. Smith communicated with and educated the staff about the need for change. The after-school program, suggested by parents was explained to the staff at a meeting at which the entire faculty and some parents were present. Next, Ms. Smith involved the teachers in planning and decision making. After selling the after-school program, Ms. Smith gave the teachers the final say on whether the program would be adopted and then involved them in planning the implementation. Her management style encourages communication and involvement. She has an open-door policy and encourages teachers to express their concerns. Ms. Smith also provides support and encouragement to her staff. This can be seen in her approach to mainstreaming the SPED (special education) students.

At the end of Part B, the school is well into the implementation phase of the change process. It must now reassess its change programs. It should examine some of the issues such as absenteeism and possible feelings of teachers being overwhelmed.

The Craig Middle School: Part B

As you studied the pattern of teacher absenteeism at the Craig Middle School, you began to share some of Ms. Smith's concerns. In your capacity as a consultant, you decided that you should do more research to find out just what was going on.

Over the past several days, you have talked with a number of teachers to find out how they feel about the changes that are taking place in the school. Some said they feel overwhelmed, but many also said they are very pleased. They told you that they like the additional freedom and enjoy the new challenge at the school. The eighth grade teachers, for example, said they are very excited about the opportunity to revamp their reading curriculum. This is something they had wanted to do but hadn't previously felt they had the authority or permission to do. Although it meant working some extra hours, they said they didn't mind because they enjoyed the challenge.

Entrepreneurial in their approach to devising a new curriculum, the eighth grade teachers said they realized that it would be beneficial to visit other schools with innovative programs. Unfortunately, visiting schools meant they would have to be out of the building during the school day, and they had heard that there was no money in the budget for additional substitutes. One eighth grade teacher had the idea to write a grant to provide money for coverage, but the grant was not funded. The alternative, they decided, was to take sick days so they could visit the other schools. They knew an excellent substitute who had worked well with their classes in the past. Since he was available only on Fridays, they arranged their school visits to coincide with his availability.

Other teachers were clearly not as energized by the longer hours and extra work needed to revise their curriculum, so they continued to follow their old ways. They were doing a good job, but they said they didn't like the subtle pressure from the principal to be more proactive in their teaching. One seventh grade teacher who had been out more than usual said she had thought about taking extra sick days but would never do it because it would hurt the children. You still wondered why she had been out so much, but you didn't ask because you didn't want to come across as if you were conducting an inquisition. You remembered someone telling you that her mother had been sick, and you figured that perhaps this was the reason for her absences. In any case, after a few more interviews, you recognized that there was some resentment about the changes in the school, and you wondered if this could be the reason for the higher than normal absentee rates. As a very astute and thorough consultant, you want to ensure that this is not a trend that might continue to increase and become more serious in the near future.

Questions for Consideration

1. Based on the information in Part B, what do you believe is the major reason for teacher absenteeism?

2. When you brought your findings to Ms. Smith and the school council, they questioned you closely as to whether there were other concerns they should look at as well. What did you tell them?

3. This case involves the management of change. Using the Continuous Change Process Model [see Moorhead and Griffin, *Organizational Behavior*, 5th ed. (Boston: Houghton Mifflin, 1998) Chapter 19], or another accepted model, determine where The Craig's change process is on the model. Explain.

4. What do you see as some of the reasons that the teachers might be resistant to change?

5. What has Ms. Smith done to help reduce resistance to change?

6. Using the model as a guide, determine and describe your next steps. Be specific.

Organizational Charts

CHAPTER 5

Louis W. Ascione

1. Introduction

Once we develop the necessary habits and attitudes to be procedural problem solvers, we can further increase our problem-solving effectiveness by taking a more organized approach to the problem-solving process. One way of doing this is to generate *organizational charts*. Organizational charts are used to create a visual representation of some aspect of a problematic situation. This visual representation helps us to go through the problem-solving process more efficiently by allowing us to keep track of our progress. A visual representation of a problem also gives us a better, and often bigger, perspective of the problem as a whole.

The use of organizational charts of one sort or another to solve problems is not a new concept, and there is no limit to the types of organizational charts that can be generated as tools for solving problems. Some of the most common organizational charts include calendars, schedules, maps, schematics, flowcharts, and graphs. Some are made for general usage while others are made for very specific instances of problem solving. In this chapter, we will look at a few common types of organizational charts to understand their basic nature and function. All of these organizational charts are versatile and can be modified to suit any problem solving need.

2. Causal Analysis

When dealing with certain types of adaptive problems, it is often necessary to determine the cause of the problem in order to solve it effectively. The types of problems being referred to here are problems that occur within a system that is functioning properly at one point in time, but begins to malfunction at some later point in time. In the simplest terms possible, we need to find causes of problems in which something is "broken." For instance, if our car will not start in the morning, we can only remedy the situation by discovering the cause of the car's malfunction. We drove the car home yesterday, so we know it was working properly then, but today it will not start. Therefore, something must have changed between yesterday and today, which is preventing the car from starting; the question is what?

Because we wish to fix the car as soon as possible, we begin asking ourselves some very normal questions such as "What's wrong with my car?" or "Why won't my car start?" These types of questions are all requests for knowledge regarding the specific cause of our car's malfunction, and it is assumed that if we determine the cause, then we can form a plan for repairing it. Clearly, we cannot even begin to fix our car until we know what is wrong with it. We call this search for causes in a mal-

In CAUSAL ANALYSIS we (1) list all the possible causes of a problem and (2) test each possible cause with the aim of eliminating those which prove not to be the actual cause.

functioning system *troubleshooting*. We can best carry out the activity of troubleshooting if we employ a simple yet effective procedure called *causal analysis*.

There are two general steps to the procedure of causal analysis: (1) listing all the possible causes of a problem and (2) testing each possible cause with the aim of eliminating those which prove *not* to be the actual cause. In this way, we narrow down all possible causes until we are left with only a single cause, which must be the actual cause. In other words, we list every alternative hypothesis as to what could have caused a problem, and then we do our best to demonstrate that each alternative is in fact false. Only the actual causes of a problem will withstand any attempts to eliminate them as false. This second step of the process of causal analysis is often referred to as the *process of elimination*.

Notice that causal analysis involves all the functions of the problem-solving process, but the focus is on understanding the problem, which in this case means discovering the cause of the problem. Causal analysis, like all problem-solving procedures, is complex in the same sense that the entire problem-solving process is complex. When undertaking a causal analysis, we do our best to list all possible causes for a specific event. However, it is neither practical nor rational to attempt to list *all* possible causes for the event. Instead, we must begin the process by listing all the possible causes that seem reasonable or apparent to us at the time. Once we start testing our list of possible causes, we can get a better idea as to whether our list of possible causes needs to be revised in any way. The results of our tests are a source of new information that must be taken into consideration. Therefore, this new information may lead us to re-evaluate the situation and develop a new understanding of the problem, which may then give us insight into new possibilities regarding possible causes.

Applying Causal Analysis

Let's look at how causal analysis works using the example, just mentioned, of a car that will not start. If we want to find out why our car is not starting—that is, if we want to discover the cause of our problem—we must first make a list of all possible reasons that our car will not start. Of course, to do this we need to know something about how cars work. If we have no mechanical understanding of a car's normal functioning, we cannot even begin a causal analysis of a malfunction. However, assuming we have a general knowledge of how a car functions normally, we can generate a list of all possible reasons why our car will not start. Certainly, we would begin compiling such a list by making a survey of all of the components in our car that are directly related to its ability to start. A list of reasons why the car will not start will thus include all statements that indicate a malfunction of one of these components.

For example, certainly a charged battery is needed for a car to start. Thus, one reason why a car might not start is a dead battery. In addition, a car must have gas to start, so another possible cause for a car to fail to start may be that it is out of gas. Of course, a complete list of all the components of a car that are involved in the starting function would be quite long, so for simplicity's sake, let's imagine that there are only three reasons why a car will not start:

1. The car is out of gas.

2. The starter is broken.

3. The battery is dead.

If these are the only possible reasons why a car will not start, then we have a complete set of possible causes for our problem, and our task is to determine which one of these is the correct one. We do this by trying to demonstrate that each one of these alternatives is false. The hypothesis that cannot be proven false will most likely be the cause of our problem.

The attempt to demonstrate that a hypothesis is false defines the most general meaning of testing, and we begin testing our three hypotheses by determining what kinds of evidence would prove them false. For example, the first hypothesis—that the car is out of gas—would be proven false simply by examining the gas tank. If gas is in the tank, then the hypothesis that the car is out of gas is false and can be eliminated as a possible cause for our problem. Now, we have only two possible causes left (2) the starter is broken and (3) the battery is dead. We might test the battery by using a simple voltage meter to see whether it has the proper charge. If it does, then the battery cannot be the cause, and the starter, being the only alternative left, must be preventing the car from starting. The faulty starter is therefore the actual cause of the problem.

Troubleshooting is thus an activity of taking all the possible causes of a problem and isolating the actual cause(s) from among them. In order to be more procedural in causal analysis, as well as to make our causal analysis more explicit for others, it is often helpful to use a *causal analysis chart*. We construct a causal analysis chart by listing in a column our hypotheses of the possible causes of a problem. Then we list the tests that can falsify each of our hypotheses. Lastly, we list the results of each test already conducted as a means of keeping track or our progress. The finished chart of our simplified causal analysis is shown in Table 5-1.

Table 5-1   *Causal Analysis Chart*

Possible Causes	Tests	Test Results
Dead Battery	Check Voltage	Negative
Out of Gas	Check Tank Level	Negative
Broken Starter	Examine the Part	Positive

Of course, the number of possible causes for a specific problem may be so large that it is not practical to list and test them all. In such instances, we must troubleshoot in stages from general to particular. In other words, we attempt to isolate the problem little by little. For example, given the true number of possible causes for a car not to start, auto mechanics may begin troubleshooting with a more general causal analysis that breaks the possible causes into categories and then, through testing, eliminates entire categories, such as electrical problems, fuel problems, or mechanical problems. Simple tests can be used to determine that the cause of the problem is not electrical in nature or not related to the fuel system. Once this is ascertained, we are left with mechanical problems as the category in which the actual problem must be contained. This more general causal analysis chart is shown in Table 5-2.

Table 5-2   *General Causal Analysis Chart*

Possible Causes	Test Results
Electrical	Negative
Fuel	Negative
Mechanical	Positive

In this fashion, a problem can be isolated into a particular category, and then each possible problem within that category can be tested and the actual cause determined. Once we have determined that the problem must be mechanical in nature, we can begin listing all the possible causes for our car's malfunction in a more limited and practically manageable way. Our next causal analysis chart would list only those possible causes of the problem that are mechanical in nature and are related to the starting function of the car so that we can determine which part(s) are defective.

It is important to note that we can only effectively determine causes by eliminating those hypotheses that turn out to be false when tested. It is *not* the case that a hypothesis that turns out to be true when tested is necessarily the sole cause of the problem, or even the most important cause of the problem. For example, if we test the battery and find that it is not fully charged, does this mean that everything else is functioning properly? Certainly not. It may be that the car is also out of gas and the starter is not working. In fact, the battery may have a low charge because we wasted a lot of the charge trying to start a car with no gas and a broken starter. Therefore, we can only be certain about causes by determining what is *not* the problem so that the problem will be what is left over at the end of causal analysis.

One thing that must be kept in mind, however, is the fact that if we are experienced enough with a particular system, we may have a pretty good idea as to what the cause of the problem is just by collecting enough data regarding the symptoms of the problem. For instance, a good auto mechanic may simply listen to what happens when we try to start the car and determine that it is probably the starter. He or she would then examine the starter to see whether it is indeed the cause of the problem. If it is, the problem is solved. However, if it is not, and the mechanic is genuinely perplexed at the cause of the problem, then the process of troubleshooting must begin in an organized and procedural fashion using causal analysis.

3. Comparison Charts

The basic function of developing solution strategies involves two specific procedures, research and brainstorming, and the primary consideration for both these activities is volume. Because the objective of research and brainstorming is to develop as many solution strategies as possible, it is important to organize them in such a way that we can keep track of what kinds of solutions we have already come up with and what kinds of solutions we have yet to generate. Organizing solution strategies is therefore often a good way to stimulate the systematic production of even more solution strategies.

One way of organizing solution strategies as we develop them is to make a *comparison chart*. In a comparison chart, we unify all solution strategies developed into a single structure so that we can create a list of all the consequences of implementing each solution strategy as we test them. The value of a comparison chart is that it facilitates the evaluation of each solution strategy by placing all the consequences of each solution strategy side by side for easy comparison. Typically, we break down the consequences of each solution strategy into advantages and disadvantages. Comparison charts are most effective when dealing with a fairly small amount of solution strategies that each have several advantages and disadvantages.

For example, given a problem, such as that the Apollo 13 faced, the first action to be taken in order to solve the problem is to state the primary and secondary objectives clearly and to identify the constraints. Then, we can develop solution strategies for achieving these objectives within the boundaries of the constraints. Lastly, we can categorize this list into an organized format. The primary objective of Apollo 13 after its accident was to return the astronauts to Earth safely. The secondary objective of the mission was to minimize any danger to the health of the astronauts. The constraint for achieving these objectives was the insufficient amount of electricity needed for the spacecraft to function properly. Therefore, the solution to the problem had to be a plan that got the astronauts home safely without using very much electricity.

Once the problem was made explicit, solution strategies were developed. Because Apollo 13 was still on the way to the moon when the accident occurred, there were two general types of solutions that could be implemented.

1. The spacecraft could be turned around and flown directly home.

2. The spacecraft could continue towards the moon, go around it, and then come back home.

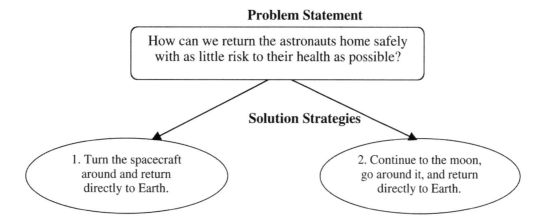

Problem Statement

How can we return the astronauts home safely
with as little risk to their health as possible?

Solution Strategies

1. Turn the spacecraft
around and return
directly to Earth.

2. Continue to the moon,
go around it, and return
directly to Earth.

ADVANTAGES TO SOLUTION STRATEGY 1	ADVANTAGES TO SOLUTION STRATEGY 2
1. The strategy uses the shortest route to Earth.	1. The strategy has already been planned and tested, therefore it is relatively safe.
DISADVANTAGES TO SOLUTION STRATEGY 1	DISADVANTAGES TO SOLUTION STRATEGY 2
1. The strategy is unplanned, has never been tested, and is therefore relatively risky. 2. The strategy is likely to require more fuel than is available, which would make a safe return to Earth impossible.	1. The strategy requires a longer time for astronauts to remain in spacecraft with unknown life-support capabilities. 2. The strategy eliminates radio communication with Earth when the spacecraft passes the far side of the moon.

Figure 5-1   Simple Comparison Chart for the Apollo 13 Mission

Essentially, then, we have two general solution strategies for getting the astronauts home safely. We can represent this situation by taking the explicit problem statement that emerged from the first function of the problem-solving process (understanding the problem) and connecting it with all potential solution strategies.

Once this is accomplished, we must simulate each option in an attempt to elaborate the consequences of implementing each solution strategy. For instance, one of the consequences of implementing the first solution strategy is that the astronauts would travel the shortest possible distance to earth, thus getting them home as soon as possible. The less time the astronauts spent in space, the less risk to their health. Another consequence of this same strategy, however, was that they ran a serious risk of burning up all their remaining fuel in attempting such a maneuver, which would make re-entry into the earth's atmosphere uncontrollable and, therefore, likely fatal. Regarding the second strategy, one consequence of its implementation was that the spacecraft would take the longest possible route back to Earth. On the other hand, it was also the most efficient use of energy since it required very few course corrections.

Once we have identified the consequences of each solution strategy, we can further categorize them in terms of advantages and disadvantages with regards to their potential for attaining the primary and secondary objectives. Figure 5-1 shows what a simple comparison chart for the Apollo 13 mission would look like.

4. Fishbone Diagrams

Not all sets of solution strategies are small enough for us to use a comparison chart effectively. There may be a large number of general solution strategies to a given problem, or general solution strategies may include several different means for achieving them. In such cases, we would adopt a more complex method of representing potential solution strategies. For example, given the problem of how to get from New York to Los Angeles, we can imagine several general means for accomplishing this goal. Basically, we can travel by (1) land, (2) air, or (3) sea.

For each mode of transportation, we can imagine various alternatives. For instance, if we decide to travel to Los Angeles by land, we can drive a car, take a bus, take a train, hitchhike, and so on. Similarly, if we decide to go by air, we can use any number of commercial airlines, or we can hire a private jet to take us. Let's imagine a cruise is the only available means to travel from New York to Los Angeles by sea. Clearly, our choice to travel by land, air, or sea will be affected by the nature of the specific methods of transportation that are available to us in each category. Therefore, we must examine the advantages and disadvantages of each specific means of transportation in order to make an intelligent decision. This requires a more elaborate form of organization than a comparison chart.

One common method for organizing such a large array of alternative solution strategies is a *fishbone diagram*. An example of a fishbone diagram is shown in Figure 5-2.

Fishbone diagrams allow us to effectively narrow down the number of options we have for solving a problem by providing a means for eliminating whole categories or parts of categories from our list of solution strategies. For example, let's imagine we have specific constraints regarding the time and money available to us for accomplishing our goal. Therefore, going to Los Angeles by sea is probably not a viable alternative because it requires a long and expensive cruise from New York to Central America, through the Panama Canal, back up along the coast of Mexico and Southern California to Los Angeles. Given the time and money needed for such a journey, we would eliminate the idea of going to Los Angeles by sea, leaving land and air travel as the only alternative means.

Of course, any method of organizing a list of solution strategies is acceptable. Fishbone diagrams are only one method for organizing ideas. The point is that by organizing and categorizing our potential options, we put ourselves in a better position to systematically eliminate those solution strategies that are clearly unacceptable. This, in turn, makes evaluating solution strategies more efficient. If we know exactly what our options are, it is easier to make a rational decision as to which one is preferable.

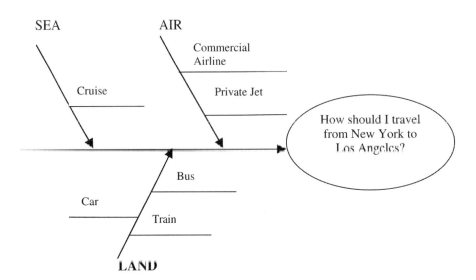

Figure 5-2   Fishbone Diagram

5. Decision Charts

The reason for organizing solution strategies is to facilitate their evaluation, which is the third function of the problem-solving process. Once we have developed a sufficient number of reasonable solution strategies, the next step is to evaluate them by testing each solution strategy against the criteria for success established in our understanding of the problem—namely, the problem objectives and constraints. The final aim of problem solving is to make a rational decision regarding action, and it is in the evaluating function of the problem-solving process that we get around to actually solving the problem.

Let us now look at the process of rational decision making by creating a *decision chart* based on the previously given problem of trying to get from New York to Los Angeles. Although a decision chart is not always necessary for making rational decisions, it is an excellent model of the process we undergo when we make a rational decision. In order to begin a decision chart, we need to understand the problem objectives and constraints because these establish the criteria by which we set up tests for solution strategies and, therefore, decide on a course of action.

We know the primary objective of the problem in question is to get from New York to Los Angeles. What we do not yet know are the secondary goals and the constraints that define the problem as a whole. We can imagine the secondary objectives being to get to Los Angeles as soon as possible and to minimize travel time. Our constraints are that we cannot spend more than three hundred dollars, and we must be there within a week.

Given these objectives and constraints, we have begun to understand the problem and can now use this understanding to produce the criteria with which to evaluate our solution strategies. Again, the best way to illustrate this is by constructing a decision chart in which the criteria are related to the alternative solution strategies in such a way that simple procedure will help us to determine which of the alternatives is the best and should therefore be pursued. We accomplish this by listing all the alternative solution strategies in a row across the top of the chart, all the primary objectives and constraints in the left column, and all the secondary objectives directly below them. A blank decision chart is shown in Figure 5-3.

When evaluating a list of alternative solution strategies, we first use the process of elimination to narrow down the alternatives by discarding any solution strategies that do not fulfill the necessary requirements set by the primary objectives and constraints. Remember, we call the primary objectives and the constraints of a problem "necessary requirements" because if they are not satisfied, the problem (by definition) will not be solved. For instance, in the above stated problem, no solution strategy can be successful if it does not result in the achievement of our primary objective, to get to Los Angeles. Furthermore, no solution strategy can be successful if it costs more than we can afford or if it requires more time than we can spare. Therefore, we can effectively eliminate any solution strategies that either would not result in the achievement of our primary objectives or would surpass the boundaries of any of our constraints.

We can represent this on our decision chart by determining whether each alternative satisfies all the necessary requirements. In this case, we have to find out the cost of each alternative as well as the travel time involved. For example, if there are any solution strategies that cost more than three hundred dollars, they must be immediately eliminated from consideration as potential solutions because they do not satisfy the necessary requirements for solving the problem. Likewise, any solution strategies that cannot achieve the goal within a week must also be eliminated. If a solution strategy satisfies the necessary requirement, we write "YES" in that column and continue to check the rest of the criteria. If a solution strategy does not satisfy a necessary requirement, we eliminated it and write "NO" in that column and cross out the rest of it.

		ALTERNATIVE SOLUTION STRATEGIES				
		Private Jet	Commercial Jet	Bus	Train	Car
PRIMARY OBJECTIVES AND CONSTRAINTS (NECESSARY REQUIREMENTS)	1. Must be a reasonable means of travelling from New York to Los Angeles.					
	2. Must cost less than 300 dollars.					
	3. Must get us to destination within the current week.					

SECONDARY OBJECTIVES (DESIRED CRITERIA)	Weight	Rating	Rating	Rating	Rating	Rating
1. Minimize travel time.						
2. Get us there as soon as possible.						
SCORE (Weight × Rating)						

Figure 5-3   A Blank Decision Chart

Let's imagine that after researching the situation, we discover that all the solution strategies we generated are in fact methods for getting from New York to Los Angeles. Next, we research the cost of each and determine that every mode of transportation except the private jet can be utilized for under three hundred dollars. At this point, we would eliminate the private jet idea because it fails to satisfy this necessary requirement regardless of how well it satisfies any secondary objectives. We can now complete the check of necessary requirements by determining how soon each means of transportation can get us from New York to Los Angeles. Let's imagine that all methods of transportation could get us to Los Angeles within a week, but that to book any commercial flight within the week would cost much more than three hundred dollars. Perhaps we could only get a ticket to Los Angeles for less than three hundred dollars if we book our reservation at least ten days in advance. Therefore, we would now eliminate this option from our list of alternatives as well. Our decision chart, at this point, looks like that shown in Figure 5-4.

Once we have eliminated any solution strategies that do not satisfy the necessary requirements, we are free to decide from among the remaining solution strategies according to how well they satisfy secondary objectives. The first thing to do is determine the relative importance of each secondary objective. We can refer to this importance as its *weight*. Usually, we establish the weight of secondary objectives on a scale of 1 to 10, but any scale can be used. Let's imagine that we weigh our secondary objectives by reasoning that minimizing travel time is important to us but not as important to us as getting to our destination as soon as possible. Therefore, we might give the first secondary objective a relative weight of 4, while we give the second secondary objective a relative weight of 7.

We fill in these weights, and then we *rate* each alternative solution strategy according to how well it satisfies each secondary objective. For example, taking a bus

		ALTERNATIVE SOLUTION STRATEGIES				
		Private Jet	Commercial Jet	Bus	Train	Car
PRIMARY OBJECTIVES AND CONSTRAINTS (NECESSARY REQUIREMENTS)	1. Must be a reasonable means of travelling from New York to Los Angeles.	YES	YES	YES	YES	YES
	2. Must cost less than 300 dollars.	NO	YES	YES	YES	YES
	3. Must get us to destination within the current week.	X	YES	YES	YES	YES

SECONDARY OBJECTIVES (DESIRED CRITERIA)	Weight	Rating	Rating	Rating	Rating	Rating
1. Minimize travel time.		X	X			
2. Get us there as soon as possible.		X	X			
		X	X			
SCORE (Weight × Rating)		X	X			

Figure 5-4   A Partially Completed Decision Chart

from New York to Los Angeles would rate low in terms of minimizing travel time. On a scale of 1 to 10, it would probably rate 3. Furthermore, buses may not leave from New York bound for Los Angeles very frequently, so we might have to wait to get the bus. Thus, taking a bus to Los Angeles might rank fairly low with regards to the second secondary objective as well; let's give it another 3.

A train would be a little faster than a bus, and we could rank it as a 6 for the first secondary objective, but it would also involve some waiting for the departure time just as would a bus, so it rates as a 4 regarding the second secondary objective. Lastly, taking a car to Los Angeles would be a little faster than a bus but slower than a train, so we give it a rating of 4 for minimizing travel time. However, we can leave whenever we want to if we drive ourselves. A train may be faster, but we can leave sooner in the car. Hence, it gets a rating of 4 for getting there as soon as possible. Now all we have to do is determine a score for each alternative and it would be rational to choose the option with the highest score, which in this case turns out to be taking the train. A finished decision chart would thus look something like that shown in Figure 5-5.

If, upon completing a decision chart, it turns out that two or more solution strategies attain an equal or close to equal score, and their score is higher than the other solution strategies, then those solution strategies are essentially equivalent or close to equivalent in consequence. Therefore, it is equally rational to choose either of these solution strategies.

The importance of organizational charts ties in the fact that many problems can only be solved by exact and thorough organization. The following case study is an example of such a problem—namely, the construction of the Empire State Building.

		ALTERNATIVE SOLUTION STRATEGIES				
		Private Jet	Commercial Jet	Bus	Train	Car
PRIMARY OBJECTIVES AND CONSTRAINTS (NECESSARY REQUIREMENTS)	1. Must be a reasonable means of travelling from New York to Los Angeles.	YES	YES	YES	YES	YES
	2. Must cost less than 300 dollars.	NO	YES	YES	YES	YES
	3. Must get us to destination within the current week.	X	NO	YES	YES	YES

SECONDARY OBJECTIVES (DESIRED CRITERIA)	Weight	Rating	Rating	Rating	Rating	Rating
1. Minimize travel time.	3	X	X	3	6	4
2. Get us there as soon as possible.	5	X	X	3	4	4
SCORE (Weight × Rating)		X	X	24	38	32

Figure 6-5   A Finished Decision Chart

Chapter Review Questions

1. What is the basic function of an organizational chart?

2. What are the two most important things to remember when creating a causal analysis chart?

3. For what kinds of problems would a decision chart be valuable?

4. For what kinds of problems would a comparison chart or a fishbone diagram be valuable?

Definitions

Causal Analysis: In causal analysis we (1) list all the possible causes of a problem and (2) test each possible cause with the aim of eliminating those which prove *not* to be the actual cause.

Case 5

Martha Stewart: Insider-Trading Scandal[1]

Martha Stewart is one of the latest chief executive officers to become embroiled in a widening series of corporate scandals across the United States. She founded Martha Stewart Living Omnimedia Inc., a company with interests in publishing, television, merchandising, electronic commerce, and related international partnerships. Along the way, she became America's most famous homemaker and one of its richest women executives. In late 2001, however, she became the center of headlines, speculations, and eventually a federal investigation and indictment on charges related to her sale of four thousand shares of ImClone stock one day before that firm's stock price plummeted. Although Stewart's case had not come to trial at the time of this writing, the scandal harmed the empire she created in her name.

Evolution of a Media Empire

Born in 1941, Martha Kostyra grew up in Nutley, New Jersey, in a Polish-American family with six children. During her childhood years, she developed a passion for cooking, gardening, and home keeping. She learned the basics of cooking, baking, canning, and sewing from her mother; her father introduced her to gardening at a very early age. While earning a bachelor's degree in history and architectural history at Barnard College, she worked as a model to pay her tuition. She became Martha Stewart when she married in her sophomore year. Although she became a successful stockbroker on Wall Street, she left to open a gourmet-food shop that later became a catering business in Westport, Connecticut. She used the distinct visual presentations and stylish recipes she developed for her catering business as a source for her first book, the best-selling *Entertaining,* which was first published in 1982.

Stewart's natural business instincts and leadership skills helped her make smart choices as she transformed her small business into a media empire and her name into a well-recognized brand. She joined Kmart as an image and product consultant in 1987, and persuaded the retailer to sell her growing line of products. She eventually became partners with the firm. This partnership helped her gain the capital necessary to break free of Time Warner, publisher of her highly successful *Martha Stewart Living magazine.* When Stewart and Time Warner disagreed over her plan to cross-sell and market her publishing, television, merchandising, and Web interests, she used everything she owned to buy back the brand rights of her products and publishing for an estimated $75 million. In 1999, she took her rapidly growing business public. Martha Stewart Living Omnimedia, the company she created, now owns three magazines, a TV and cable program, thirty-four books, a newspaper column, a radio program, a Web site, and a merchandising line, as well as the Martha by Mail catalog business. The company earns 65 percent of its revenues from publishing, and its media properties reach 88 million people a month around the world, which allows Martha Stewart Living Omnimedia to command top advertising rates.

---

[1] This case was prepared by Leyla Baykal and Debbie Thorne McAlister for classroom discussion, rather than to illustrate either effective or ineffective handling of an administrative, ethical, or legal decision by an individual or management. Reprinted with the permission of Debbie Thorne McAlister.

Martha Stewart's successes have been widely recognized. Her television show has won an Emmy, and *Adweek* named her "Publishing Executive of the Year" in 1996. She has been named one of "New York's 100 Most Influential Women in Business" by *Forbes 400*, one of the "50 Most Powerful Women" by *Fortune*, and one of "America's 25 Most Influential People" by *Time*. In 1998, she was the recipient of an Edison Achievement Award from the American Marketing Association, among many other national awards and honors.

Martha Stewart Living Omnimedia is clearly a classic success story: the small catering business transformed into a well-known brand, in the process making its founder synonymous with stylish living and good taste. Even those who have ridiculed Stewart's cheery perfect-housewife image acknowledge her confidence and business acumen. One author commented, "To the degree that her business partners were prepared to help advance the success of Martha Stewart, she was prepared to work with them. To the degree that they got in her way, she was willing to roll right over them." Another admired her hard-working nature by saying, "Anyone who spends more than a few minutes with America's most famous homemaker learns that she is one heck of a juggler."

The Insider-Trading Scandal

Despite her reputation and business successes, Stewart was indicted in 2003 on criminal charges and faced several civil lawsuits related to her sale of the ImClone stock. Stewart sold the stock on December 27, 2001, one day before the Food and Drug Administration refused to review ImClone System's cancer drug Erbitux; the company's stock tumbled following the FDA's announcement. The scandal also touches a number of other ImClone insiders, including the company's counsel, John Landes, who dumped $2.5 million worth of the company's stock on December 6; Ronald Martell, ImClone's vice president of marketing, who sold $2.1 million worth of company stock on December 11; and four other company executives who cashed in shares between December 12 and December 21.

Developments in the Scandal. After learning that FDA would refuse to review Erbitux, Sam Waksal, the CEO of ImClone and a close friend of Stewart's, instructed his broker Peter Bacanovic, who is also Stewart's broker, to transfer $4.9 million in ImClone stock to the account of his daughter Aliza Waksal. His daughter also requested that Bacanovic sell $2.5 million of her own ImClone stock. Sam Waksal then tried to sell the shares he had transferred to his daughter, but was blocked by brokerage firm Merrill Lynch. Phone records indicate that Bacanovic called Martha Stewart's office on December 27 shortly after Waksal's daughter dumped her shares. Stewart's stock was sold ten minutes later.

Sam Waksal was arrested on June 12, 2002, on charges of insider trading, obstruction of justice, and bank fraud in addition to previously filed securities fraud and perjury charges. Although he pleaded innocent for nine months, Sam Waksal eventually pleaded guilty to insider trading and another six out of thirteen charges. In his plea, Waksal said that, "I am aware that my conduct, while I was in possession of material non-public information, was wrong. I've made some terrible mistakes and I deeply regret what has happened." He was later sentenced to more than seven years in prison—the maximum allowed by federal sentencing guidelines—and ordered to pay a $3 million fine. Prosecutors continue to investigate whether he tipped off others, including family members and an individual who sold $30 million of the biotechnology company's shares. Sam Waksal's father and daughter also face a criminal investigation and the possible forfeiture of nearly $10 million that the government contends were obtained from illegal insider trading.

Martha Stewart denied that she engaged in any improper trading when she sold her shares of ImClone stock. On December 27, Stewart says she was flying in her private jet to Mexico for a vacation with two friends. En route, she called her office to check her messages, which included one from her broker Peter Bacanovic, with news that her ImClone stock had dropped below $60 per share. Stewart claims she had previously issued a "stop-loss" order to sell the stock if it fell below $60 per share. Stewart called Bacanovic and asked him to sell her 3,928 shares; she also called her friend Sam Waksal, but could not reach him. Stewart's assistant left a message for Sam Waksal saying, "Something's going on with ImClone, and she wants to know what it is. She's staying at Los Ventanos." Waksal did not call her back. Investigators are also looking into the sale of another ten thousand shares of ImClone stock by Dr. Bart Pasternak, a close friend of Stewart. At about the time Stewart made her sale, she was on her way to Mexico with Pasternak's estranged wife, Mariana.

However, Stewart's explanation that she unloaded her stock because of a pre-arranged sell order collapsed when Douglas Faneuil, the broker's assistant who handled the sale of the ImClone stock for Stewart, told Merrill Lynch lawyers that his boss, Peter Bacanovic, had pressured him to lie about a stop-loss order. Although Faneuil initially backed Stewart's story, he later told prosecutors that Bacanovic prompted him to advise Stewart that Waksal family members were dumping their stock and that she should consider doing the same. During interviews with law enforcement officials, Faneuil said, "I did not truthfully reveal everything I knew about the actions of my immediate supervisor and the true reason for the sales." He reportedly received money or other valuables for hiding his knowledge from investigators. Faneuil pleaded guilty to a misdemeanor charge on October 2 and is expected to testify against Stewart, who resigned from her board membership of the New York Stock Exchange a day after Faneuil pleaded guilty. Merrill Lynch fired Faneuil after he pleaded guilty; Bacanovic was also fired for declining to cooperate with investigators looking into trading activity of ImClone's shares.

The Probe. In August 2002, investigators requested Stewart's phone and e-mail records on the ImClone stock trade and her Merrill Lynch account as well as those of her business manager. Stewart and Bacanovic have yet to provide investigators with proof that a stop-loss order existed. Congressional investigators for the U.S. House of Representatives' Energy and Commerce Committee could not find any credible record of such an order between Stewart and her broker. However, portions of the documents presented to the committee were unreadable because they were blacked out. Stewart's lawyers later agreed to return to Capitol Hill with unedited documents. The committee did not call Martha Stewart to testify as her lawyers had made it clear that she would invoke her Fifth Amendment right to remain silent. Investigators, who had been negotiating unsuccessfully with Stewart's lawyers to arrange for her voluntary testimony, came to believe that Stewart was "stonewalling" and would not cooperate. Many wondered, "If Ms. Stewart has been straight about her story, then why wouldn't she tell it under oath?" After the scandal broke, however, Stewart and her spokespeople declined to comment or could not be reached. The House Energy and Commerce Committee ultimately handed the Martha Stewart/ImClone investigation over to the U.S. Justice Department, with a strong suggestion that it investigate whether Stewart had lied to the committee.

Additionally, the SEC indicated that it was ready to file civil securities fraud charges against Stewart for her alleged role in the insider-trading scandal and her public statement about the stop-loss arrangement with her broker. Federal prosecutors soon widened their investigation to include determining whether Stewart had tampered with a computerized phone log to delete a message from her broker as well as whether she had made her public statements about why she sold ImClone shares in order to maintain the price of her own company's stock. Federal law bars officers of public corporations from knowingly making false statements that are material in effect—meaning they have the potential to shape a reasonable investor's decision to buy or sell stock in a particular company. If prosecutors could prove that Stewart made a deceptive statement to repair her credibility and keep her firm's stock price from falling, it could charge her with securities fraud. Already, one shareholder has filed suit against Stewart.

The Charges. Finally, on June 4, 2003, a federal grand jury indicted Stewart on charges of securities fraud, conspiracy (together with Peter Bacanovic), making false statements, and obstruction of justice. Although the forty-one page indictment did not specifically charge Stewart with insider trading, it alleged that she lied to federal investigators about the stock sale, attempted to cover up her activities, and defrauded Martha Stewart Living Omnimedia shareholders by misleading them about the gravity of the situation and thereby keeping the stock price from falling. The indictment further accused Stewart of deleting a computer log of the telephone message from Bacanovic informing her that he thought ImClone's stock "was going to start trading downward." Peter Bacanovic was also indicted on charges of making false statements, making and using false documents, perjury, and obstruction of justice. The indictment alleged that Bacanovic had altered his personal notes to create the impression of a prior agreement to sell Stewart's ImClone shares if the price fell below $60/share. Both Stewart and Bacanovic pleaded "not guilty" to all charges. If convicted, Martha Stewart could be sentenced to up to thirty years in prison and fined up to $2 million.

Additionally, the SEC filed a civil lawsuit accusing both Stewart and Bacanovic of insider trading, demanding more than $45,000 in re-compensation, and seeking to bar Stewart from being an officer or director of a public company. Although Stewart denied the charges, she resigned her positions as chief executive officer and chairman of the board of Martha Stewart Living Omnimedia just hours after the indictment, avowing, "I love this company, its people and everything it stands for, and I am stepping aside as chairman and CEO because it is the right thing to do." She retains a seat on the firm's board of directors and remains its chief shareholder. Sharon Patrick, the company's president and chief operating officer, replaced Stewart as CEO, while Jeffrey Ubben, the founder of an investment group that owns Omnimedia stock, was named chairman.

Ironically, Martha Stewart could have sold her ImClone stock on December 31 instead of December 27 and collected $180,000 in profit without raising any concerns. That's just $48,000 less than what she gained through the earlier sale. That $48,000 gain has already cost Stewart $261,371,672 plus legal fees, an amount that grows daily due to the damage the scandal may create for her image and brand. Despite Stewart's denials of any wrongdoing, the scandal has sliced more than 70 percent off the stock price of Omnimedia and according to one estimate, washed away more than a quarter of her net worth. Before the scandal Stewart had an estimated net worth of $650 million.

After the indictment and Stewart's resignation, she took out a full-page newspaper ad in which she reiterated her innocence and appealed to her customers to remain loyal. Stewart insisted in the ad that, "I simply returned a call from my stockbroker. . . . Based in large part on prior discussions with my broker about price, I authorized a sale of my remaining shares in a biotech company called ImClone. I later denied any wrongdoing in public statements and voluntary interviews with prosecutors. The government's attempt to criminalize these actions makes no sense to me." Stewart also retained a public-relations firm to help her firm weather the crisis and set up a Web site, www.marthatalks.com, to update her customers and fans about the case.

Implications of the Scandal

After the scandal became public, Martha Stewart began a campaign to detach herself from the events. However, she couldn't escape questions about the insider-trading scandal. Even in her regular weekly cooking segment on CBS's *The Early Show,* host Jane Clayson attempted to ask about the scandal, but Stewart responded: "I want to focus on my salad . . ." Her appearances on the morning program have since been put on hold.

If convicted on all charges, Stewart could face a prison sentence and be forced to give up her seat on the board of directors. Separating Martha Stewart from Omnimedia, the company she personifies, would be no simple task. Her most important role in the company is as its highly recognizable spokesperson, brand, and television personality. Finding someone to replace her in that role would be far more difficult than finding a replacement chairwoman and CEO.

The Future of Stewart's Image and Business

There are few companies so closely identified with their founders as Martha Stewart Living Omnimedia Inc. Although many companies have survived scandals and the exit of their founders, Martha Stewart has a one-of-a-kind relationship with her company, its brands, and products. Regardless of whether she is convicted, the insider-trading scandal has affected Stewart's company: the stock price has fallen by 50 percent, and magazine revenues and subscription renewals have declined. Many wonder whether the firm can truly recover without Stewart's presence. Organizational psychologist Ken Siegel, commenting for CBS *News,* suggested that, "Even if she is legally exonerated, her image as the mistress of homeyness is significantly tarnished. She's playing this a little too close to the vest. It's a contradiction of the marketplace image of open, warm, and domestic." On CBS *News,* Steven Fink, president of Lexicon Communications, likewise questioned Stewart's choice of avoiding the questions: "Someone as culturally prominent as Stewart would be expected to address the public, and she has not really done that, resulting, rightly or wrongly, in the perception that she has something to hide. She branded herself as the ultimate last word on perfect living but now her image is looking like a complete act, and the dishonored reputation of its creator is sure to have severe costs for Omnimedia."

The scandal occurred at an unfortunate time for Martha Stewart Living Omnimedia. The company's publishing arm was in its mature stage, its television show was suffering declining ratings, and the Internet operation was taking heavy losses. Moreover, some market analysts have expressed concern that the company depends too heavily on the name and image of its celebrated founder. One shareholder voiced the concern felt by many: "Without Martha, the company is only a shell. She's it." Stewart personifies the brand that is associated with her credibility and honesty—traits the public and investigators now question. In this case, the strength of the brand also becomes its weakness, as it is hard to tell where the person ends and the brand begins. Market analysts agree that Stewart needs to take steps to ensure that the brand can go beyond the person. With the tremendous growth of her company, Stewart has surrounded herself with a group of trustworthy professionals to deal with the fine points who are as detail oriented as she is. She believes that her business can live on without her because it is now a combination of her artistic philosophy and spirit and the creativity of others. Although Stewart has taken strides to make the brand more independent, there are lingering doubts about the long-term effects of the scandal.

Others, however, believe that Martha Stewart's drive and spirit will help her overcome this setback. Jerry Della Femina, an advertising executive, said, "The brand will survive because Martha has gone beyond being a person who represents a brand." She built an empire and became famous by making the most discouraging circumstances seem neat and elegant. The question now is whether the billionaire "diva of domesticity" can survive an insider-trading scandal that has already resulted in the convictions of two people. Before the scandal broke, Stewart was asked about her close ties with her brand. She replied, "I think that my role is Walt Disney. There are very few brands that were really started by a person, with a person's name, that have survived as nicely as that. Estee Lauder has certainly survived beautifully, despite Mrs. Lauder's absence from the business in the last, maybe, 15 years. I would like to engender that same kind of spirit and same kind of high quality."

Questions

1. Martha Stewart has repeatedly denied any wrongdoing, despite the indictment. Why is her company being damaged by the scandal?

2. What role has Stewart's image played in the insider-trading scandal?

3. Will Martha Stewart Living Omnimedia survive if Stewart is convicted? In order to survive, what changes will need to be made at the company?

Sources: These facts are from Christopher M. Byron, *Martha Inc.: The Incredible Story of Martha Stewart Living Omnimedia* (New York: John Wiley & Sons, Inc., 2002); Diane Brady, "Martha Inc. Inside the Growing Empire of America's Lifestyle Queen," *Business Week,* Jan. 17, 2000; Julie Creswell, "Will Martha Walk?" *Fortune,* Nov. 25, 2002, pp. 121–124; Mike Duff, "Martha Scandal Raises Questions, What's in Store for Kmart?" *DSN Retailing Today,* July 8, 2002, pp. 1, 45; Anne D'Innocenzio, "Charges Imperil Stewart Company," *[Fort Collins] Coloradoan,* June 5, 2003, pp. D1, D7; Shelley Emling, "Martha Stewart Indicted on Fraud," *Austin American-Statesman,* June 5, 2003, www.statesman.com; Shelley Emling, "Stewart Defends Her Name with Ad," *Austin American-Statesman,* June 6, 2003, www.statesman.com; "Feds Tighten Noose on Martha," CNN/Money, Feb. 6, 2003, http://money.cnn.com/2003/02/06/news/companies/martha/index.htm; Charles Gasparino and Kara Scannell, "Probe of Martha Stewart's Sale of Stock Enters Its Final Phase," Wall Street Journal, Jan. 24, 2003, p. C7; Constance L. Hays, "Stiff Sentence for ImClone Founder," *Austin American-Statesman,* June 11, 2003, http://www.statesman.com; "ImClone Founder Pleads Guilty," CBS News, Oct. 15, 2002, www.cbsnews.com/stories/2002/08/12/national/main518354.shtml; "ImClone Probe Costly for Martha Stewart," MSNBC, Jan. 27, 2003, http://stacks.msnbc.com/news/864675.asp; Charles M. Madigan, "Woman Behaving Badly," *Across the Board,* July/Aug. 2002, p. 75; Jerry Markon, "Martha Stewart Could Be Charged As 'Tippee,'" *Wall Street Journal,* Oct. 3, 2002, pp. C1, C9; "Martha Stewart Enters Not Guilty Plea to Charges," *Wall Street Journal,* June 4, 2003, http://online.wsj.com; "Martha's Mouthpiece: We'll Deliver," CBS News, Aug. 20, 2002, www.cbsnews.com/stories/2002/08/20/national/main519320.shtml; "Martha Stewart Living Slides into Red, Expects More Losses," *Wall Street Journal,* Mar. 4, 2003, http://online.wsj.com/article/0,,SB1046721988332486840,00.html; Erin McClam, "Martha Stewart Indicted in Stock Scandal," Coloradoan, June 5, 2003, p. A1; Amy Merrick, "Can Martha Deliver Merry?" *Wall Street Journal,* Oct. 8, 2002, pp. B1, B3; Keith Naughton, "Martha's Tabloid Dish," *Newsweek,* June 24, 2002, p. 36; Keith Naughton and Mark Hosenball, "Setting the Table," *Newsweek,* Sept. 23, 2002, p. 7; "New Witness in Martha Probe," CBSNews, Aug. 9, 2002, www.cbsnews.com/stories/2002/08/12/national/main518448.shtml; Marc Peyser, "The Insiders," *Newsweek,* July 1, 2002, pp. 38–53; Thomas A. Stewart, "Martha Stewart's Recipe for Disaster," *Business2.com,* July 3, 2002; Jeffrey Toobin, "Lunch at Martha's," *New Yorker,* Feb. 3, 2003, pp. 38–44; Thor Valdmanis, "Martha Stewart Leaves NYSE Post," *USA Today,* Oct. 4, 2002, p. 3B.

Flow Charts

CHAPTER 6

Louis W. Ascione

1. Introduction to Flowcharts

Logic, in the broadest sense of the term, refers to the structural relationship between inputs and outputs. When a technological structure is designed to produce specific outputs given specific inputs, we call this technological structure a *logical procedure*. For instance, all digital circuits or computer programs are types of logical procedures. Logic is therefore the central focus of their design.

One of the most important tools for designing logical procedures is an activity called *flowcharting*. Essentially, flowcharting is a method for modeling logical procedures by using specific symbols to represent its various parts. These symbols, in turn, are connected by arrows to indicate the proper direction of logical flow through the various parts of the procedure. Figure 6-1 is an example of a very basic flowchart. This particular flowchart represents the logical procedure for converting a Fahrenheit temperature into a Celsius temperature.

2. The Use of Flowcharts

There are two general uses for flowcharts that make them valuable tools for problem solving:

1. Flowcharts create a visual representation of a logical procedure in its entirety. This enables people to clearly understand the function of a logical procedure, and it provides a medium for effective communication between people regarding this function. Flowcharts are especially valuable for comparing logical procedures.

2. Flowcharts allow us to test the design of a logical procedure to determine whether it functions as intended *before* we use it to structure some form of technology. We do this by entering as many different types of inputs into a model of the logical procedure as is practical, and then we check to see whether the outputs of this procedure are always exactly what we would like them to be.

For example, given the flowchart that represents a logical procedure for converting a Fahrenheit temperature into a Celsius temperature in Figure 6-1, we can test this procedure before we create a circuit or program based on this design. We do this by inputting random Fahrenheit temperatures into the logical procedure, and then physically carrying out this logical procedure to generate outputs. Once we have generated outputs, we check them against a known source, such as an existing chart that tells us the correct Celsius temperature for any Fahrenheit temperature. If our outputs are 100 percent correct, then our logical procedure functions properly; if not, then we must re-design the logic of the procedure until out outputs are 100 percent correct. The more precisely inputs and outputs correspond,

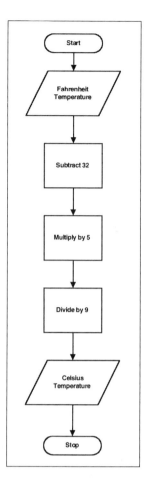

Figure 6-1   A Basic Flowchart Representing a Logical Procedure for Converting Fahrenheit to Celsius

the more logical the procedure is said to be. However, only 100 percent precision regarding the correspondence between inputs and outputs defines a properly functioning logical procedure.

Flowcharting can thus help us to avoid making the mistake of building technology based on untested logical procedures. It is extremely costly to commit resources such as time and money to the development of technology based on untested designs. After all, if a technological device is produced but does not function as intended because it was designed around an inappropriate logical procedure, all the time and money that went into its production will have been wasted.

Furthermore, an even greater amount of time and money will be spent trying to troubleshoot a device that has a fundamentally flawed design. First, the flaw will have to be detected, which is often very difficult to discover because it is assumed that the design itself is valid. Even if the design flaw is detected, even more time and money will have to be invested in re-designing the device so that it does function as originally intended. And, unless this new design is tested before production of a new technological device commences, there is no guarantee that the new device will function any better than the first. Solving one problem may simply cause new problems in technology if the logical design of a device is not checked before production. Now let's look at how flowcharts are developed.

3. Flowcharting Symbols

Any logical procedure is comprised of three basic components: *inputs/outputs*, *processes*, and *decisions*. The specific nature and design of these components defines the function of any form of technology. If these components are organized in a design that guarantees specific outputs given specific inputs, the form of technology that results is valid, meaning that it functions properly, or in more common terms, it works. If these components are organized in a design that does not guarantee specific outputs given specific inputs, the form of technology that results is not valid, meaning it does not function properly and simply does not work. This is why it is extremely important to use flowcharts to determine whether a form of technology involving a logical procedure works before it goes into production.

Specific symbols are used to construct flowcharts, and these symbols fall into two general categories: functional and organizational. *Functional symbols* represent the basic components that make up any logical procedure—namely, inputs and outputs, decisions and processes. *Organizational symbols* are used to indicate the structural design of the basic components and therefore make the logic of the entire process easily comprehensible. Because flowcharting is used in a variety of ways, many symbols can be used. However, for the purpose of understanding the fundamental nature and value of flowcharts, only nine symbols will be used: three functional symbols and six organizational symbols. When constructing flowcharts, it is a good idea to keep a chart containing all the symbols in front of you such as that shown in Figure 6-2.

Let's now look at the three functional symbols used to represent the basic components of any logical procedure.

Input/Output

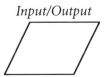

A parallelogram is used to represent both the inputs and outputs of a logical procedure. While all logical procedures have some sort of input that is used to initiate a pro-

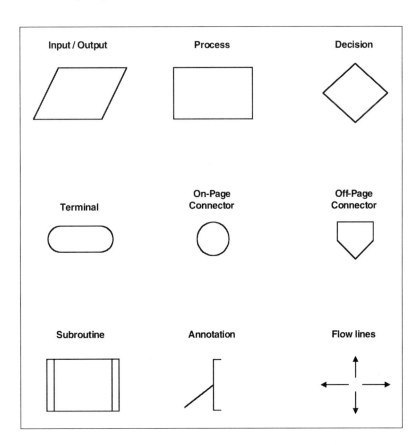

Figure 6-2   Flowcharting Symbols

cedure, not all logical procedures have an output because not all logical procedures terminate. This is because some logical procedures continue indefinitely, once initiated, through the use of a feedback mechanism called a *loop*. All inputs and outputs in a flowchart should have a single entry point and a single exit point for the logical flow. The preferable direction of flow is from top to bottom.

Process

A rectangle is used to represent any process within a logical procedure. Processes are simply activities that must be carried out in order to complete the procedure. As with inputs and outputs, a process should have a single entry point and a single exit point for logical flow, and once again, the preferred direction of flow is from top to bottom.

Decision

A diamond is used to represent decisions, which are questions that can be answered by either "yes" or "no." All decisions should have a single entry point and exactly two exit points. The two exit points represent the two alternative answers to the question being asked. The single entry point for a decision is always from the top, and the preferred direction of logical flow regarding the two exit points is either down and to the right or left and right. Reasons for choosing one or the other will be discussed later.

The remaining six symbols are those used to organize the design of the functional symbols to make the flowchart easier to read and understand.

Terminal

A terminal is represented by an oval. It tells us where logical procedures begin and end. Terminals that are used to tell us where a logical procedure begins are usually labeled "start," while terminals that tell us where logical procedures end are usually labeled "stop." Terminals are also used to indicate the beginning and the end of a subroutine in which the beginning terminal is labeled with the name of the subroutine, and ending terminal is labeled "return." This will be illustrated in more detail when we discuss subroutines. Terminals that begin a logical procedure or a subroutine always have a single exit point from the bottom, and terminals which end a logical procedure or a subroutine always have a single entry point from the top.

On-Page and Off-Page Connectors

Connectors help organize large flowcharts by allowing them to continue on either another point of the same page or on another page when there is a lack of space. We use on-page connectors to continue a flowchart on the same page when there is not enough vertical space to represent the entire flowchart in a single sequence. We use off-page connectors to continue a flowchart on another page when there is not enough space on a page to represent the entire flowchart. Like terminals, connectors have either a single entry point or a single exit point depending on whether they mark the bottom of a page or the top of a page.

Subroutine

A subroutine is represented by a rectangle with two vertical lines on each side. Subroutines are extremely valuable when it come to organizing complex logical procedures because they allow us to reduce any smaller logical procedures contained within a larger logical procedure to a mere process. In this way, we can "bracket" a logical procedure contained within a larger logical procedure and represent it separately on another page. The use of subroutines greatly simplifies any flowchart and allows us to show the connections between one logical procedure and other, related logical procedures.

Annotation

Annotations are used to more fully explain particular functional symbols in a flowchart, but they should only be used as a means to clarify the function of a logical procedure. Use of annotations should be limited to the explanation of functional symbols that may be confusing or unclear. The unnecessary use of annotation almost always hinders more than helps the clarity of a flowchart.

Flow lines

Flow lines are used in all flowcharts to indicate the proper direction of flow within a logical procedure. It is preferable to have all flow lines travel downward except when a decision forces them to go a different direction, in which case it is preferable for them to travel to the right. However, even in such a case, flow lines should return to a downward direction as soon as possible. The only time a flow line should travel upward is when it is part of a loop that is contained in the logical procedure, in which case it is best for the flow lines to travel left and then up. This maintains a clockwise flow of logic within a flowchart. To get a better understanding of flowcharts, it is best if we look at several different examples.

4. Building Flowcharts: Example 1

Our first example of a flowchart represents the simple logical procedure of converting a Fahrenheit temperature into a Celsius temperature, which we already had a brief look at in Figure 6-1. The procedure for converting Fahrenheit into Celsius requires that we take a Fahrenheit temperature, subtract 32, then multiply that number times the fraction 5/9. We would multiply a number by 5/9 by first multiplying that number by five and then dividing by nine.

This flowchart begins, as do all flowcharts, with a terminal (start), which indicates that the following step initiates the logical procedure. The first actual step in this logical procedure is to input a Fahrenheit temperature. This temperature then goes through the process of having 32 subtracted from it. The result of the subtraction process is multiplied by 5, and is then divided by 9. Once this is accomplished, the corresponding Celsius temperature is printed as the output, and the procedure is completed as indicated by the final terminal (stop). Notice that this procedure is so simple that no decisions were necessary.

As we will soon see, however, most flowcharts represent procedures that are more complex than this and therefore include decisions as well. Whenever decisions are involved in flowcharts, the direction of flow necessarily changes at least once because decisions involve at least two alternatives. A flowchart that includes a decision must branch off into at least two directions of flow. Therefore, it is not possible to maintain a single direction of flow in a flowchart that contains a decision. This is why arrows are used in flowcharts. Arrows ensure a clear indication of the direction of flow through a logical procedure.

5. The Rule of Clarity

Regarding the format of flowcharts, there is only one rule that must never be broken. It is called the *rule of clarity* and it states:

> Clarity is the primary criterion for designing any flowchart and ultimately informs us as to the selection of any flowcharting options.

Apart from this rule, there are only general guidelines regarding the proper format of flowcharts. However, the rule of clarity always takes precedence over any flowcharting guidelines. Therefore, if there is ever a point in the construction of a flowchart in which following any of the guidelines would contradict the rule of clarity, always sacrifice the guidelines in favor of the rule of clarity. Indeed, the guidelines only exist as means for maximizing clarity; they are aimed at supporting the rule.

6. Flowcharting Guidelines

1   Try to maintain the direction of flow from top to bottom and from left to right.

2   When there is a loop built into a flowchart, try to have it move right to left and then up so that the general flow of the logic remains clockwise.

3   A single flow line should enter every input/output and process symbol from the top, and should have a single flow line exiting from the bottom.

4   Decisions should have a single flow line entering from the top and two flow lines exiting from the bottom and one or both of the sides. One exit flow line should be labeled "yes" and the other "no."

5   Be as consistent as possible regarding the use of any symbols or structures without sacrificing clarity.

6   Avoid crossing lines at any time (it inevitably reduces clarity).

7. Building Flowcharts: Example 2

Let's now look at a few more examples of flowcharts to get a better understanding of these guidelines as well as the other symbols. The next flowchart we will look at is a representation of a basic temperature control procedure that might be used in a house or car to maintain a specific temperature. The logic of the procedure is as follows:

A temperature reading is taken every minute. If the temperature exceeds 75 degrees Fahrenheit, then the air-conditioning unit will be turned on unless it is already on, in which case nothing is done. If the temperature is 75 degrees or less, then the air-conditioning unit will be turned off unless it is already off, in which case nothing is done.

Figure 6-3 shows what this procedure looks like when it is represented in a flowchart.

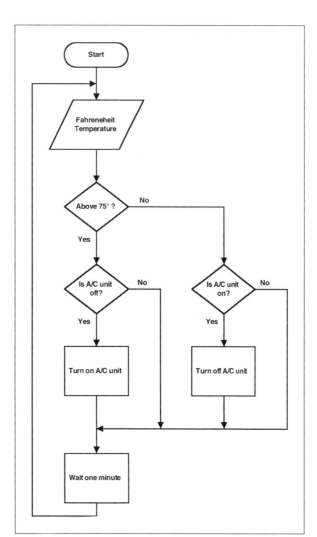

Figure 6-3   Flowchart Representing a Logical Procedure for Automatic Temperature Control

In this particular flowchart, all the guidelines are met: The logic of the procedure flows from top to bottom except when it passes through a decision, and immediately after making a decision, the logical flow travels downward once again. All functional symbols (other than decisions) have a single flow line entering from the top and exiting from the bottom. All decisions have a single flow line entering from the top and exactly two flow lines exiting from it, one from the bottom and one from the right.

The flow lines that exit decisions from the bottom are both labeled "yes," and those that exit from the right are labeled "no." Although there are many ways to represent decisions, such as having "yes" go to the right and "no" go down or to the left, this flowchart is effective because it is consistent with itself and maintains a single structure for decisions throughout. It therefore conforms to the rule of clarity as well as the flowcharting guidelines.

Notice that this flowchart begins with a terminal but does not end with one. This is because this procedure has no end but continues indefinitely until it is stopped manually. As you'll recall, the logical function that permits such a continuous flow is called a loop. In this flowchart, the loop begins at the bottom-most process (wait one minute), and it brings the logical flow back to the beginning of the procedure every time it gets to this point. Because of loops, not every logical procedure has an end, although all have beginnings. Loops are extremely common and helpful for designing complex circuits and programs because they allow for complete automation.

8. Differences in Style: Form and Function

At this point, we need to explain certain differences in flowcharting style that often emerge in accordance with the various uses for which flowcharts are developed. Flowcharts are used for many different purposes, and the nature of the purpose for which they are used may influence flowcharting style. The reason for this is that different purposes require different types and degrees of clarity, and the rule of clarity asserts that we style our flowcharts to maximize clarity. Therefore, different uses of flowcharts will lead to different flowcharting styles.

For example, an electrical engineer may use a flowchart as the first step in designing an electronic circuit. In such cases, the flowchart is used as a sort of "drawing board" with which to test a logical procedure to make sure that it achieves the desired function; that is, it establishes the proper relationship between inputs and outputs. Only after the logic of a circuit is tested should it be physically built. To build a circuit without first knowing the exact function of its design is to risk wasting valuable time, money, and other resources. Because the flowcharts electrical engineers use are often representations of logical procedures that are designed to be built into some sort of circuitry, the format of these flowcharts tends to more closely resemble circuitry than a flowchart created by a computer programmer. It is this resemblance to circuitry that defines clarity for an electrical engineer, and he or she will thus use this definition to guide the format of a flowchart.

Computer programmers, on the other hand, tend to build flowcharts differently than electrical engineers because they define "clarity" differently. A clearly structured flowchart, for a computer programmer, is one that makes it easier to understand how to translate or "code" the logical procedure represented in the flowchart into a programming language. This definition of clarity therefore guides the formatting decisions that are made when developing flowcharts. For example, electrical engineers might prefer a decision to be structured as is shown in Figure 6-4.

A computer programmer would most likely prefer a decision to be structured like Figure 6-5.

The distinction between these two styles of decision structure is the following: The first decision structure (Figure 6-4) makes it possible to clearly discern a straight

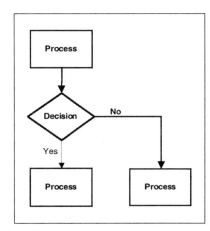

Figure 6-4   A Decision Structure Preferred by Electrical Engineers

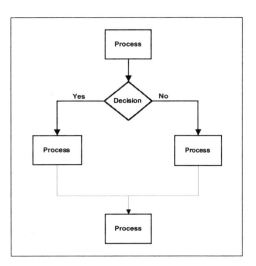

Figure 6-5 ⋯ Flowchart Preferred by Computer Programmers

line from the beginning to the end of a logical procedure, while the second decision structure (Figure 6-5) makes it possible to clearly discern distinct modules within a logical procedure. The value of clarifying a straight line of flow through a logical procedure is that it establishes a "main flow," which is important when using a flowchart to design an electronic circuit of some sort. Therefore, electrical engineers prefer this type of structure when flowcharting. The value of clarifying distinct modules within a logical procedure is that it makes the function of any structure within a logical procedure easy to understand, and it allows a section of a logical procedure to be isolated, evaluated, and modified independently without affecting the rest of the procedure. This is particularly important for programmers who are developing very large and complex programs so that only sections of the program can be evaluated and modified at any time. Therefore, computer programmers prefer to flowchart in such a way that modularization of a logical procedure is facilitated.

As an example of this difference in style, compare Figure 6-3 with Figure 6-6. below. Both flowcharts represent the same logical procedure, namely, the temperature control function that was discussed earlier. What was not mentioned was that the style of flowcharting in Figure 6-3 is more representative of electrical engineers than computer programmers. Notice that it maintains a main flow from top to bottom by making all "yes" decisions travel downward.

Figure 6-6, on the other hand, is more representative of the style of flowcharting used by computer programmers. Notice that both "yes" and "no" alternatives of a decision eventually terminate at a single point regardless of whether

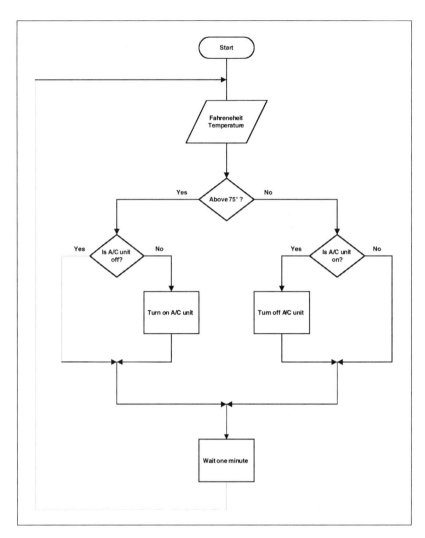

Figure 6-6   A Flowchart Structured for Computer Programmers

any activity takes place in between. For a computer programmer, this flowchart-ing style makes the decision structure clear and it is therefore used consistently. For an electrical engineer, this flowcharting style contains flow lines that do not clearly represent the actual function of the structure and therefore should be replaced with a more realistic flowcharting structure. In either case, it is the rule of clarity that should ultimately determine how to structure a flowchart, and it is the purpose of the flowchart that defines the meaning of clarity. In summary, any style of flowcharting is perfectly acceptable as long as it does not go against the rule of clarity, but those styles of flowcharting that conform *both* to the rule of clarity *and* to the flowcharting guidelines are best.

9. Building Flowcharts: Example 3

The next flowchart we are going to look at is not like most flowcharts in that it is not created to test the function of a logical procedure as a means to develop some form of technology. Instead, this flowchart is created to better illustrate and teach a specific logical procedure to people who are learning a new activity. In this instance, the activity being learned is part of the sport of skydiving—namely, using a parachute after you jump out of an airplane.

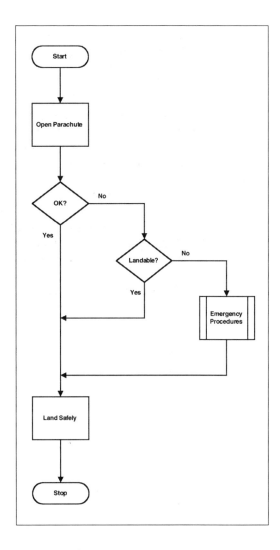

Figure 6-7   A Flowchart Representing a Logical Procedure for Using a Parachute

The important feature of this flowchart is that it makes use of subroutines. As we mentioned earlier, a subroutine is a logical procedure that is being used as part of a larger logical procedure. Because subroutines are themselves logical procedures, they can be represented independently as a separate flowchart. Therefore, whenever we include a subroutine in a flowchart, we represent it as one symbol that refers to another flowchart that fully represents the structure of that logical procedure. This allows us to greatly simplify a flowchart, thus following the rule of clarity.

For example, the logical procedure this flowchart represents begins with a skydiver attempting to open his or her parachute. A decision then has to be made as to whether it opened properly (OK?). If it did, then the skydiver simply lands the parachute. However, if the parachute does not open properly, an entirely different sequence of activities must take place. First, the skydiver must determine whether it is still possible to land the parachute safely. If it is determined that the problem is minor, meaning the parachute can still be landed safely, then this is the best course of action to take and the skydiver should proceed to land carefully. If, however, the problem is major, meaning that the parachute cannot be landed safely, then the situation becomes classified as an emergency, and emergency procedures should go into effect.

Emergency procedures for a malfunctioning parachute begin by disconnecting or "cutting away" the problematic parachute and opening a reserve parachute. The reason that the main parachute is cut away is that it might, and often does, interfere with the proper opening of the reserve parachute. If a reserve parachute is opened without cutting away a malfunctioning main parachute, the two parachutes are most likely going to tangle, leaving the skydiver with no parachute. Needless to say, this is a bad thing.

It is for this reason that it is rational to land a parachute with only minor problems as long as it can be landed safely. It is better to stick with a known problem that will definitely get you to the ground unharmed than to cutaway the parachute and gamble with your last resort. In a situation with such high risk constraints, it is not rational to trade a known, reasonably safe situation for one that is unknown and possibly more dangerous.

Getting back to the flowchart, notice that "emergency procedures" constitute a subroutine. This subroutine is represented by the subroutine symbol, and the use of this symbol greatly simplifies the flowchart because it eliminates the need to represent the contents of that subroutine in the flowchart. The subroutine symbol is therefore a product of the rule of clarity. It allows us to temporarily bracket large portions of a logical procedure and represent them on a separate but related flowchart.

This subroutine is represented in our flowchart only as a single process, but since this process is itself a logical procedure, it is represented in its entirety, on a separate sheet of paper as is shown in Figure 6-8.

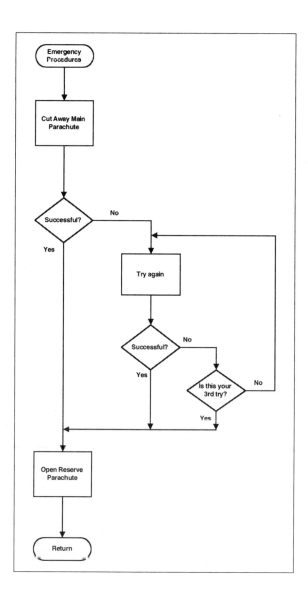

Figure 6-8   Subroutine Representing a Logical Procedure for Emergencies when Using a Parachute (See Figure 6-7)

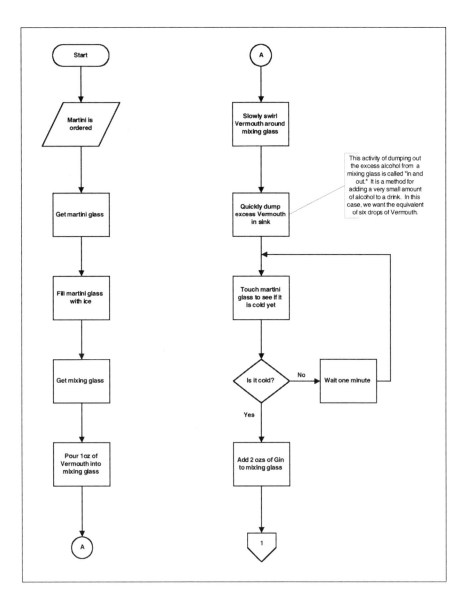

Figure 6-9   A Flowchart Representing a Logical Procedure for Making a Martini

Notice that this subroutine begins and ends with a terminal: the initial terminal is the name of the subroutine and the final terminal says "return." As we mentioned earlier, the use of such a subroutine greatly simplifies this flowchart and maximizes the rule of clarity. In general, the more complex a logical system, the more subroutines are used to make it comprehensible.

10. Building Flowcharts: Example 4

The final flowchart we will examine resembles the previous flowchart in that it is not intended to represent a logical procedure for the purpose of technology but is designed only to train people to perform a task in a procedural manner. The logical procedure represented here is designed to guide bartenders in making a Martini, and while it is a not a complex procedure, it is a somewhat long procedure to flowchart. Therefore, it requires the use of connectors, both on-page and off-page. In this flowchart, shown in Figures 6-9 and 6-10, we also see the use of annotations which can be used to further explain brief symbol labels as yet another means to enhance clarity.

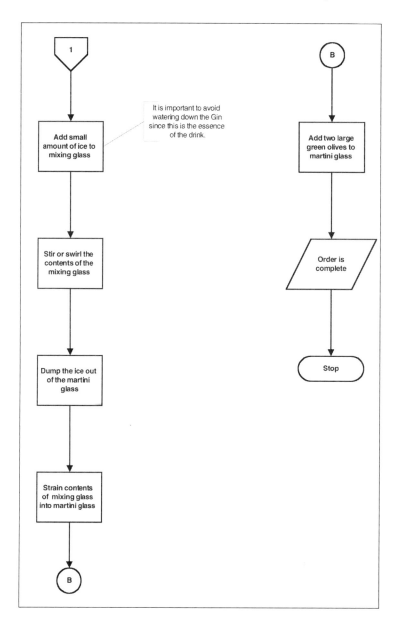

Figure 6-10   A Flow-chart Representing a Logical Procedure for Making a Martini

Notice that the on-page connectors use letters to connect breaks in the flow-chart and the off-page connectors use numbers. This is by no means essential; on-page connectors can certainly use numbers and off-page connectors can certainly use letters—and it is even possible to use a single system of either numbers or letters for both. Once again, the point is to keep things as clear as possible, and it is most often a good idea to use one identification system for on-page connectors and another for off-page connectors.

When using annotations, it is important to use them sparingly. Too many annotations is a surefire way to make a flowchart confusing and cluttered. However, it is equally important to make sure that all labels are completely understood in a flowchart. Being concise is great as long as the meaning is clear, but sometimes the need for brevity detracts from clarity. This is where annotations come in handy. For example, in Figures 6-9 and 6-10, it is important for a bartender to understand the nature of certain processes such as the "in and out" method for adding small amounts of alcohol to a drink. Once this method is understood, it may be used to make other drinks as well. Therefore, it is best to supply a little extra information regarding this step in the martini-making process, and an annotation was used to do so.

Case 6

Exxon Valdez: Revisited[1]

In 1989, Exxon Corporation and Alyeska Pipeline Service Co., an eight-company consortium that operates the Trans-Alaska pipeline and the shipping terminal in Valdez, Alaska, were severely criticized for their handling of a major oil spill from an Exxon tanker. The *Exxon Valdez* ran aground near Valdez, Alaska, on March 24, 1989, and spilled two hundred forty thousand barrels—eleven million gallons—of crude oil, which eventually covered twenty-six hundred square miles of Prince William Sound and the Gulf of Alaska. Although the Exxon spill was not the largest ever, it was the worst in terms of environmental damage and disruption of industry, and it jeopardized the future of oil production in environmentally sensitive areas of Alaska. The effects of the spill could still be seen more than ten years after the wreck.

The Wreck

At 12:04 A.M. on March 24, 1989, the *Exxon Valdez* was under the command of Third Mate Gregory Cousins, who was not licensed to pilot the vessel through the waters of Prince William Sound. The ship's captain, Joseph Hazelwood, apparently was asleep below deck. In an effort to dodge floating ice in the sound, Cousins performed what officials later described as an unusual series of right turns. The ship ran aground on Bligh Reef, spilling much of its cargo through the ruptured hull. The spill spread rapidly during the next few days, killing thousands of sea birds, sea otters, and other wildlife; covering the coastline with oil; and eliminating the fishing season in the sound for several years.

The Prince William Sound area was home to abundant wildlife. More than two hundred species of birds had been reported there, including one-fifth of the world's trumpeter swans. The fishing industry derived annual sales of $100 million from the sound's herring, salmon, Pacific cod, Alaska pollock, rockfish, halibut, flounder, and sharks, as well as crabs and shrimp. The world's largest concentration of killer whales and about one-fourth of the total U.S. sea otter population had inhabited the sound at the time of the wreck.

Response to the Disaster

The events following the March 24 spill reveal what some observers say was a pattern of unpreparedness, mismanagement, and negligence. According to the transcripts of radio conversations between Captain Hazelwood and the Coast Guard immediately after the accident, the captain tried for an hour to rock the tanker free from the reef, an action that Coast Guard officials claim might have sunk the ship and spilled more oil. They say that Hazelwood ignored their warnings that rocking the ship might make the oil spill almost five times as bad.

When Coast Guard officers boarded the tanker at 3:30 A.M., they reported that 138,000 barrels of crude oil had already been spilled. According to a contingency plan

---

[1] This case was prepared by O. C. Ferrell, John Fraedrich, and Gwyneth Vaughn Walters for classroom discussion rather than to illustrate either effective or ineffective handling of an administrative, ethical, or legal decision by management.

filed when the Valdez terminal first began operations, Alyeska crews should have arrived at the ship with containment equipment within a very short period of time; they did not. A frantic Coast Guard officer radioed, "We've got a serious problem. . . . She's leaking and groaning. There's nobody here. . . . Where's Alyeska?"

After being notified of the accident, Alyeska Pipeline Service initiated the first line of defense against oil spills: sending an observation tug to the scene and beginning to assemble its oil-spill containment equipment, much of which was in disarray. It loaded containment boom and lightering equipment (emergency pumps to suction oil from the *Exxon Valdez* onto other vessels) onto a damaged barge. The Coast Guard decided, however, that the barge was too slow and the need for the lightering equipment more urgent, so Alyeska crews had to reload the lightering equipment onto a tugboat, losing still more time.

The first Alyeska containment equipment did not arrive at the scene until 2:30 in the afternoon; the rest of the equipment came the next morning. Neither Alyeska nor Exxon had enough containment booms and chemical dispersants to fight the spill. They were not ready to test the effectiveness of the dispersants until eighteen hours after the spill, and then they conducted the test by tossing buckets of chemicals out the door of a helicopter. The helicopter's rotor dispersed the chemicals, and they missed their target. Moreover, the skimmer boats used to scoop oil out of the sea were old and kept breaking down. The skimmers filled up rapidly and had to be emptied into nearby barges, taking them out of action for long periods of time. Some of the makeshift work crews were assigned to boats without any apparent mission. Cleanup efforts were further hampered by communication breakdowns between coordinators on shore and crews at the scene caused by technical problems and devices' limited range. Instead, messages had to be relayed through local fishermen. In addition, although a fleet of private fishing boats was standing by ready to assist with the containment and cleanup, Exxon and Alyeska failed to mobilize their help. Exxon has admitted that the early efforts were chaotic but says that they were no more so than the usual response to any major disaster.

The *Exxon Valdez* was not fully encircled by containment booms until Saturday afternoon, thirty-six hours after the accident. By then the oil spill covered an area of twelve square miles. Exxon conducted more tests with chemical dispersants Saturday night, but the tests were inconclusive because conditions were too calm. (The chemical dispersants require wave action to be effective.) On Sunday afternoon the Coast Guard gave Exxon permission to use the dispersants on the spill. But that night a storm with winds as high as seventy-three miles an hour drove the oil slick thirty-seven miles into the southwestern section of the sound. All cleanup efforts were halted until the next afternoon because of the weather. Exxon eventually applied 5,500 gallons of chemical dispersants. However, by then, because of the delay caused by the storm, the oil had become too emulsified for dispersants to work properly. By the end of the week, the oil slick had spread to cover twenty-six hundred miles of coastline and sea.

Coast Guard officers tested Captain Hazelwood for alcohol nine hours after the wreck. They apparently did not realize that the ship was equipped with a testing kit. The test showed that Hazelwood had a blood-alcohol content of 0.061. It is a violation of Coast Guard regulations for a person operating a ship to have a blood-alcohol level in excess of 0.04. Four other crewmen, including the third mate, tested negative for alcohol. Exxon officials later admitted that they knew the captain had gone through an alcohol detoxification program, yet they still gave him command of the *Exxon Valdez*, Exxon's largest tanker.

Alyeska's Containment Plan

Since the early 1970s, Alaskan officials and fishermen had expressed concern that a major oil spill was inevitable. In response, Alyeska Pipeline Service, its eight oil company owners, and federal officials promised in 1972 that the tanker fleet operating out of Valdez would incorporate safety features such as double hulls and protective ballast tanks to minimize the possibility of spills. By 1977, however, Alyeska had convinced the Coast Guard that the safety features were not necessary, and only a few ships in the Valdez fleet incorporated them. The E*xxon Valdez* did not.

Alyeska Pipeline Service had filed a comprehensive contingency plan detailing how it would handle spills from the pipeline or from the Valdez terminal. In the event of an oil spill from a tanker, emergency crews were to encircle the spill with containment booms within five hours—yet it took them a day and a half to encircle the *Exxon Valdez.* Alyeska's contingency plan further specified that an emergency crew of at least fifteen people would be on hand at all times. However, in 1981 much of the team had been disbanded to cut costs. In 1989 Alyeska maintained a crew of eleven to monitor terminal operations, but because the *Exxon Valdez* spill occurred at the beginning of the Easter holiday weekend, the company had trouble rounding up the team. Furthermore, Exxon's staff of oil-spill experts had been reduced since 1985. At least nine oil-spill managers, including Exxon's chief environmental officer, had left or retired. An Exxon spokesman said that he was not aware that the cutbacks affected Alyeska's initial readiness to combat a spill.

A state audit of Alyeska's equipment demonstrated that the company was unprepared for the spill. It was supposed to have three tugboats and thirteen oil skimmers available but had only two and seven, respectively. Furthermore, the company had only fourteen thousand feet of boom for containing spills rather than the twenty-one thousand feet specified in the contingency plan. Moreover, the barge that carried the booms and stored skimmed oil was out of service because it had been damaged in an earlier storm. However, even if it had been available, the required equipment would not have been enough because a tanker like the *Exxon Valdez* is almost one thousand feet long and holds 1.2 million barrels of oil. The booms available could barely encircle the giant ship, much less a sizable slick.

Alyeska violated its own contingency plans when it failed to notify state officials that the barge was out of service. A key piece of equipment in the contingency plan, the barge should have been loaded with seven thousand feet of boom. But the boom had been removed during the repair. A replacement barge had been ordered and was on its way from Texas. On March 24, it was in Seattle.

Although Alyeska conducted regular "spill drills," state monitors said that drills in the previous few years had been bungled and were considered unsuccessful. Among other things, the drills showed that crew members often did not know how to operate their assigned equipment. It was also noted that Alyeska's equipment and the crew's responses were inadequate for a real spill. Reporters Ken Wells and Charles McCoy wrote in the *Wall Street Journal:* "The oil companies' lack of preparedness makes a mockery of a 250-page containment plan, approved by the state, for fighting spills in Prince William Sound." Arlon R. Tussing, a Seattle oil consultant, commented, "The system that was set up early on has disintegrated."

Cleaning Up

Exxon's chairman, Lawrence Rawl, apologized to the public for the spill in full-page advertisements in many newspapers and in a letter to Exxon shareholders. The company accepted liability for the spill and responsibility for its cleanup. By summer, Exxon had ten thousand people, one thousand vessels, thirty-eight oil skimmers, and seventy-two aircraft working to clean up beaches and wildlife.

Exxon hoped to have completed its cleanup before September 15, 1989, but a 1990 survey showed that much work remained to be done. Shoreline surveys and limited cleanup efforts were made in 1991, 1992, 1993, and 1994. In 1992 crews from Exxon and the state and federal governments reported that an estimated 7 miles of the 21.4

miles of shoreline surveyed still showed some surface oiling. The surveys also indicated that subsurface oil remained at many of the sites that were heavily oiled in 1989. The surveys determined that the potential environmental impact of further cleanup, as well as the cost, was greater than the problems caused by leaving the oil in place. The 1992 cleanup and the 1993 shoreline assessment were concentrated in those areas where oil remained to a greater degree: Prince William Sound and the Kenai Peninsula. In 1994 restoration workers cleaned a dozen important subsistence and recreation beaches in western Prince William Sound.

Exxon claims that it saved $22 million by not building the *Exxon Valdez* with a second hull. During the period of the oil spill, Exxon spent more than $2.2 billion for cleanup and for reimbursements to the federal, state, and local governments for their expenses in response to the oil spill. In addition, thirty-one lawsuits and thirteen hundred claims had been filed against Exxon within a month of the spill. On August 15, 1989, the state of Alaska also filed a suit against Exxon for mismanaging the response to the oil spill. The suit demanded both compensatory and punitive damages that would exceed $1 billion. Captain Hazelwood, who was fired by Exxon soon after the accident, was found guilty in March 1990 of negligent discharge of oil, a misdemeanor. He was acquitted on three other more serious charges, including drunk driving.

Exxon also faced heated criticism from the public and from state and federal officials, who believed the cleanup efforts were inadequate. A Coast Guard spokesman in Valdez said, "We're running into a problem with the definition of the word 'clean.' The concept of being clean makes you think no oil is there. The oil is still there, but it may be three feet or two feet beneath the surface." Lee Raymond, Exxon's president, said, "Assuming that we can have people working till mid-September, we have a good shot at having all the beaches treated. But not clean like Mr. Clean who shows up in your kitchen. Our objective is to make sure the ecosystems are back in shape." Many Alaskans and environmentalists did not believe Exxon's idea of "clean" was clean enough. In addition, there were disputes as to how much oil had actually been cleaned up. By 1989 six hundred miles of shoreline had been "treated," but another two hundred miles still required treatment. Moreover, incoming tides often brought new oil slicks to cover just-treated beaches, slowing cleanup efforts considerably.

In addition, Exxon came under fire for the way it had managed the crisis. Chairman Lawrence Rawl did not comment on the spill for nearly six days, and then he did so from New York. Although Rawl personally apologized for the spill, crisis-management experts say that it is important for the chief executive to be present at the site of an emergency. Harry Nicolay, a Boston crisis-management consultant, said, "When the most senior person in the company comes forward, it's telling the whole world that we take this as a most serious concern." The crisis-management experts believe that Rawl's delayed response and failure to appear on the scene angered the public even despite Exxon's efforts to clean up the spill.

Some of Exxon's statements to the public have also been criticized as bad public relations moves. For example, one Exxon executive told reporters that consumers would pay for the costs of the cleanup in the form of higher gas prices. Although that statement may have been truthful, it did nothing to placate already angry consumers. The public also reacted skeptically to Exxon officials' attempts to blame cleanup delays on the Coast Guard and Alaskan officials. Gerald C. Meyers, a specialist in corporate crisis management, said that Exxon's newspaper apology was "absolutely insincere. They were ill advised to say they sent 'several hundred people' to the scene. This is a company with more than 100,000 employees." Furthermore, Exxon insisted that it would stop all cleanup operations on September 15, 1989, regardless of how much shoreline remained to be cleaned. In a memorandum released in July 1989, that September deadline was said to be "not negotiable." After much public and government protest, however, the company's president promised that Exxon would return in the spring of 1990 if the Coast Guard determined that further cleanup was warranted. "It's our best guess that there will be a lot less oil than people think," he said. "But if the conclusion is reached by the Coast Guard that something needs to be made right and it can be made right, we'll be there. We're not trying to run off." Exxon did return that spring and the next four years for further cleanup efforts.

Exxon's response to the crisis certainly hurt its reputation and credibility with the public. National consumer groups urged the public to boycott all Exxon products, and nearly twenty thousand Exxon credit card holders cut up their cards and returned them to the company to express their dissatisfaction with its cleanup efforts. Indeed, anger and resentment toward Exxon linger more than a decade after the disaster, and some consumers still refuse to patronize the company because of its handling of the spill.

The Effects of the Exxon Valdez Disaster in the Twenty-First Century

Many changes have occurred since the *Exxon Valdez* incident. Because Captain Hazelwood was found to have had a high blood-alcohol content after the spill, three of Alyeska's largest owners (including Exxon) began mandatory random drug and alcohol searches of all ships using the Valdez port. In 1999, Captain Hazelwood began serving a sentence of one thousand hours of community service after he failed in a nine-year appeal of his 1990 conviction for negligent discharge of oil. Alaska's Governor Steve Cowper ordered Alyeska Pipeline to restock the Valdez terminal with all the booms, skimmers, and other equipment that were required by the original contingency plan. Alyeska was also ordered to form an emergency crew to respond immediately to spills. Governor Cowper demanded that Alyeska stock enough additional equipment to allow it to respond within two hours to a ten-million-gallon spill in Prince William Sound. Alyeska is now required to encircle all tankers with containment booms as they are loading and unloading, and it also had to change other procedures. The state of Alaska also eliminated many of the tax exemptions granted to oil companies producing in many Alaskan oil fields. The elimination of the tax breaks was expected to cost the affected oil companies about $2 billion over the next twenty years. The *Exxon Valdez* was renamed the SeaRiver Mediterranean, but the new name failed to prevent environmentalists from regularly protesting the ship in ports along its new Middle East–Europe route. Prevented by law from entering Alaskan waters and too large and expensive for the Middle Eastern route, the ship was retired from service in the early 2000s.

In a civil settlement with the state of Alaska and the federal government, Exxon agreed to make ten annual payments—ending in the twenty-first century—totaling $900 million, for injuries to natural resources and services and for the restoration and replacement of natural resources. In addition, $5 billion was awarded in punitive damages, which must be divided evenly among the fourteen thousand commercial fishermen, natives, business owners, landowners, and native corporations that were part of the class-action suit. Exxon appealed this judgment, but in late 2000, the Supreme Court refused to free the company from having to pay the $5 billion in damages; a U.S. District Judge later reduced the punitive damages to $4 billion.

In a criminal plea agreement, Exxon was fined $150 million, of which $125 million was remitted in recognition of its cooperation in cleaning up the spill and paying private claims. Of the remaining $25 million, $12 million went to the North American Wetlands Conservation Fund and $13 million to the Victims of Crime Fund. In addition, Exxon agreed to pay restitution of $50 million to the United States and $50 million to the state of Alaska.

But the court debate has not ended. Exxon is involved in a highly contested lawsuit with its numerous insurance providers over their refusal to pay Exxon for its spill-cleanup efforts. The insurance companies, led by Lloyd's of London, refused to pay Exxon because (1) the cleanup efforts engaged in were not required by law; (2) the efforts were conducted in substandard fashion; (3) Exxon's level of liability coverage was well below the expenses sought; and (4) the spill itself was a result of "intentional misconduct," thus disqualifying insurance coverage of the accident. In short, the insurance companies contend that Exxon's cleanup activities were little more than "an expensive public relations exercise," designed to make the public think of Exxon as an ethical and socially responsible corporation. Claiming that it had incurred between $3.5 billion and $4 billion in expenses for the cleanup, Exxon in turn filed suit against the 250 insurance companies, originally seeking around $3 billion in compensation, though it was covered for only $850 million. Most of the original amount Exxon sought from the insurers, $2.15 billion, was for their "bad-faith" conduct in initially refusing to pay as well as interest charges and attorneys' fees. The original figure of $3 billion was later reduced to about $1 billion, and insurers agreed to pay Exxon $300 million as a partial settlement of claims related to cleanup activities.

The one positive consequence of the *Exxon Valdez* oil spill has been better industry response to spills. According to one analyst, "We're still seeing the same number of spills. What has improved is the response to those spills." However, this hardly compensates for the harm inflicted by Exxon's negligent spillage of eleven million gallons of crude oil into the Prince William Sound area. Exxon, now called ExxonMobil, insists the area has completely recovered. However, a study by the National Marine Fisheries Service found that toxins leaching from Valdez oil that remains on the beaches continued to harm sea life more than twelve years after the disaster.

Questions

1. In the context of this incident and the circumstances that led up to it, discuss the role of individual moral development, organizational factors, and significant others in the decisions made after the spill.

2. If Exxon had had an ethics program, would this have prevented the wreck of the *Exxon Valdez*?

3. Should Exxon and Alyeska be held responsible for cleaning up the spill, or should taxpayers and consumers pay for it (in the form of higher gasoline prices and taxes)? Why?

4. In future oil-production efforts, which should take precedence: the environment or consumers' desires for low-priced gasoline and heating oil? Why?

5. Create a flow chart that lists the main problem, decisions, and processes you would use to solve the clean-up problem.

Sources: These facts are from Scott Allen, "Oil Spills: A Fossil-Fuel Fact of Life," *Boston Globe,* Jan. 27, 1996, p. 13; Ronald Alsop, "Corporate Reputations Are Earned with Trust, Reliability, Study Shows," *Wall Street Journal,* Sept. 23, 1999, http://interactive.wsj.com; American Petroleum Institute, "Oil Spill Prevention and Response: It's in Everyone's Best Interest," www.api.org/resources/valdez/ (accessed June 14, 1999); Reed Abelson, "Tax Reformers, Take Your Mark," *New York Times,* Feb. 11, 1996, sec. 3, p. 1; Scott Allen, "Oil Spills. A Fossil-Fuel Fact of Life," *Boston Globe,* Jan. 27, 1996, p. 13; Wayne Beissert, "In *Valdez*'s Wake, Uncertainty," *USA Today,* July 28, 1989, p. 3A; Amanda Bennett, Julie Solomon, and Allanna Sullivan, "Firms Debate Hard Line on Alcoholics," *Wall Street Journal,* Apr. 13, 1989, p. 131; CNN, Mar. 22, 1990; Carrie Dolan, "Exxon to Bolster Oil-Cleanup Effort After Criticism," *Wall Street Journal,* May 11, 1989, p. A10; Carrie Dolan and Charles McCoy, "Military Transports Begin Delivering Equipment to Battle Alaskan Oil Spill," *Wall Street Journal,* Apr. 10, 1989, p. A8; Stuart Elliot, "Public Angry at Slow Action on Oil Spill," *USA Today,* Apr. 21, 1989, pp. B1, 132; "Exxon Mobil Must Pay *Valdez* Fine," *USA Today,* Oct. 2, 2000, www.usatoday.com/news/court/nsco1379.htm; "Exxon Valdez Disaster Haunts Alaska 14 Years On," *Sydney Morning Herald,* Jan. 16, 2003, www.smh.com.au/articles/2003/01/15/1042520672374.html; "Exxon Will Pay $3.5 Million to Settle Claims in Phase Four of *Valdez* Case," *BNA State*

Environment Daily, Jan. 19, 1996; Aliza Fan, "Exxon May Still Get More Than $3 Billion in Dispute with Lloyd's," *Oil Daily,* Jan. 22, 1996, p. 3; Tony Freemantle, "Billion-Dollar Battle Looms over Spill Costs: Exxon Corp. Trying to Collect from Its Insurance Companies," *Anchorage Daily News,* Sept. 5, 1995, p. IA; William Glasgall and Vicky Cahan, "Questions That Keep Surfacing After the Spill," *Business Week,* Apr. 17, 1989, p. 18; Kathy Barks Hoffman, "Oil Spill's Cleanup Costs Exceed $1.3B," *USA Today,* July 25, 1989, p. B1; *Institute for Crisis Management Newsletter,* 4 (March 1995): 3; "Judge Cuts Exxon Valdez Punitive Damage Award," *Alaska Journal,* Dec. 16, 2002, www.alaskajournal. com/stories/121602/loc_20021216003.shtml; Dave Lenckus, "Exxon Seeks More Spill Cover: Oil Giant Reaches Partial Agreement with Insurers," *Business Insurance,* Jan. 22, 1996, p. 1; Charles McCoy, "Alaska Drops Criminal Probe of Oil Disaster," *Wall Street Journal,* July 28, 1989, p. A3; Charles McCoy, "Alaskans End Big Tax Breaks for Oil Firms," *Wall Street Journal,* May 10, 1989, p. A6; Charles McCoy, "Heartbreaking Fight Unfolds in Hospital for Valdez Otters," *Wall Street Journal,* Apr. 20, 1989, pp. A1, A4; Charles McCoy and Ken Wells, "Alaska, U.S. Knew of Flaws in Oil-Spill Response Plans," *Wall Street Journal,* Apr. 7, 1989, p. A3; Peter Nulty, "The Future of Big Oil," *Fortune,* May 8, 1989, pp. 46–49; Wayne Owens, "Turn the Valdez Cleanup Over to Mother Nature," editorial, *Wall Street Journal,* July 27, 1989, p. A8; Natalie Phillips, "$3.5 Million Settles Exxon Spill Suit," *Anchorage Daily News,* Jan. 18, 1996, p. 113; "In Ten Years You'll See 'Nothing'" (interview with Exxon chairman, Lawrence Rawl), *Fortune,* May 8, 1989, pp. 50–54; Lawrence G. Rawl, letter to Exxon shareholders, Apr. 14, 1989; "Recordings Reveal Exxon Captain Rocked Tanker to Free It from Reef," [Texas A&M University] *Battalion,* Apr. 26, 1989, p. 1; Michael Satchell, with Steve Lindbeck, "Tug of War Over Oil Drilling," *U.S. News & World Report,* Apr. 10, 1989, pp. 47–48; Richard B. Schmitt, "Exxon, Alyeska May Be Exposed on Damages," *Wall Street Journal,* Apr. 10, 1989, p. A8; Stratford P. Sherman, "Smart Way to Handle the Press," *Fortune,* June 19, 1989, pp. 69–75; Caleb Solomon and Allanna Sullivan, "For the Petroleum Industry, Pouring Oil Is in Fact the Cause of Troubled Waters," *Wall Street Journal,* Mar. 31, 1989, p. A4; Allanna Sullivan, "Agencies Clear Exxon Oil-Cleanup Plan Despite Coast Guard Doubts on Deadline," *Wall Street Journal,* Apr. 19, 1989, p. A2; Allanna Sullivan, "Alaska Sues Exxon Corp., 6 Other Firms," *Wall Street Journal,* Aug. 16, 1989, pp. A3, A4; Allanna Sullivan and Amanda Bennett, "Critics Fault Chief Executive of Exxon on Handling of Recent Alaskan Oil Spill," *Wall Street Journal,* Mar. 31, 1989, p. B1; Kim Todd, "Last Voyage of the Valdez?" *Sierra,* Jan./Feb. 2003, www.sierraclub.org/sierra/200301/lol6_printable. asp; "*Valdez* Captain Serves Sentence," Associated Press, June 22, 1999; Ken Wells, "Alaska Begins Criminal Inquiry of Valdez Spill," *Wall Street Journal,* Mar. 30, 1989, p. A4; Ken Wells, "Blood-Alcohol Level of Captain of Exxon Tanker Exceeded Limits," *Wall Street Journal,* Mar. 31, 1989, p. A4; Ken Wells, "For Exxon, Cleanup Costs May Be Just the Beginning," *Wall Street Journal,* Apr. 14, 1989, pp. B1, B2; Ken Wells and Marilyn Chase, "Paradise Lost: Heartbreaking Scenes of Beauty Disfigured Follow Alaska Oil Spill," *Wall Street Journal,* Mar. 31, 1989, pp. A1, A4; Ken Wells and Charles McCoy, "How Unpreparedness Turned the Alaska Spill into Ecological Debacle," *Wall Street Journal,* Apr. 3, 1989, pp. A1, A4; Ken Wells and Allanna Sullivan, "Stuck in Alaska: Exxon's Army Scrubs the Beaches, but They Don't Stay Cleaned," *Wall Street Journal,* July 27, 1989, pp. A1, A5.

Leadership In Groups

CHAPTER 7

Isa N. Engleberg and Dianna Wynn

Chapter Outline

What Is Leadership?

All groups need leadership. Without leadership, a group may be nothing more than a collection of individuals lacking the coordination and motivation to achieve a common goal. Cathcart and Samovar maintain, "There are no successful groups without leaders. . . . Leaders lead because groups demand it and rely on leaders to satisfy needs."[1] **Leadership** is the ability to make strategic decisions and use communication to mobilize group members toward achieving a shared goal.

A leader and leadership are not the same. *Leader* is the title given to a person; *leadership* refers to the action that a leader takes to help group members achieve shared goals. Some groups have no official leader but instead have one or more members who engage in leadership behaviors. Other groups may have designated leaders who fail to behave in ways typically associated with leadership.

Another way to understand the nature of leadership is to contrast it with the functions of management. Whereas managers often focus on efficiency, leaders are

TOOLBOX 7.1 Chairing a Meeting

The person who chairs a meeting may not be the same person who serves as a group's leader. Although a leader often calls and conducts meetings, that responsibility may also be delegated to someone other than the leader, particularly when a group breaks into subcommittees or when a leader wants to be a more active participant in a group's deliberations. Maintaining order during a meeting and facilitating a productive discussion are the primary responsibilities of the chairperson.

concerned with effectiveness. Whereas managers become absorbed in getting an assigned job done, leaders focus on the ultimate direction and goal of the group. Note how the employee in the following situation describes the difference between a manager and a leader.

> Lee is the manager of our department, so he's technically our leader. Lee always follows procedures and meets deadlines for paperwork, so I guess he's a good manager. But we don't get much guidance or motivation from him. I just think managing tasks and real leadership of people are somehow different. Allison supervises the other department. She seems to inspire her workers. They're more innovative and work closely with each other. We do our job, but they seem to be on a mission. I've always thought that working for Allison would be more fulfilling and fun.

Leadership and Power

It is impossible to understand effective leadership and the skills of an effective leader without understanding the importance of power. Bennis and Nanus contend that power is "the quality without which leaders cannot lead."[2] In the hands of a just and wise leader, power is a positive force; in the hands of an unjust and foolish leader, power can be destructive.

Power is the ability or authority to influence and motivate others. One of the traditional ways to analyze power in a group is found in the categories of power developed by French and Raven.[3] They divide power into five categories: reward power, coercive power, legitimate power, expert power, and referent power.

Reward Power

Reward power derives from the leader's authority to give group members something they value. Whether the reward is a cash bonus, a promotion, or a convenient work schedule, its effectiveness depends on whether group members value the reward. Some leaders may think they have power because they control group rewards, only to discover that those rewards have little value for members. Employees may not want a promotion if the new job is less appealing than their current job. Only when the reward is worthwhile will group members respond to a leader who uses this kind of power.

Coercive Power

If the carrot approach doesn't work, a leader may resort to using a stick: **coercive power.** Another way to describe coercive power is to call it punishment

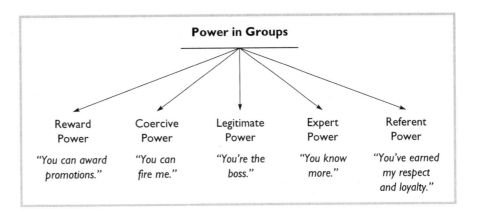

FIGURE 7.1 Power in Groups

power. When leaders can discipline, demote, or dismiss group members, they have coercive power. Hackman and Johnson contend that "coercion is most effective when those subject to this form of power are aware of expectations and are warned in advance about the penalties for failure to comply. Leaders using coercive power must consistently carry out threatened punishments."[4] However, coercive power can be counterproductive. A skillful leader uses coercive power sparingly and only when all other means of influence have failed to mobilize group members toward achieving their shared goal.

Legitimate Power

Legitimate power resides in a job, position, or assignment rather than in a person. For example, elected officials have the power to vote on the public's behalf; committee chairpersons are authorized to take control of their assigned tasks; supervisors have authority over their workers. The word *legitimate* means "lawful" or "proper." Most people believe it is lawful and proper that a judge make decisions and keep order in a courtroom. Group leaders may call meetings, assign tasks, and evaluate members as part of their legitimate duties.

Expert Power

Expert power is assigned to someone who has demonstrated a particular skill or special knowledge. Just as we may accept the advice of a doctor when we're ill or that of an auto mechanic when we've broken down on the highway, we are more likely to grant power to an expert. When, however, the advice of supposed experts proves incorrect, their power will fade and even disappear. A leader can rely on expert power only if the group has recognized the leader as a well-informed and reliable authority.

Referent Power

Hackman and Johnson explain that **referent power** is role model power—the ability to influence others that arises when one person admires another.[5] Referent power is the personal power or influence held by people who are liked, admired, and respected. When certain individuals demonstrate that they are effective communicators, talented organizers, shrewd problem solvers, and good listeners, we are more likely to be influenced by them. We often feel honored to work with someone who has strong referent power. Referent or personal power is very influential because it is recognized and conferred by the group rather than by an outside source.

In most groups, a leader employs several kinds of power, depending on the needs of the group and the situation. Some leaders may have the power to reward and coerce as well as having legitimate, expert, and referent power. In other groups, a leader may depend entirely on one type of power to get a group to work cooperatively toward a goal. The more power a leader has, the more carefully the use of that power must be balanced with the needs of the group. If you exert too much power, your group may lose its energy and enthusiasm. If you don't exert enough power, your group may flounder and fail. Gaining power is not the same as using it wisely.

Becoming a Leader

Anyone can become a leader. Abraham Lincoln and Harry S. Truman rose from humble beginnings and hardship to become U.S. presidents. Corporate executives have worked their way up from the sales force (Ross Perot) and secretarial pools (Ardis Krainik, former General Director of the Lyric Opera of Chicago) to become chief executive officers. Yet as inspiring as these examples may be, leaders are not necessarily the hardest workers or the smartest employees. The path to a leadership position can be as easy as being in the right place at the right time or being the only person willing to take on a difficult job. Becoming the leader of a group occurs in many different ways.

Designated Leaders

Designated leaders are deliberately and purposely selected by a group or an outside authority. You may be hired for a job that gives you authority over others. You may be promoted or elected to a leadership position. Your boss may create a special work team or subcommittee and assign you to be its leader. In all these cases, the selection of the leader depends on an election or an appointment. Unfortunately, less-than-deserving people are sometimes appointed or elected to powerful positions. Electing a compromise candidate or appointing a politically connected member as a leader is too common a practice and no guarantee of leadership ability. Is it possible, then, for a designated leader to be an effective leader? Of course it is. When a leader's abilities match the needs of the group and its goal, there is a greater likelihood of success.

Unique challenges face a leader chosen by a source outside the group. When a new leader enters a well-established group, there can be a long and difficult period of adjustment for everyone. One student described this difficult process as follows:

Kweisi Mfume gave up his seat in the U.S. Congress to become President and CEO of the National Association for the Advancement of Colored People (NAACP). What factors motivate individuals to seek such leadership positions?
(© Getty Images)

For five summers, I worked as a counselor at a county day camp for underprivileged children. Harry was our boss and all of us liked him. We worked hard for Harry because we knew he'd look the other way if we showed up late or left early on a Friday. As long as the kids were safe and supervised, he didn't bother us. When Harry was promoted into management at the county government office, we got Frank. The first few weeks were awful.

Frank would dock us if we were late. No one could leave early. He demanded that we come up with more activities for the kids. Weekend pool parties were banned. He even made us attend a counselors' meeting every morning rather than once every couple of weeks. But, in the end, most of us had to admit that Frank was a better camp director. The camp did more for the kids and that was the point.

Both Harry and Frank were leaders with legitimate power. What made them different were the various kinds of power available to them. Because Harry had earned the admiration and respect of the staff, he could rely on his personal, or referent, power. Frank, however, had to use coercive power to establish order.

When a leader is elected or appointed from within a group, the problems can be as difficult as with a leader from outside the group. If the person who once worked next to you becomes your boss, the adjustment can be problematic. Here is the way a business executive described how difficult it was when she was promoted to vice president:

> When I was promoted, I became responsible for making decisions that affected my colleagues, many of whom were close friends. I was given the authority to approve projects, recommend salary increases, and grant promotions. Colleagues who had always been open and honest with me were more cautious and careful about what they said. I had to deny requests from people I cared about while approving requests from colleagues with whom I often disagreed. Even though I'm the same person I was as a manager, I was treated differently and, as a result, I behaved differently.

Being plucked from a group in order to lead it can present problems because it changes the nature of your relationship with the other group members. Even though the members know you well, you still must earn their trust as a leader. Initially, try involving the group in decision making as much as possible. Discuss ground rules for interaction with friends within the group while assuring them of your continued friendship. Finally, openly and honestly addressing leadership concerns with group members and seeking their suggestions may resolve many potential problems.[6]

Emergent Leaders

Very often, the most effective leadership occurs when a leader emerges from a group rather than being promoted, elected, or appointed. The leaders of many political, religious, and neighborhood organizations emerge. **Emergent leaders** gradually achieve leadership by interacting with group members and contributing to the achievement of the group's goal. The leader who emerges from within a group has significant advantages. He or she does not have to spend time learning about the group, its goals, and its norms. In addition, a leader who emerges from within a group has some assurance that the group wants him or her to be the leader rather than having to accept leadership because an election or outside authority says it must. Such leaders usually have referent power—a significant factor in mobilizing members toward the group's goal.

Strategies for Becoming a Leader

Although there is no foolproof method, there are strategies that can improve your chances of emerging or being designated as a group's leader. The following strategies require a balanced approach, one that takes advantage of opportunities without abusing the privilege of leadership:

▶ Talk early and often (and listen).

▶ Know more (and share it).

▶ Offer your opinion (and welcome disagreement).

Talk Early and Often (and Listen).   Of all the strategies that can help you attain the position of group leader, the most reliable have to do with when and how much you talk. According to Hollander, the person who speaks first and most often is more likely to emerge as the group's leader.[7] The number of contributions is even more important than the quality of those contributions. The quality of contributions becomes more significant after you become a leader. The link between participation and leadership "is the most consistent finding in small group leadership research."[8] Although talking early and often does not guarantee you a leadership position, failure to talk will keep you from being considered as a potential leader. Don't overdo it, though. If you talk too much, members may think that you are not interested in or willing to listen to their contributions. As important as it is to talk, it is just as important to demonstrate your willingness and ability to listen to group members.

Know More (and Share It).   Leaders often emerge or are appointed because they are seen as experts—people who know more about an important topic. Even if a potential leader is only able to explain ideas and information more clearly than other group members, she or he may be perceived as knowing more. Groups need well-informed leaders; they do not need know-it-alls. Know-it-alls see their own comments as most important; leaders value everyone's contributions. Knowing more than other members may require hours of advance preparation. Members who want to become leaders understand that they must demonstrate their expertise without intimidating other group members.

Offer Your Opinion (and Welcome Disagreement).   When groups are having difficulty making decisions or solving problems, they appreciate someone who can offer good ideas and informed opinions. Very often leaders will emerge when they help a group out of some difficulty. Offering ideas and opinions, however, is not the same as having those ideas accepted. Criticizing the ideas and opinions of others runs the risk of causing resentment and defensiveness. Bullying your way into a leadership position can backfire. If you are unwilling to compromise or listen to alternatives, the group may be unwilling to follow you. Effective leaders welcome constructive disagreement and discourage hostile confrontations. "They do not suppress conflict, they rise and face it."[9]

Implications.   The strategies for becoming a leader are not necessarily the same strategies needed for successful leadership. Once you become a leader, you may find it necessary to listen more than talk, welcome better-informed members, and criticize the opinions of others. Once you have emerged as leader, your focus should shift from becoming the leader to serving the group you lead.

TOOLBOX 7.2 Listening and Leadership

Effective listening is one of the hallmarks of successful leadership. If you talk early and often but ignore or misinterpret what other group members say, you will not emerge or be highly successful as a leader. Effective leaders devote their full attention to making sure that they comprehend what is said. They also follow the golden listening rule: Listen to others as you would have them listen to you. In other words, suspend your own needs in order to listen to someone else's.

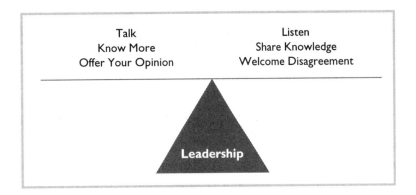

FIGURE 7.2 Becoming a Leader: A Balanced Approach

Leadership Theories

Leadership is a quality that seems to defy accurate measurement. Bennis and Nanus point out that "no clear and unequivocal understanding exists as to what distinguishes leaders from non-leaders, and perhaps more important, what distinguishes effective leaders from ineffective leaders. . . ."[10] Despite such inconclusive results, there is a lot to be learned from the many theories of leadership. In the following sections, we explain five different theoretical approaches to leadership.

Trait Theory

The trait theory is often called the "Great Man" theory. It is based on what many people now believe is a myth—that leaders are born, not made. **Trait theory** attempts to identify and prescribe individual characteristics and behaviors needed for effective leadership.

Think of some of the leaders you most admire. What traits do they have? Most of us can come up with a list of desirable leadership traits that includes intelligence, ability to communicate, confidence, enthusiasm, organizational talent, and good listening skills. Most of us would gladly follow a leader with these qualities. The problem is that there is no guarantee that someone possessing these traits will be an effective leader. Furthermore, there are many effective leaders who possess only a few of these traits. Harriet Tubman, an illiterate runaway slave, did little talking but

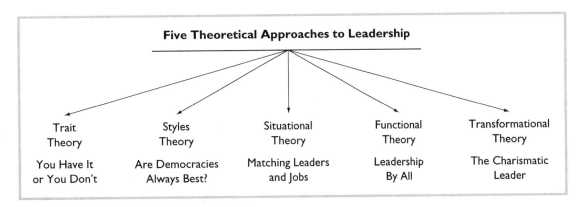

FIGURE 7.3 Leadership Theories

led hundreds of her people from bondage in the South to freedom in the North. Ross Perot, a little guy with big ears and a squeaky voice, became a business leader and serious contender for the U.S. presidency. Depending on the group and its circumstances, one set of traits may be less effective than another. Yet some important implications of this theory are of value to anyone seeking and gaining a leadership position.

Implications of Trait Theory.   According to proponents of the Myers-Briggs Type Indicator®, there is a set of traits that characterize "life's natural leaders." These "extroverted thinkers" (the ENTJ type) use reasoning ability to control and direct those around them.[11] They are usually enthusiastic, decisive, confident, organized, logical, and argumentative. They love to lead and can be excellent communicators.

However, although they often assume or win leadership positions, they may not necessarily be effective leaders. Extroverted thinkers may intimidate and overpower others. They may be insensitive to the personal feelings and needs of group members. Women with such traits, moreover, are often perceived as arrogant and confrontational. Although many extroverted thinkers become leaders, they may need a less intense, more balanced approach in order to be effective leaders.

Styles Theory

As a way of expanding the trait approach to the study of leadership, researchers began reexamining the traits they had collected. Rather than looking for individual leadership traits, they developed the **styles theory** of leadership—a collection of specific behaviors that could be identified as unique leadership styles. Actors work in different styles—tough or gentle, comic or tragic. Even sports teams differ in style; the South American soccer teams are known for their speed and grace, the European teams for their technical skill and aggressiveness. Different styles are attributed to leaders, too.

One of the first attempts to describe different leadership styles yielded three categories: autocratic, democratic, and laissez-faire.[12]

An autocrat is a person who has a great deal of power and authority, someone who maintains strict control over the group and its discussion. The **autocratic leader** tries to control the direction and outcome of a discussion, makes many of the group's decisions, gives orders, expects followers to obey orders, focuses on achieving the group's task, and takes responsibility for the results.

A **democratic leader** promotes the interests of group members and believes in and practices social equality. This type of leader shares decision making with the group, helps the group plan a course of action, focuses on the group's morale as well as on the task, and gives the entire group credit for success.

Laissez-faire is a French phrase that means "to let people do as they choose." A **laissez-faire leader** lets the group take charge of all decisions and actions. In mature and highly productive groups, a laissez-faire leader may be a perfect match for the group. Such a laid-back leadership style can generate a climate in which open communication is encouraged and rewarded. Unfortunately, there are laissez-faire leaders who do little or nothing to help a group when it needs decisive leadership.

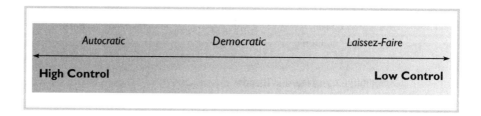

FIGURE 7.4 The Leadership Style Continuum

Mayor Giuliani met with President Bush and Governor Pataki immediately following the September 11th tragedy. What leadership qualities led Time magazine to choose Giuliani as its 2001 Person of the Year? (© *Reuters New Media, Inc./Corbis*)

Implications of Styles Theory.   Many people assume that democratic leadership is always the best. There are, however, circumstances in which an autocratic style may be more effective. During a serious crisis there may not be enough time to discuss issues or consider the wishes of all members. In an emergency, a group may want its leader to take total responsibility.

In groups with democratic leadership, members are often more satisfied with the group experience, more loyal to the leader, and more productive in the long run. Whereas members often fear or distrust an autocratic leader, they usually enjoy working with a democratic leader. Autocratic leaders may stifle critical opinions and creativity whereas a democratic leader can create a climate in which members' opinions and ideas are welcome. Not surprisingly, groups led by democratic leaders exhibit lower levels of stress and conflict along with higher levels of innovation and creative problem solving.[13]

It may be worthwhile to assess your own leadership style. If you have a tendency to interrupt group members who seem to be wasting time, to start meetings on time regardless of the social interaction occurring in the group, or to confront members with terse questions, you may be more of an autocratic than a democratic leader. There are costs to using the autocratic approach. By exerting too much control, autocratic leaders may lower group morale and sacrifice long-term productivity. Unfortunately, many autocratic leaders defend such authoritarian actions by arguing that the group can't get the job done without the strict control of the leader.

Dr. Sandy Faber, a world-renowned astronomer, wrote about her experience as the leader of a group of six astronomers who developed a new theory about the expansion of the universe. An unfortunate back injury made her take a new look at her leadership style:

My usual style would have been to take center stage . . . and control the process. My back problem was at its worst . . . and instead I found myself lying flat on a portable cot in Donald's office. It is very hard to lead a group of people from a prone position. My energies were at a low ebb anyway. I found it very comfortable to lie back and avoid taking central responsibility. . . . It was the best thing that could have happened to us. The resultant power vacuum allowed each of us to quietly find our own best way to contribute. This lesson has stood me in good stead since. I now think that in small groups of able and motivated individuals, giving orders or setting up a well-defined hierarchy may generate more friction than it is designed to cure. If a good spirit of teamwork prevails, team leadership can be quite diffuse.[14]

If you have a tendency to ask open and general questions of the group as a whole, encourage participation from all members regardless of their status, and avoid dominating the group with your own opinion, you may be a democratic leader. Here, too, there are costs. Democratic leaders may sacrifice productivity by avoiding direct leadership. Many democratic leaders defend this approach by arguing that, regardless of the circumstance, the only way to make a good decision is to involve all group members. However, by failing to take charge in a crisis or curb a discussion when final decisions are needed, democratic leaders may be perceived as weak or indecisive by their followers.

Laissez-faire leaders are most effective in groups with very mature and productive members. Whether for lack of leadership skill or interest, laissez-faire leaders avoid taking charge or taking the time to prepare for complex and lengthy discussions.

Knowing whether your primary leadership style is autocratic, democratic, or laissez-faire is helpful only if you also understand the ways in which that style affects the members of your group and the goal your group is working to achieve. Effective leadership cannot be classified like a chemical molecule or a style of automobile. Effective leaders must seek a balance between their instinctive style and their ability to use other leadership strategies adapted to different group situations.

Situational Theory

The situational approach assumes that leaders are made, not born, and that nearly everyone can be an effective leader under the right circumstances. Moreover, **situational theory** explains how leaders can become more effective once they have carefully analyzed themselves, their group, and the circumstances in which they must lead. Rather than describing traits or styles, the situational approach seeks an ideal fit between leaders and leadership jobs.

The most influential theory of situational leadership was developed by the researcher Fred Fiedler. **Fiedler's Contingency Model of Leadership Effectiveness** is based on his study of hundreds of groups in numerous work settings.[15] The contingency model of situational leadership suggests that effective leadership occurs only when there is an ideal match between the leader's style and the group's work situation.

Leadership Style.   Rather than classifying leaders as autocratic or democratic, Fiedler characterizes them as either task-motivated or relationship-motivated. **Task-motivated leaders** want to get the job done; they gain satisfaction from completing a task even if the cost is bad feelings between the leader and group members. Task-motivated leaders may be criticized for being too bossy and too focused on the job rather than on the morale of the group. Sometimes task-motivated leaders take on the jobs of other group members because they're not satisfied with the quality or quantity of work done by others.

Relationship-motivated leaders gain satisfaction from working well with other people even if the cost is neglecting or failing to complete a task. Relationship-motivated leaders may be criticized for paying too much attention to how members feel and for tolerating disruptive members; they may appear inefficient and weak. Sometimes relationship-motivated leaders take on the jobs of other group members because they can't bring themselves to ask their colleagues to do more.

The Situation. Once you have determined your leadership style, the next step is to analyze the way in which your style matches the group's situation. According to Fiedler, there are three important dimensions to every situation: leader-member relationships, task structure, and power.

Fiedler claims that the most important factor in analyzing a situation is understanding the relationship between the leader and the group. Because **leader-member relations** can be positive, neutral, or negative, they can affect how a leader goes about mobilizing a group toward its goal. Are group members friendly and loyal to the leader and the rest of the group? Are they cooperative and supportive? Do they accept or resist the leader?

The second factor is rating the structure of the task. **Task structure** can range from disorganized and chaotic to highly organized and rule-driven. Are the goals and task clear? Is there an accepted procedure or set of steps for achieving the goal? Are there well-established standards for measuring success?

The third situational factor is the amount of power and control the leader has. Is the source of that power an outside authority, or has the leader earned it from the group? What differences would the use of reward, coercive, legitimate, expert, and/or referent power have on the group?

Matching the Leader and the Situation. Fiedler's research suggests that there are ideal matches between leadership style and the group situation. Task-motivated leaders perform best in extremes—such as when the situation is highly controlled or when it is almost out of control. Task-motivated leaders shine when there are good leader–member relationships, a clear task, and a lot of power. They also do well in stressful leadership jobs where there may be poor leader–member relationships, an unclear and unstructured task, and little control or power. Task-motivated leaders do well in extreme situations because their primary motivation is to take charge and get the job done.

Relationship-motivated leaders do well when there is a mix of conditions. They may have a structured task but an uncooperative group of followers. Rather than taking charge and getting the job done at all costs, the relationship-motivated leader uses diplomacy and works with group members to improve leader–member relationships. If there are good leader–member relations but an unstructured task, the relationship-motivated leader may rely on the resources of the group to develop a plan of action. Whereas a task-motivated leader might find these situations frustrating, a relationship-motivated leader will be quite comfortable.

Implications of Situational Theory. According to the situational approach, once you know your leadership style and have analyzed the situation in which you must lead, you can begin to predict how successful you will be as a leader. If you are a task-motivated leader, you should feel confident if asked to take on a highly structured or highly unstructured task. If completing the group's task is your major concern and motivation, you should feel confident if asked to lead a group that is unable and unwilling to pursue its goal.

Relationship-motivated leaders have different factors to consider. If there is a moderate degree of structure, a relationship-motivated leader may be more successful. If people issues are your major concern, you should feel confident if asked to lead a group that is able but somewhat unwilling to complete its task.

Unfortunately, you cannot always choose when and where you will lead. You may find yourself assigned or elected to a leadership situation that does not match your leadership style. Rather than trying to change your leadership style, you may find it easier to change the situation you are leading. For example, if leader–member relations are poor, you may decide that your first task is to gain the group's trust and support. You can schedule time to listen to members' problems or take non-meeting time to get to know key individuals in the group.

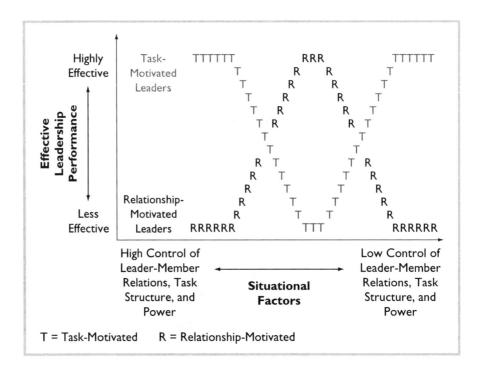

FIGURE 7.5 Contingency Model of Leader Effectiveness

If your task is highly unstructured, you can exert your leadership by providing structure or by dividing the task into smaller, easier-to-achieve subunits. On the other hand, you may find yourself in a leadership situation where the task is so highly structured there is almost no need for leadership. The group knows exactly what to do. Rather than allowing the group to become bored, ask for or introduce new and less structured tasks to challenge the group.

Finally, you may be able to modify the amount of power you have. If you are reluctant to use coercive power or if you don't have enough legitimate power, you can earn referent power by demonstrating your leadership ability. If you have a great deal of power and run the risk of intimidating group members, you may want to delegate some of your duties and power.

All the preceding strategies rely on leaders who understand who they are, who recognize the way in which they are motivated to lead, and who have analyzed the group's situation. Rather than wishing you were born with leadership traits or waiting for situations that match your style, the situational approach suggests ways to improve your leadership ability.

Functional Theory

Like the situational approach, the **functional theory** of leadership assumes that people are not born as leaders but learn to function as leaders. Unlike the situational approach, the functional approach focuses on what a leader *does* rather than who a leader is. Even more significant, the functional approach does not assume that leadership is the sole responsibility of the leader. Instead, it assumes that anyone in a group can and should help the group achieve its goal. There are no rules dictating that only the leader can motivate group members, provide procedural suggestions, or solve group problems. Leadership is a job, not a person. And, according to the functional approach to leadership, any capable group member can assume leadership functions when necessary.

Implications of Functional Theory. Although the functional approach can shift leadership responsibilities to anyone capable of performing them, doing so

TOOLBOX 7.3 Functional Theory and Participation

Because functional theory maintains that any group member can assume specific leadership tasks, it may be more of a participation theory than a leadership theory. As a theory of participation, functional theory assumes that the behavior of every member is critical to the group's success or failure. The theory divides group members' behaviors into three categories: (1) group task functions such as information giver, evaluator, and energizer; (2) group maintenance functions such as compromiser, tension releaser, and gatekeeper; and (3) self-centered functions such as blocker, dominator, and recognition seeker. An effective leader would assume most task and maintenance roles described by functional theory while minimizing or avoiding self-centered functions.

does not mean that leadership is unnecessary. Just the opposite may be true. If one participant is better at motivating members while another member excels at keeping the group on track, the group may be better off with both members assuming such leadership functions than if it relies on a single person to assume these important responsibilities.

Another significant implication to the functional approach to leadership is its focus on communication strategies and skills. Rather than relying on a leader's natural traits, styles, or motivation, the functional approach concentrates on what a leader says and does in a group situation. An information-giver, a compromiser, or even a dominator functions by communicating. Given the nature of group discussions, most of these functional leadership behaviors require effective communication skills.

Transformational Leadership Theory

In the late 1970s, researchers took a new and more sophisticated look at a special set of leadership traits. What qualities, they asked, are common to leaders who change the world in which they live—leaders such as Abraham Lincoln, Martin Luther King Jr., Mother Teresa, and the "giants" of corporate industries? The result of this investigation was the development of **transformational leadership theory,** which looks at the ways in which leaders *transform* followers into a unified group with an inspired purpose. House and Shamir describe the effects that transformational leaders have on followers:

> Such leaders transform the needs, values, preference, and aspirations of followers from self-interests to collective interests. Further, they cause followers to become highly committed to the leader's mission, to make significant personal sacrifices in the interests of the mission, and to perform above and beyond the call of duty.[16]

Several terms describe the characteristics of transformational leaders: charismatic, creative, empowering, inspirational, interactive, intellectually stimulating, passionate, and perhaps most important of all, visionary.

Bennis and Goldsmith list four qualities that most group members want from their leaders: vision, trust, optimism, and action.[17] The ability to create and communicate a compelling vision or purpose for the group separates transformational leaders from most other leaders. And it can't be "any old purpose, either, but must be one that galvanizes, energizes, and enthralls people."[18] In addition to having an inspiring vision, transformational leaders generate and maintain trust and openness, twin qualities that strengthen member commitment and loyalty. Transformational leaders are also optimistic and hopeful. According to Bennis and Goldsmith, "their optimism stems from their clear vision of the future and their commitment to get there and bring everyone on their team along for the ride."[19] Last but not least, transformational leaders are doers—they convert their vision into action. They take risks, learn from their mistakes, and never lose sight of or faith in their vision.

Implications of Transformational Leadership Theory.   Most of us will never be world-famous transformational leaders. We can, however, learn a great deal from such leaders. The most essential feature of the transformational puzzle is a compelling vision. President John F. Kennedy envisioned the United States putting a man on the moon. Walt Disney's famous quotation—"If you can dream it, you can do it"—sits high atop a sign at the Epcot Center at Disney World Orlando. Developing answers to the following questions can help you form the images that can shape a compelling vision.

1. What, if anything, is unique or special about your group and/or its purpose?

2. What are your values, and how do they shape your priorities for the future?

3. What do the people or group members you serve really need that you could provide?

4. What would make you personally commit your mind and heart to this vision for the foreseeable future?

5. What do you really want your group to accomplish so that you and they will be committed to and proud of their association with the group?[20]

With a compelling vision, trust and openness among group members, confident optimism, and purposeful action, a leader can transform a group into a remarkable and productive team of colleagues.

The 4-M Model of Leadership Effectiveness

Given the millions of words published about leadership by scholars, management gurus, and popular press writers, you may have difficulty sorting out the "dos and don'ts" of effective leadership. To help you understand and balance the contributions made by these many differing approaches, we offer an integrated model of leadership effectiveness that emphasizes specific communication strategies and skills.

The **4-M Model of Leadership Effectiveness** divides leadership tasks into four interdependent leadership functions: (1) **M**odeling leadership behavior, (2) **M**otivating members, (3) **M**anaging group process, and (4) **M**aking decisions. These strategies incorporate the features of several theories and provide a set of behaviors characteristic of effective leadership.[21]

Modeling Leadership Behavior

All of us have expectations about what an ideal leader should say and do. Model leaders project an image of confidence, competence, trustworthiness, and optimism. They rely on referent or role model power to influence others. Chemers refers to this function as *image management* and notes that when "image management is particularly successful, the leader may be described as charismatic."[22] Yet no matter how much you may *want* to be seen as a model leader, only your followers can grant you that honor. We recommend the following strategies for modeling effective leadership:

1. Publicly champion your group and its goals.

2. Speak and listen effectively and confidently.

3. Behave consistently and assertively.

4. Demonstrate competence and trustworthiness.

5. Study and improve your own leadership skills.

Motivating Members

Motivating others is a critical skill for leaders. Effective leaders guide, develop, support, defend, and inspire group members. They develop relationships that "match the personal needs and expectations of followers."[23] Five leadership skills are central to motivating members:

1. Secure member commitment to the group's shared goal.

2. Appropriately reward the group and its members.

3. Help solve interpersonal problems and conflicts.

4. Adapt tasks and assignments to member abilities and expectations.

5. Provide constructive and timely feedback to members.

Managing Group Process

From the perspective of group survival, managing group process may be the most important function of leadership.[24] If a group is disorganized, lacks sufficient information to solve problems, or is unable to make important decisions when they are called for, the group cannot be effective. Five leadership skills can enhance this important function:

1. Be well organized and fully prepared for group meetings and work sessions.

2. Understand and adapt to member strengths and weaknesses.

3. Help solve task-related and procedural problems.

4. Monitor and intervene to improve group performance.

5. Secure resources and remove roadblocks to group effectiveness.

Making Decisions

A leader's willingness and ability to make appropriate, timely, and responsible decisions characterizes effective leadership. Too often we hear disgruntled group members talk about their leader's inability to make critical decisions. A high school teacher described this fatal leadership flaw as follows:

> Everyone agrees that our principal is a "nice guy" who wants everyone to like him. He doesn't want to "rock the boat" or "make waves." As a result, he doesn't make decisions or take decisive action when it's most needed. He patiently listens to a request or both sides of a dispute, but that's all he does. Our school comes to a standstill because he won't "bite the bullet." The teachers have lost respect for him, students and their parents know that they'll get what they want if they yell loudly enough or long enough, and the superintendent has to intervene to fix the mess that results.

When you assume or are appointed to a leadership role, you must accept the fact that some of your decisions may be unpopular, and some may even turn out to be wrong. But you still have to make them. Robbins and Finley contend that it's often better for a group leader to make a bad decision than no decision at all, "For if

Leadership in Virtual Groups

Leadership is both pervasive and necessary in successful virtual groups. But, according to Lipnack and Stamps, "although virtual teams may have single leaders, multiple leaders are the norm rather than the exception."[25] Why? Consider some of the added responsibilities required of someone who organizes and leads a virtual group—be it a simple teleconference, an email discussion, or an intercontinental videoconference.

Long before the actual meeting, someone must set up the unique logistics for a virtual get-together. When participants live in different cities or time zones, arranging a meeting is much more difficult than calling a regular staff meeting in a conference room down the hall. In order to make sure that members are fully prepared for a virtual meeting, a detailed agenda must be prepared and sent to all members well in advance. At the same time, someone must make sure that the technology required for the conference is up and running when it's needed. Finally, someone must lead a discussion in which participants may neither see nor hear each other in real time. Effective virtual groups manage these added tasks by sharing leadership roles rather than by assuming that one superhuman leader can handle all of these complex challenges.

The 4M Model of Leadership Effectiveness

also applies to the unique responsibilities of a virtual group leader. When virtual groups first "meet," they often depend on a leader to model appropriate behavior. The leader must demonstrate effective participant behavior for other virtual group members. Motivating a virtual group can be more difficult than motivating participants in a face-to-face discussion. Unmotivated members may ignore messages or respond infrequently. When this happens, a group is vulnerable to miscommunication, poor quality of work, missed deadlines, lack of cohesion, inefficiencies, and disaffected team members.[26]

A virtual group leader also has additional managerial duties. Resources may be needed to train group members on specialized software. A leader may need to set guidelines for how and when the virtual group will do its work. Finally, making decisions in a virtual group can be difficult when group members are not communicating in real time. In virtual groups, the leader may be responsible for determining when the virtual group will "meet," the rules of interaction, and the criteria for group decision making.

By sharing leadership functions, virtual group members have the opportunity to become a highly cohesive and democratic team of coworkers, all of whom embrace the challenge of leading and working in groups to achieve a worthy goal.

you are seen as chronically indecisive, people won't let you lead them."[27] The following five leadership strategies can help you determine when and how to intervene and make a decision.

1. Make sure that everyone has and shares the information needed to make a quality decision.

2. If appropriate, discuss your pending decision and solicit feedback from members.

3. Listen to members' opinions, arguments, and suggestions.

4. Explain the rationale for the decision you intend to make.

5. Make and communicate your decision to everyone.

When President Harry S. Truman said that "the buck stops here," he was describing the penultimate responsibility of a leader. Hersey and Blanchard contend that effective leaders intervene and *tell* members what to do when a group lacks confidence, willingness, and an ability to make decisions. When, however, group members are confident, willing, and skilled, a leader can usually turn full responsibility over to the group and focus on helping members implement the group's decision.[28] As a leader, you can make decisions yourself with little or no group input when time and efficiency are important, or you can engage group members in the decision-making process, particularly when the support and involvement of group members takes priority over efficiency. In short, as a leader, you have to *decide* what decision-making strategies best serve your group and its purpose.

When it's time to assess your leadership ability, the way in which you make and implement decisions will be the basis on which you will be judged. As the leader, you have the right and the responsibility to decide which strategies will be most effective in achieving your group's goal. If you want to be an effective leader, act like one, support your members, make sure that your group has the resources it needs, and be decisive.

Diversity and Leadership

Until recently, most leadership studies concentrated on the traits, styles, and functions of white male leaders. However, the global economy and the increasing diversity of the American population have made a white-males-only leadership perspective a thing of the past. Today, successful organizations and groups must understand, respect, and adapt to diversity if they hope to tap the potential of their members. At the same time, female and culturally diverse leaders must understand that, even under the best of circumstances, negative stereotypes about them can still handicap their ability to lead.

Gender and Leadership

In the early studies of leadership, there was an unwritten but additional prerequisite for becoming a leader: Be a man. Yet, despite the achievements of exceptional women leaders, some people still question the ability of women to serve in leadership positions. These doubts are based on long-held prejudices rather than on valid evidence.

In 2001, Congresswoman Nancy Pelosi was elected House Democratic Whip, making her the highest-ranking woman in the history of the U.S. Congress. Why did it take so long for a woman to achieve this status?
(© Joe Marquette/AP-Wide World Photos)

In a summary of the research on leadership and gender, Shimanoff and Jenkins conclude that "women are still less likely to be preselected as leaders, and the same leadership behavior is often evaluated more positively when attributed to a male than a female."[29] In other words, even when women talk early and often, are well prepared and always present at meetings, and offer valuable ideas, a man who has done the same things is more likely to emerge as leader. After examining the research on gender and leadership, Napier and Gershenfeld conclude that "even though male and female leaders may act the same, there is a tendency for women to be perceived more negatively or to have to act differently to gain leadership."[30]

Deborah Tannen has described the difficulties that women have in leadership positions.[31] If their behavior is similar to that of male leaders, they are perceived as unfeminine. If they act "like a lady," they are viewed as weak or ineffective. One professional woman described this dilemma as follows:

> I was thrilled when my boss evaluated me as "articulate, hard-working, mature in her judgment, and a skillful diplomat." What disturbed me were some of the evaluation comments from those I supervise or work with as colleagues.
>
> Although they had a lot of good things to say, a few of them described me as "pushy," "brusque," "impatient," "has a disregard for social niceties," and "hard-driving." What am I supposed to do? My boss thinks I'm energetic and creative while other people see the same behavior as pushy and aggressive.

The preference for male leaders may come down to a fear of or an unwillingness to adjust to different kinds of leaders. Because many people have worked in groups that were led by men, they may feel uncomfortable when the leadership shifts to a woman. Even though extensive research indicates only slight differences between men and women leaders, stereotypical, negative expectations still persist. These expectations make it more difficult for women to gain, hold, and succeed in leadership positions.[32] Our best advice is that instead of asking whether a female leader is different from a male leader, it is more important to ask whether she is an effective leader.

Cultural Diversity and Leadership

Groups are now using technology to communicate not only with the enormous proliferation of ethnic minorities in America, but also with colleagues around the globe. Effective leaders in the twenty-first century must be able to meet the many challenges inherent in working with diverse groups. Cultural diversity impacts leadership in two ways: Leaders, regardless of their cultural background, must know how to lead groups composed of diverse members. At the same time, group members must learn to respect and adapt to culturally diverse leaders.

The ways in which a leader models leadership behavior, motivates group members, manages group process, and makes decisions may not match the cultural dimensions of all group members. For example, if as a leader, you model leadership behavior by strongly and publicly advocating group goals, you may be upsetting members from high-context cultures who would be less direct and open about such matters. Your way of modeling leadership behavior may not reflect *their* view of a model leader.

A member's cultural background can also influence a leader's choice of motivational strategies. For example, Western cultures (United States, Canada, Europe) assume that members are motivated by personal growth and achievement. However, when group members' cultural backgrounds suggest a more collective, long-term, and high-context perspective, the same motivational strategies may not work. A collective-oriented member might desire a close relationship with the leader and other group members rather than personal gain or growth. The same member may act out of loyalty to the leader and the group rather than for personal achievement or material gain.[33] Another member with a long-term perspective may become frustrated when a leader pursues short-term objectives.

Managing group process in a group composed of culturally diverse members can be difficult if, for example, you want to give the group the freedom to decide how to structure a task. Members from uncertainty-avoidance cultures will want

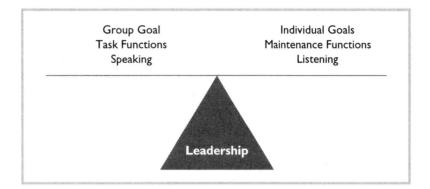

FIGURE 7.6 Balanced Leadership

more structure and instruction from a leader. If your leadership style is more feminine (nurturing, collaborative, caring), you may find yourself fighting a losing leadership battle with more masculine members who are competitive, independent, and aggressive. Your feminine leadership style may be interpreted as weakness or indecision.

Finally, the decision-making style of a leader may not match that of a culturally diverse group. If members come from a low-power-distance culture, they will not welcome an authoritarian leader who takes control of all decision making. Conversely, a leader who prefers a more democratic approach to decision making may frustrate members who come from high-power-distance cultures in which leaders make all the decisions with little input from group members.

Stereotypes about a culturally diverse leader can diminish a group's effectiveness. Unfortunately, we do not have a lot of research on American ethnic minority leaders (such as African Americans, Latino Americans, Asian Americans, Native Americans, Jewish Americans, or Muslim Americans). The research that is available indicates that minority leaders, like women leaders, do not differ from dominant-culture leaders in behavior, performance, or satisfying member expectations. Nonetheless, negative stereotypes about minority leaders are prevalent, and such individuals have more difficulty moving up the leadership ladder.[34]

Culturally diverse groups and leaders are here to stay. An effective leader helps group members work together, achieve their potential, and contribute to the group's shared goal. Balancing the needs of culturally diverse group members may be difficult, but the ability to do so is essential to providing effective leadership in the twenty-first century.

Balanced Leadership

The leader performs the most difficult balancing act in a group. Much like a tightrope walker who juggles during a death-defying walk across open space, a group leader must juggle many interests and issues while propelling a group toward its goal. The leader must exert control without stifling creativity. The leader must balance the requirements of the task with the social needs of group members. The leader must resolve conflict without losing the motivation and energy that results from conflict and must encourage participation from quiet members without stifling the enthusiasm and contributions of active members. The effective leader juggles all of these variables while mobilizing a group's resources in pursuit of a common goal that unifies both leaders and followers. The job of a juggling tightrope walker may seem easy compared to balancing all of these leadership tasks.

Kevin Freiberg claims that effective "leaders have both the desire and ability to create an environment where the wants and needs of followers can be satisfied. They are particularly adept at using their skills and insight to establish a balance between cooperative common action and the fulfillment of individual goals."[35] Achieving balanced leadership does not depend on developing a particular trait or style but depends rather on a leader's ability to analyze a situation and select leadership strategies that help mobilize a group to achieve its goal.

Summary Study Guide

▶ A leader mobilizes group members toward a goal shared by the leader and followers. Leadership is a process that requires the ability to make strategic decisions and use communication to mobilize others toward achieving a shared goal.

▶ Leadership power can be categorized as reward power, coercive power, legitimate power, expert power, and referent power.

▶ Designated leaders are selected by an outside authority or elected by a group; emergent leaders come from within a group and gradually assume leadership functions.

▶ Strategies for becoming a leader include talking early and often, knowing more, and offering opinions.

▶ Trait theory attempts to identify individual characteristics and behaviors needed for effective leadership.

▶ Styles theory describes the strengths and weaknesses of autocratic, democratic, and laissez-faire leaders.

▶ Situational theory seeks an ideal fit between a leader's style (task or relationship motivated) and three dimensions of the group's work situation (leader-member relations, the task structure, and the leader's power).

▶ Functional theory focuses on what leaders do rather than on who leaders are; anyone in a group can assume leadership functions.

▶ Transformational leadership theory focuses on the characteristics of extraordinary leaders whose transcendent vision motivates followers to devote unprecedented time and effort to achieving the group's goal.

▶ The 4-M Model of Leadership Effectiveness includes four essential functions of leadership: modeling leadership behavior, motivating members, managing group process, and making decisions.

▶ Virtual groups often require multiple leaders because of the added dimensions of setting up and facilitating virtual interaction, arranging and maintaining technical support, and motivating members to contribute from a distance.

▶ Women are less likely to be selected as leaders; the same leadership behavior is often evaluated more positively when attributed to a man rather than to a woman.

▶ Cultural diversity presents special challenges for leaders and group members that require an understanding of, respect for, and adaptation to different cultural dimensions and behaviors.

GroupWork

Wanted: A Few Good Leaders

Goal
To analyze and discuss different perceptions of effective leadership

Participants   Groups of three to seven members

Procedure

1. Each student should complete *The Least-Preferred Coworker Scale* that follows this GroupWork exercise.

2. After all students have completed the scale, they should form groups based on similar individual results, e.g., all relationship-motivated students in one set of groups and all task-motivated students in another set of groups.

3. Each group should then work to write a description of the desired characteristics, skills, and/or duties of a potential leader in the form of a want ad for the employment section of a newspaper. Each advertisement should begin with "WANTED: LEADER The ideal candidate for this job should . . ."

4. Each group should post its leadership want ad and have a spokesperson explain it to the class.

5. The class should then discuss the following questions:

   ▶ What are the similarities among the want ads?

   ▶ What are the differences among the want ads?

   ▶ Which leadership theories apply to each want ad?

   ▶ In what ways did group members' preferences for relationship motivation or task motivation affect the words they chose to include in each want ad?

   ▶ Who was the leader in each group? Did the group designate a leader or did one emerge?

Assessment

The Least-Preferred Coworker Scale

Directions   All of us have worked better with some people than with others. Think of the one person in your life with whom you have worked least well, a person who might have caused you difficulty in doing a job or completing a task. This person may be someone with whom you have worked recently or someone you have known in the past. This coworker must be the single individual with whom you have had the most difficulty getting a job done, the person with whom you would least want to work.

On the scale below, describe this person by circling the number that best represents your perception of this person. There are no right or wrong answers. Do not omit any items, and circle a number for each item only once.

Pleasant	8	7	6	5	4	3	2	I	Unpleasant
Friendly	8	7	6	5	4	3	2	I	Unfriendly
Rejecting	I	2	3	4	5	6	7	8	Accepting
Tense	I	2	3	4	5	6	7	8	Relaxed
Distant	I	2	3	4	5	6	7	8	Close
Cold	I	2	3	4	5	6	7	8	Warm
Supportive	8	7	6	5	4	3	2	I	Hostile
Boring	I	2	3	4	5	6	7	8	Interesting
Quarrelsome	I	2	3	4	5	6	7	8	Harmonious
Gloomy	I	2	3	4	5	6	7	8	Cheerful
Open	8	7	6	5	4	3	2	I	Guarded
Backbiting	I	2	3	4	5	6	7	8	Loyal
Untrustworthy	I	2	3	4	5	6	7	8	Trustworthy
Considerate	8	7	6	5	4	3	2	I	Inconsiderate
Nasty	I	2	3	4	5	6	7	8	Nice
Agreeable	8	7	6	5	4	3	2	I	Disagreeable
Insincere	I	2	3	4	5	6	7	8	Sincere
Kind	8	7	6	5	4	3	2	I	Unkind

Scoring

Obtain your Least-Preferred Coworker (LPC) score by adding up the numbers you circled on the preceding scale. Your score should range between 18 and 144.

Relationship-Motivated Leader. If your score is 73 or above, you derive satisfaction from good relationships with group members. You are most successful when a situation has just enough uncertainty to challenge you: moderate leader-member relations, moderate task structure, and moderate power.

Task-Motivated Leader. If your score is 64 or below, you derive satisfaction from getting things done. You are most successful when a situation has clear guidelines or no guidelines at all: excellent or poor leader-member relations, highly structured or unstructured tasks, and high or low power.

Relationship- and Task-Motivated Leader. If your score is between 65 and 72, you may be flexible enough to function in both leadership styles.

Source: "The Least-Preferred Coworker Scale" from *Improving Leadership Effectiveness: The Leader Match Concept,* 2nd edition, Fiedler, F. E. and Chemers, M. M. (John Wiley & Sons: 1984), pp. 17–42. Reprinted by permission of Fred Fiedler.

Notes

1. Cathcart, R. S., & Samovar, L. A. (Eds.). (1992). Small group communication: A reader (6th ed.). Dubuque, LA: Wm. C. Brown, p. 364.

2. Bennis, W., & Nanus, B. (1985). Leaders: The strategies for taking charge. New York: HarperPerennial, p. 15.

3. French, J. R. P., Jr., & Raven, B. (1968). The bases of social power. In D. Cartwright & A. Zander (Eds.), Group dynamics: Research and theory (3rd ed). New York: Harper & Row, pp. 259–269.

4. Hackman, M. Z., & Johnson, C. E. (2000). *Leadership: A communication perspective* (3rd ed.). Prospect Heights, IL: Waveland, p. 131.

5. Hackman & Johnson, p. 137.

6. Lloyd, S. R. (1996). *Leading teams: The skills for success.* West Des Moines, IA: American Media Publishing, p. 13.

7. Hollander, E. P. (1978). *Leadership dynamics: A practical guide to effective relation-ships.* New York: Macmillan, p. 53.

8. Hackman & Johnson, p. 201.

9. Jesuino, J. C. (1996). Leadership: Micro-macro links. In E. H. White and J. H. Davis (Eds.), *Understanding group behavior, Vol. 2.* Mahwah, NJ: Erlbaum, pp. 93, 119.

10. Bennis & Nanus, p. 4.

11. Kroeger, O., with Thuesen, J. M. (1992). *Type talk at work: How the 16 personality types determine your success on the job.* New York: Dell, p. 385.

12. Lewin, K., Lippit, R., & White, R. K. (1939). Patterns of aggressive behaviour in experimentally created social climates. *Journal of Social Psychology, 10,* pp. 271–299.

13. Jesuino, p. 99.

14. Dressler, A. (1994). *Voyage to the great attractor: Exploring intergalactic space.* New York: Alfred A. Knopf, pp. 193–194.

15. Fiedler, F. E., & Chemers, M. M. (1984). *Improving leadership effectiveness: The leader match concept* (2nd ed.). New York: Wiley. In addition to Fielder's Contingency Model of Leadership Effectiveness, several other situational theories offer valuable insights into the ways in which leaders must find a match between their styles and the needs of their group. See Chapter 4 in M. M. Chemers (1997), *An integrative theory of leadership* (Mahwah, NJ: Erlbaum), for a discussion and analysis of the following theories: House's Path-Goal Directive, Vroom and Yetton's Normative Decision Theory, and Hersey and Blanchard's Situational Leadership.

16. House & Shamir (1993). In M. M. Chemers & R. Ayman (Eds.), *Leadership theory and research: Perspectives and directions.* San Diego: Academic Press, p. 82.

17. Bennis, W., & Goldsmith, J. (1997). *Learning to lead: A workbook on becoming a leader* (Updated ed.). Cambridge, MA: Perseus Books, pp. xiv–xvi.

18. Bennis & Goldsmith, p. xv.

19. Bennis & Goldsmith, p. xvi.

20. Questions are adapted from those suggested by Bennis & Goldsmith, pp. 107–108.

21. The 4-M Model of Effective Leadership is based, in part, on Martin M. Chemers' integrative theory of leadership that identifies three functional aspects of leadership: image management, relationship development, and resource utilization. We have added a fourth function—decision making—and have incorporated more of a communication perspective into Chemers' view of leadership as a multifaceted process. See Chemers, M. M. (1997). *An integrative theory of leadership.* Mahwah, NJ: Earlbaum, pp. 151–173.

22. Chemers, p. 154.

23. Chemers, p. 155.

24. Chemers, p. 160.

25. Lipnack, J., & Stamps, J. (2000). *Virtual teams* (2nd ed.). New York: Wiley, p. 177.

26. Rees, F. (2001). *How to lead work teams: Facilitation skills* (2nd ed.). San Francisco: Jossey-Bass/Pfeiffer, p. 108.

27. Robbins, H., & Finley, M. (2000). *The new why teams don't work: What goes wrong and how to make it right.* San Francisco: Berrett-Koehler, p. 107.

28. Hersey, P., & Blanchard, K. H. (1988). *Management of organizational behavior: Utilizing human resources* (5th ed.). Englewood Cliffs, NJ: Prentice Hall.

29. Shimanoff, S. B., & Jenkins, M. M. (1996). Leadership and gender: Challenging assumptions and recognizing resources. In R. S. Cathcart, L. A. Samovar, and L. D. Henman (Eds.), *Small group communication: Theory and practice* (7th ed). Madison, WI: Brown & Benchmark, p. 327.

30. Napier, R. W., & Gershenfeld, M. K. (1993). *Groups: Theory and experience.* Boston: Houghton Mifflin, p. 371.

31. Tannen, D. (1994). *Talking from 9 to 5: Women and men in the workplace: Language, sex and power.* New York: Avon.

32. Chemers, p. 150.

33. Chemers, p. 126.

34. Chemers, M. M., & Murphy, S. E. (1995). *Leadership for diversity in groups and organizations: Perspectives on a changing workplace.* Newbury Park, CA: Sage.

35. Freiberg, K. L. (1992). Transformation leadership. In R. S. Cathcart & L. A. Samovar (Eds.), *Small group communication: A reader* (6th ed.). Dubuque, IA: Wm. C. Brown, pp. 526–527.

COLL 147
Groupthink Exercise

On July 12th, 2004, the Senate Intelligence Committee, a bipartisan committee, released a report stating that one of the reasons the U.S. invaded Iraq in March 2003 was a result of groupthink.

Now that you have an understanding of what grouthink is, use the Internet to read either the report itself, or many of the articles and editorials that were written in response to the report.

Using your own words, summarize whether or not you feel groupthink was one of the reasons why the U.S. went to war with Iraq.

Be sure to use proper citation if you are going to quote or paraphrase someone else's words or ideas.

Case 7

Cyril and Edna: The Manager as Mediator

Group Size: Any number of groups of three to six.

Recommended Time: 90 minutes recommended minimum (5 minutes to set up; 10 minutes for student preparation; 30–40 minutes for role play; 15 minutes for Worksheet 1 and small group discussion; 10 minutes for Worksheet 2 and small group discussion; 20 minutes or more for report out and large group discussion).

Provided: Instructions, manager's role, worksheets, and Observation Sheet in the student edition. Roles for Cyril and Edna are in the *Instructor's Resource Manual.*

Also Required: Enough photocopies of Cyril's and Edna's roles to provide one of each for each group. No other materials required.

Facilities: Moveable chairs. Enough room for approximately six feet between groups.

Objectives

▶ To help students develop skills for managing and mediating conflict in the workplace

▶ To help students practice the skills of active listening

▶ To help students practice the skills of making one's needs understood

▶ To help students recognize the superordinate goals common to both parties to a conflict

Background

"Cyril and Edna" is a classic case of unaddressed interpersonal conflict in the workplace. Lack of communication around small differences continues until a larger issue, possible racism by one party, brings both parties into the arena armed not only with the present issue but with a slew of unresolved historical ones, real and/or imagined, as well. Since both parties have approached the manager for help, it provides a wonderful opportunity for the manager to use mediation techniques to help the parties resolve their differences and build a better relationship.

Students should be familiar with the philosophy and steps of the mediation process before trying this exercise. It will also be useful for them to review the process of active listening.

Two things are likely to be especially difficult for students to manage in this role play: the issue of racism and the tendency of angry people to repeat themselves. In the first, it is going to be important for the manager to allow Cyril to talk about how he feels when he hears racist jokes or remarks. The manager will probably have to reframe Cyril's comments more than once to focus the issue on the feelings raised in Cyril rather than Edna's blame. Not doing this will likely push Edna into a defensive stance rather than into a position of being able to listen to and understand Cyril's feelings.

With regard to the tendency of angry people to repeat themselves, many managers find it difficult to interrupt and refocus a disputant who is ranting and raving without a break and generally monopolizing the floor. In addition, that kind of behavior may elicit anger in the manager who may then try to control the situation by belittling the disputant and/or his or her concerns. Those managers who are successful at redirecting the angry disputant should be encouraged to share how they did it and what their feelings were.

While observers are not critical in this exercise, they tend to be extremely useful.

Suggested Outline and Timing

1. *Set-up (full class: 5 minutes)*

In setting up this exercise, briefly review the steps in the mediation process. Suggest that this includes:

▶ Setting out the reasons for the meeting and the role of the manager.

▶ Clarifying the process and the guidelines.

▶ Getting agreement from the disputants to keep open minds.

▶ Helping the disputants to find their common interests.

▶ Focusing on the future relationship.

▶ Reaching a specific agreement on resolving the problem.

Do the following:

▶ Briefly review the instructions for the exercise.

▶ Ask for and answer any questions on how to proceed.

▶ Divide students into their groups.

▶ Distribute the roles of Cyril and Edna to those who have been assigned to play them.

2. *Student preparation, role play, and small group debrief (small groups: approximately 65 minutes)*

During the role play, be available to answer any questions that might arise. Flag four time periods:

▶ After the first 10 minutes, remind students to stop preparation and begin the role play.

▶ After the next 30–40 minutes, ask students to stop role play, and complete Worksheet 1.

▶ After the next 15 minutes, ask students to complete Worksheet 2.

▶ After the next 10 minutes, ask for small-group report outs.

3. *Report out and discussion (20-minute minimum recommended)*

During this time, debrief the exercise in the larger group. Ask a spokesperson for each of the groups to first describe the process, its successes, and areas for improvement.

Next ask each spokesperson to describe one or more of the elements of his or her solution. Handling the report out in two steps, rather than having each group report on both process and solution at the same time, helps keep the groups not reporting from losing focus. Ask the students to discuss what they see as the usefulness of the mediation process.

The discussion might include or focus on such issues as:

▶ The difficulties in handling issues around racism.

▶ The difficulties in handling angry disputants.

▶ The importance of the resolution coming from the disputants rather than the manager.

▶ In what ways the mediation process helps build better future communication.

▶ How students might use mediation techniques in their own lives.

Conclude the discussion by stressing the business benefits of helping individuals deal with their workplace disputes directly rather than allowing them to undermine productivity and morale.

Cyril

You have been employed in the technical support division of a medium-sized software development firm for slightly more than two years, having joined right after you got your undergraduate engineering degree. Despite the stresses of spending all day on the telephone talking to frustrated and sometimes abusive customers, you really like your job, your boss, and the people with whom you work. You sit in a cubicle that is separated from the adjoining cubicles by partitions that are approximately five feet high. Edna's cubicle is next to yours.

Edna, a white woman who is about twenty years older than you, has been in the division about two and a half years. She has a high, squeaky voice that is often shrill and loud when she's on the phone, and her conversations with customers seem to go on forever, sometimes making it difficult for you to concentrate.

Edna has the annoying habit of borrowing your things without asking. When you're missing a stapler, a reference book, or any of your office or personal supplies, chances are Edna has it. On more than one occasion, you have gone to her cubicle while she has been away from her desk to "borrow back" what she has taken. On the one or two occasions when you have asked Edna to stop borrowing your things, she has gotten angry and told you that they all belong to the company anyway.

Edna is really good at her job, and more than once she has been an immense help to you with a customer problem. Unfortunately, something happened yesterday that made you angry and upset with her. You had just finished a customer call when you overheard Edna talking to a coworker on the other side of her cubicle. As you wrote up your customer notes, you realized that Edna was telling a not very funny joke about two black men who stole a car. The joke was filled with racial stereotypes and bigotry. As a black man, you were offended and furious at their lack of sensitivity.

When you went to complain, your manager suggested that the three of you—you, Edna, and your manager—get together to talk things over.

Edna

You have been employed in the technical support division of a medium-sized software development firm for about two and a half years, having joined right after you got your undergraduate degree in computer science. Before going back to school for your degree, you stayed home to raise your children who are now sixteen and nineteen.

Despite stresses of spending all day on the telephone talking to frustrated and sometime abusive customers, you really like your job, your boss, and the people with whom you work. You sit in a cubicle that is separated from the adjoining cubicles by partitions that are approximately five feet high, and you often talk over the partitions to your neighbors.

Cyril, a black man who is about twenty years younger than you, has been in the division a little over two years. His cubicle is next to yours. It annoys you that he regularly hangs his coat over your common partition, but you haven't said anything because you haven't wanted to make trouble. You also know that Cyril has often gone into your cubicle when you haven't been there and taken things from your desk and from your desk drawers. When you've tried to borrow office items from Cyril, he has told you to "get your own," but in other ways he has generally been cooperative.

Occasionally you have been irked to overhear Cyril imitate you when talking to your coworker. As a result of a botched tonsillectomy when you were nine, you have a high and squeaky voice.

You have ignored most of Cyril's behavior as simply petty annoyances and have attributed most of it to his youth. After all, he isn't much older than your own son, and you're impressed by his competence on the job.

Your manager has suggested that the three of you—you, Cyril, and your manager—get together today to talk over some problems that have arisen. You're not exactly sure what this is all about, but you do see this as an opportunity to deal with some of the things that have been bothering you.

Research and Writing

CHAPTER 8

Linda Stevens Hjorth

Your written work in college will help you discover that writing is more than an assignment; it is a way of life. Think about all the things you do on a daily basis that involve writing. The papers you write, the letters you send, the reports you create, and the job applications you fill out are examples of writing that is often taken for granted. In each case, you need to know how to place thoughts on paper effectively. Words must be spelled correctly, ideas must make sense, and syntax must be grammatically correct. The success of your writing depends on your knowledge, comfort level, and ability to communicate ideas in written words.

Part of being victorious in college is knowing how to write essays, reaction papers, and research papers. With the completion of each writing assignment, your comfort level and expertise in writing increase. Possessing effective writing strategies can help you get and keep jobs, attain promotions, and achieve career goals. The writing skills that you learn in college carry over to your career. They help you to write organized business reports, letters, and memos that are grammatically correct. For example, it is difficult to get a job without sending out well-written cover letters and résumés. Recruiters often throw away résumés that have spelling errors. Promotions into positions with increased responsibility demand effective writing capability. No one wants a manager who cannot communicate properly in writing.

This chapter presents ways to clarify writing assignments, follow steps for research papers, improve writing, combat writer's anxiety, and prevent plagiarism. The main focus of this chapter is the creation of essays and research papers. However, writing is not only something you do in college but also a great way to communicate, share ideas with others, and express feelings that may not be easy to say.

Writing is a way to make your ideas come alive. Experiment with writing. Practice. You may even enjoy it.

Clarify the Assignment

You have a writing assignment. Your instructor tells you to write a 750-word paper and hand it in next week. You write the assignment down as a priority on your to-do list and go home. As you sit in front of your computer and stare at the blank screen, you wait for the writing to happen. Many ideas pass through your mind, but you do not know where to begin.

The best place to start is with the instructor's original assignment. What type of paper has been assigned? Whatever the assignment, make sure you understand the instructor's expectations. Each instructor will expect different things; by asking the right questions, you will understand more easily what you need to do.

▶ Is your paper supposed to be historical, autobiographical, biographical, theoretical, or scientific?

▶ Should your paper be informative, persuasive, informational, or research oriented?

▶ Is your paper based on fact or fiction?

▶ Will your instructor provide you with the topic, or must you pick one? If you are allowed to pick one, do you need to have it approved by your instructor?

▶ How many sources will you need? How do you cite them?

▶ How long should the paper be?

▶ What are your instructor's overall expectations for this assignment?

By clarifying the expectations of the instructor, you will find fewer roadblocks as you write. Most instructors want papers that are typed double-spaced, neat, and well organized with no spelling errors. In order to be creative in your writing endeavors, it is important to allow your creative juices to flow and not limit your writing with self-doubts.

Writing Guidelines

The following writing guidelines provide support and a basic foundation for your writing effort. As you write, use the guidelines as a gentle reminder to complete all of the steps of writing.

▶ Choose a subject.

▶ Narrow it into smaller topics.

▶ Write a thesis statement.

▶ Prepare an outline.

▶ Write a first draft. Cover all of the topics on your outline. Use headings and sub-headings.

▶ Spell the instructor's name correctly. Use the instructor's correct title (Professor, Mrs., Ms., Mr., Dr.).

▶ Proofread.

▶ Ask others for constructive criticism.

▶ Rewrite the paper (integrate suggestions).

▶ Check punctuation, grammar, and spelling.

▶ Be sure your paper is neat, organized, and understandable.

▶ Proofread, make corrections, and read again for last minute changes.

▶ Hand in your final paper.

The following section explains the possible writing steps. Try them and see how they work for you. Writing is different for everyone. After using these steps once or twice, change the order, add new ones, subtract the ones that do not work. That way, you will be able to use the steps within your own writing style. These steps are set up for writing research projects. For writing projects that are not research-based, eliminate the "research" and "research notes" steps. The rest remain the same.

Important skills are involved in the process of writing a research paper: researching in the library, reading sources, taking notes from these sources, and writing the actual paper. Enough time must be allotted for each stage of the process. There should also be time to proofread the paper and make necessary revisions. The result should be a well-researched, well-written research paper.

Maele Seau, student
Columbia College, Columbia, Missouri

Writing Steps

Choose a Subject

Imagine that the instructor has asked you to write a research paper, report, or essay based on the environment. What would you write about? Sometimes it helps to create a list of all of the topics related to the subject recommended by the instructor. For example, you might choose to write about the environment. Which topic would you choose? Recycling, reducing waste, deforestation, the effects of the Chernobyl nuclear accident on the environment, polluted water tables, extinction of species, ozone depletion, or global warming? When you choose a subject that you like and that is of interest to you, the writing process seems more pleasant and less daunting.

Narrow the Subject

What subject would be fun or interesting to write about?

How many topics can you list from your selected subject?

Most subjects that you choose initially will be very general. You will need to narrow down the subject to make it easier to write about. Otherwise, all of the available data can be overwhelming. It would be frustrating to start researching a subject and find that there are two hundred and forty articles available. Where would you begin?

Narrowing down a broad concept (a subject) into smaller parts (topics), before you begin writing will save you time and leave you less frustrated. When you narrow down your subject into smaller topics, and then choose one topic to write about, you can create a more focused paper.

Let us say, for example, that your psychology instructor assigns a five-page research paper on any theorist in the field of psychology. You could narrow your subject by choosing Sigmund Freud from a list that also includes John B. Watson, Carl Jung, B. F. Skinner, Edward B. Titchener, Carl Rogers, Abraham Maslow, and Wilhelm Wundt. After choosing Freud, you will need to narrow the topic further. You could decide to examine a few Freudian theories like unconscious conflict, dream interpretation, personality development, or psychosexual development. Finally, you could complete the narrowing process by choosing "psychosexual development" as your topic.

Write a Thesis Statement

Before you create a thesis statement, take time to read some sources on your topic, reflect, analyze, and understand the sources that you have reviewed. Write down or

A THESIS STATEMENT contains one or two sentences that state explicitly the focus of a writing assignment.

QUICK CHECK

Choose a topic.

Write a thesis statement based on your topic.

type some notes from the original sources (remember to record full source citation data): your reactions to new theory, statistics, or ideas. Your reactions to others' written words strengthen your own writing skills. Trust your own thoughts and reflect upon them.

A thesis statement consists of one or two sentences that clearly state the focus of the writing assignment. It summarizes the main concepts to be presented and lets the reader know the order in which topics will appear in the paper. It is a helpful tool because it can keep you focused as you write. It also gives the reader a brief preview of what will be featured in your writing. The only time you would not use a thesis statement is in fiction or autobiographical writing. If the instructor asks that the thesis statement not be included in the final written paper, you may still want to write one for yourself to keep you focused as you write.

You may find as you write your paper that your thesis will change. The more information that you gather, the more likely you are to change your focus. It is possible that the thesis statement may not correlate to a newly written first draft. If this happens, change the thesis statement so that it reflects the new draft.

Do Research

RESEARCHING means finding materials pertaining to your thesis statement.

Once your topic has been chosen and your thesis statement written, it is time to research. There are many ways to conduct research. Visit your library or investigate options on the Internet to see what kinds of information are available. Although the Internet provides you with a massive amount of information, it will be up to you to check resources in the library to be sure that the data you find on the Internet are accurate and factual.

Take pens, pencils, and a laptop computer (if you have one) to the library with you. In your library, you will find card catalogues, on-line catalogues, computer databases, inter-library loan, and much more.

Do not limit yourself to the written word. Also check out videos, laser disks, tapes, and CDs. A variety of community resources are also available to you. You could contact industries, art institutes, museums, village boards, chambers of commerce, zoos, and so on.

Interviews are a viable source of information. For example, if you were conducting research on the environment, you could interview someone at the local waste management company. Most companies are glad to have staff meet with you, as it is a way for them to market the good things they do. If you are not sure whom to call first, call the marketing or customer service department.

Take Research Notes

When conducting research, it is important that you record accurately *all* of the data pertaining to your sources. You may want to refer to the *MLA Handbook* (Gibaldi, 1995) or the *Publication Manual of the American Psychological Association* (1983) for citation style in your final bibliography. When creating your bibliographic information, remember that whether you find the information in books, journals, abstracts, periodicals, or specialized indexes, or on the Internet, your bibliographical notes should include the following:

▶ Journals and periodicals: subject and title of the article, author's name, magazine title, volume number, date of publication, and page number.

▶ Books and abstracts: title of book, author's and editor's names, name of publisher, place and date of publication, and page number.

▶ Internet: subject and title, author's name, and Web site address.

Both the *Publication Manual of the American Psychological Association* and *A Guide to MLA Documentation* (Trimmer, 1998) provide guidance in citing all types of references, including electronic sources.

If you use bibliography cards, one card (3″ × 5″) should be used for each source. You could use different card colors for different sources and number each bibliography card. After you have completed your bibliography cards, create 4″ × 6″ note cards. Find a large space on your desk or floor and fill it with all of the materials relating to your research. Write on each note card a main idea, a summary, relevant details, or a quote that you want to present in your paper. Place a brief source citation on each note card, or indicate the number of the bibliography card listing that source, so that you will not confuse various sources when you start your paper. Another option would be to use computer software that can organize bibliographical information.

Outline and Organize

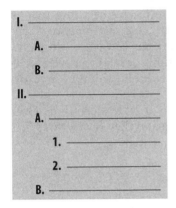

Now that your research is done, one of the best ways to organize your collected information is to create an outline (see Chapter 3). Like thesis statements, outlines allow you to organize your paper without really writing it. They provide a quick look at whether your paper will flow, and how main and subordinate ideas will fit within the body of your paper. Like thesis statements, outlines can always be changed. However, the fundamental parts of the paper listed in the outline usually remain the same.

Place your notes in a topical order that makes sense to you. Use your notes to create your outline. The headings and subheadings included in your outline (based on the main ideas from your notes) will organize the paper for both the writer and the reader. Even if you eventually remove them from your final draft, they remain an important part of the organizing process.

Write a First Draft

Instructors Have Different Ideas about Outlines. Be Sure to Ask Your Instructor for Guidelines

Using your organized notes and outline, write the first draft of your assignment. Do not let this become a difficult or frustrating process. Record all ideas that come to mind. Do not edit or delete at this point. Just get something down on paper for each main and subordinate idea. This will generate a quantity of further ideas that will help you complete the project. You can always delete and elaborate later. Remember, this is not your final draft.

Write and write and write until you feel that you have filled in your outline with written material. Then go back and reorganize the writing until you are satisfied with the content. After you have done this, leave your paper for a period of at least twenty-four hours. Meanwhile, allow your mind to come up with new creative ideas to improve the quality of your work.

Proofread

Proofread your paper for correct spelling, punctuation, grammar, capitalization, and so on. Then leave it alone for another period of time. Review it again later. If you find no blatant errors, ask someone else, such as a family member, a friend, or a professional in the tutoring center at your college, to proofread it for you.

Seek Constructive Criticism

Others can provide you with pertinent feedback regarding your writing. Many professional writers belong to writing groups in which group members provide positive and negative feedback on each of the members' written pieces. Although it is difficult to hear criticism, comments from others will improve the quality of your writing. Study groups can increase writing awareness and skill. However, to offer group feedback effectively, it is important to focus the responses. One way to do this is to ask group members to respond to your writing by answering the following questions:

1. Does the introduction and conclusion reflect the essence of the entire work?

2. Are the ideas that are presented clear and concise? Are any parts of the writing confusing or in need of clarification?

3. Are more transitions needed? If so, what suggestions would you offer?

By answering these questions, the group can stay focused on the essentials of writing and not get lost in details or in ineffective criticism.

Seek Answers to Questions

There are many places to receive support when writing. Most campuses have writing centers or hotlines for quick questions. You can also receive help through the Internet, writer's reference guides [e.g., *The Rinehart Guide to Grammar Usage* (1993) and *The Chicago Manual of Style* (1993)] or various computer programs. Some academic support centers will also answer questions or help you solve writing problems. Ask your instructor what support services are available on your campus for writers.

Some instructors are willing to look over a draft and provide suggestions. Others like to look at your outline before you begin writing and then review your first draft. This is a good idea if you are unsure initially of your writing.

Students need to realize no piece of writing is ever perfect and that revisions can only help. They should be able to express their thoughts and ideas effectively on paper. This helps students project their ideas clearly to their reader.

Robin Marie Carpenter, student
McHenry County College, Crystal Lake, Illinois

Revise

Make the appropriate revisions and get ready for the final draft. At some point, you have to become comfortable enough with the paper to move on. If you find yourself revising and revising, and never feeling satisfied with your product, stop. Put your paper away for a few hours, and if you find no major imperfections, get ready to write your final draft.

Write a Final Draft

This is it. The end of the road. All of the hours that you have put into this writing assignment will now pay off. Make your final content corrections, and lay the paper aside. Check it later for grammatical errors, awkward sentences, paragraph transitions, and completion of topic coverage. Review the writing checklist at the beginning of this chapter to make sure that you have effectively scrutinized the entire paper. Make appropriate corrections, and hand it in.

Some students are never happy with the finished product and thus never finish the paper. It may never be perfect in your eyes, but it *must* be handed in. You have given it your best.

It took a while to get through the first draft. Now let's start the next one.

EXERCISE

Writing Assignment

The purpose of this exercise is to provide you with practice in following the steps for writing assignments.

Choose a subject about which you would like to write a two to three page paper. Narrow the subject. Create a thesis statement. List two bibliographical sources that you will integrate into your paper. Create an outline of your paper, and organize your material. Write the first draft of the paper, ask for constructive criticism (include written feedback in your final paper), revise, and hand in a final draft.

Manage Your Attitude

It is easy to give up on writing when it does not seem to be happening as fast as you think it should. Take a quick break, but do not give up. When you stick with it, the writing ideas will begin to flow. Find ways to keep yourself motivated. Use positive reinforcers when you complete tasks (a walk, lunch with a friend, a sporting event). When you have a thought such as "I will never finish this paper," turn the negative thought into a positive one. Think, "I will finish two pages tonight and then see how much I can do tomorrow night."

Do not be hard on yourself when you write. Creativity comes from the heart and the mind. If you constantly censor your work, you will be stifling your creativity and productivity. Let your thoughts flow, and allow yourself to write.

Know that each time you complete a writing project successfully you are building skills to help you achieve your life goals. Writing is a part of school, of business, and of creativity. Believe in your ability to write and create, learn from your mistakes, and try again. The more confidence you have in yourself, the more confidence will be expressed in your writing.

Combat Writer's Anxiety

WRITER'S ANXIETY is a physical, fearful reaction to any attempt to write.

Writer's anxiety is what you might be experiencing as you stare at the blank screen and try to put your thoughts into words. Your heart might palpitate, and you might wonder to yourself, "Can I really do this?" Writer's anxiety sometimes includes writer's block. That is the experience of feeling that no matter what you write, it is not right, or that no new creative ideas come into your mind as you write. Not everyone experiences writer's anxiety, but if you do, the following tips could help.

Free-writing

Free-writing is writing without censoring. If your mind seems frozen, try free-writing. Sit at the computer, or grab some paper and a pen, and write, write, write. Write for fifteen minutes (minimum) without stopping. Let every idea from the recesses of your mind get recorded on paper. Later, you can edit the information, but during the free-writing experience, no editing is allowed. It is an enjoyable way to unfreeze thoughts and create ideas of which you might not have been aware. This technique combats anxiety because it allows creative ideas to surface without censorship.

Free-talking

If you do not have time to sit and write down your free-floating ideas, then find a tape recorder, and while you are doing the dishes, working on the car, or sitting and enjoying a sunset, record all of the thoughts relating to your topic. Later, as you are writing, you can listen to the tape and take notes on any ideas that pertain to your paper. Free-talking is a great technique for busy people who do not have time to free-write. It also works well for people who create best when not focusing on just one task.

Write Yourself a Letter about Your Topic

This is a technique that gives you permission to write anything you want. It works because you know that no one but you will see it.

Read about the Topic

Record any ideas that come to mind as you read about the topic. Use those ideas later in your paper, remembering to cite sources. By reading and pondering others' ideas, your own creativity can be stimulated.

Change Your Writing Technique

If you are using the computer, take out a pen and paper. If you are writing in sentence form, change to sentence fragments, poems, or rap. This change often sparks new ideas. Just by changing the tools or place in which you write you may find that new ideas can be created.

Take a Break

If nothing else works, leave the writing and do something enjoyable. Go for a walk, work on a hobby, get a good night's sleep. When you return to your writing, the ideas might flow more easily. It is almost as if your brain is working on the ideas while you are physically doing something else. A break provides a fresh start on an old project.

EXERCISE

Combating Writer's Anxiety

The purpose of this exercise is to practice strategies that will decrease writer's block or writer's anxiety.

Choose three of the following strategies, and follow the directions within each one.

1. *Free-writing:* Choose a topic. Free-write for three minutes about the topic without censorship. After you have done this, list the concepts that are good enough to use in a paper.

2. *Free-talking:* Choose a topic. Tape record, for five minutes, all of your ideas about the topic. Create a list of ideas from free-talking that you could incorporate in a writing assignment. Hand in the tape and your written paper.

3. *Write yourself a letter:* Choose a topic that causes you to have mixed emotions or conflicting feelings. Write to yourself about them. What did you learn?

4. *Read about a topic:* Choose a topic. Find a source that relates to the topic on the Internet or in the library. Read for fifteen minutes and then correlate what you read to your topic. Write the correlations on a separate sheet of paper to be included in a writing assignment later.

5. *Change your writing technique:* Choose a topic, and see if writing in a different place or using different tools makes a difference in your creativity, productivity, or writing. Try writing in three different places.

6. *Take a break:* After you have been writing for a long time, leave the writing alone for twenty-four hours. Come back to it, and start to write again. Then record if the break made a difference.

PLAGIARISM

When you decide to present someone else's ideas as your own without giving the source, it is plagiarism.

► **When you use another's work, word for word, without providing the source, it is plagiarism.**

► **When you copy a report (full or partial) from another student, it is plagiarism.**

► **When you insufficiently paraphrase a paragraph without citing the source, it is plagiarism.**

Plagiarism is morally wrong, and most colleges and universities punish students who plagiarize. Sometimes, however, plagiarism occurs because you are not sure what should be cited and what should not. By following the Modern Language Association of America (MLA) or the American Psychological Association (APA) guidelines you will be less likely to make mistakes.

Before you plagiarize, remember that there is a tremendous pride that comes from creating a work that is totally your own. If you make the decision to plagiarize, you must also take personal responsibility for the punishment that could include failure on that specific project or failure in that class. Some colleges and universities dismiss or suspend students for repeated offenses.

Plagiarism is not only wrong, it does not allow you to create, learn, or advance. By choosing to plagiarize you are preventing yourself from participating in the educational system that you have worked so hard to enter. Professors do not like "cheats" and neither do employers.

PLAGIARISM is presenting someone else's ideas and words as your own, without source citations

---

This chapter has presented a variety of techniques that you can use in all of your writing endeavors. You will find that your writing improves as you read, research, outline, create, free-write, edit, rewrite, edit, and write again. Good writing comes from being willing to practice your writing skills until excellence permeates each written product.

Evaluating the Internet

Now that you are familiar with the library's databases, please complete the following:

Go to Ebscohost and find an article using "critical thinking" as your search term. Feel free to use an advanced search and use critical thinking combined with another topic/search term. When you find an article that looks interesting, read and evaluate it based on the following criteria:

1. What do you know about the author and his/her credibility on the topic?

2. How current is the information?

3. Was the article well-written? Did you find any typos, errors in logic, or obvious spelling or gramatical errors?

4. Did you find the information useful?

5. Did you find the information relevant to what you were looking for?

Now go to the Internet and use any search engine you like—e.g. Google, Yahoo, or Proquest, and complete the same exercise, responding to the above questions.

When you have finished, use your critical thinking skills to respond to the following questions:

How would you summarize the major differences between the two articles? How will this information help you when you go to research your next term paper?

Case 8

Critical Analysis Allison

Break into groups of four or five, and read aloud the setting and case. You will need to create the ending of this case through discussion and collaboration in your group. You may change the dialogue and add new characters. Your conclusion should demonstrate that you have reflected on the character's perspective and her circumstances. Answer the questions at the end of the case.

Setting: *Allison and Xi are drinking coffee in the student center.*

Allison is a first-semester college student. In three of her courses, term papers have been assigned. Allison hates writing papers. She had her sister help her with a mandatory English paper her senior year in high school. This semester, one of her term papers has been returned with a large, red D at the top. Allison has two more papers to write.

Xi is in her sophomore year at the same college. Allison knows her from high school. Xi has always received good grades. She wrote for the high school newspaper.

Allison: Thanks for meeting me, Xi.

Xi: Well, anything for a graduate of Everett High. So, how can I help you?

Allison: I am having lots of trouble with my classes. I never knew there would be so much writing involved. I am really good at Scantron tests, but putting a paragraph together is tough.

Xi: You just have to practice writing. The more you write, the easier it becomes.

Allison: I wanted to show you a paper I just got back. [*Hands her the paper*] I got a D. The instructor also wrote the word *plagiarism*. What does that mean?

Xi: Well, *plagiarism* means you have stolen someone's words or ideas.

Allison: I don't get it. How are you supposed to write on a topic you have no knowledge about without using someone else's information?

Xi: That's where citing sources and paraphrasing comes in.

Allison: I don't get it; I had a bibliography at the end.

Continue the dialogue. Xi can clarify source citations and paraphrasing, and she can give Allison more tips on writing research papers.

Questions

1. When is it important to cite sources?

2. What role do note cards play in the writing of a research paper?

3. How would you answer Allison's question: How are you supposed to write on a topic you have no knowledge about without using someone else's information?

4. What resources should Allison use?

Study Strategies

Linda Stevens Hjorth

OBJECTIVES

By the end of this appendix, you will be able to . . .

1. Improve your reading study strategies with PQ4R.

2. Master basic study skills.

3. Improve your study environment.

4. Develop more effective ways to learn while in the classroom.

5. Acquire new ways to study math.

6. Study science more effectively.

7. Become more knowledgeable in using a computer as an aid to studying.

STUDY STRATEGIES CHECKLIST

The purpose of the following checklist is to help you evaluate the effectiveness of your study strategies.

Check the appropriate answer:

1. Do you always study in the same area? YES _____ NO _____

2. Do you set up your study area with paper, pencils, erasers, etc., before you begin? YES _____ NO _____

3. Do you preview your materials before you begin? YES _____ NO _____

4. Do you ask yourself questions as you study? YES _____ NO _____

5. Have you found satisfactory ways to stay focused as you study? YES _____ NO _____

6. When you read, do you visualize pictures, words, and ideas associated with your reading? YES _____ NO _____

7. Do you recite terms out loud as you study? YES _____ NO _____

8. Do you review notes within twenty-four hours of taking them? YES _____ NO _____

9. Do you reflect on lessons learned when you have finished studying? YES _____ NO _____

10. Do you study your most difficult subjects first YES _____ NO _____

If you are using effective study strategies, your answer to most of these questions will be yes. If you said yes to most or all of them, write the reasons for your success.

_____

_____

If you said no to several questions, record specifically what you need to learn from this chapter to improve your study skills. Pick a study strategy that you would like to try, and write about its limitations and advantages.

_____

_____

Choose a study area that is compatible with your learning style.
© Jon Feingersh/THE STOCK MARKET—CORBIS

If you have ever explained the plot of a movie, described a recently read book to a friend, or prepared for an upcoming exam, you have participated in the learning process. The acquisition of knowledge—an integral part of the learning process—is achieved primarily through study. Through the mastery of study skills you can begin to control the future course of your education, career, and life.

Study skills mastery is not simply memorization. It is understanding, comprehending, questioning, and learning. Learned information is stored in long-term memory, ready for retrieval when necessary. Your study strategies should allow you to remember vital information and retrieve it in the future.

Studying means taking responsibility for the acquisition of knowledge. Making the most of your study time, focusing as you study, and accepting the responsibility to learn make college victories achievable.

When working through this appendix, choose and practice the study techniques you think will make a difference in your current study efforts. This appendix will strengthen your current study habits whether you are reading, attending lectures, or participating in lab. With the application of each study strategy, your confidence will increase, and you will begin to study more wisely (not necessarily harder) and learn more.

Improve Your Reading Study Strategies with PQ4R

PQ4R is an efficient study technique that was pioneered by Francis P. Robinson (1970) in his work *Effective Study*. It requires you to focus, get involved, and learn. If you are a student who finds him- or herself staring blankly at a reading assignment without comprehension, you can use PQ4R as a way to get started and to maintain interest in reading assignments.

▶ Preview

▶ Question

▶ Read

▶ Reflect

▶ Recite

▶ Review

PQ4R is effective because it provides structure to the study process. When you begin to use PQ4R, you may feel that it takes too much time. Be patient, keep working, and you will begin to experience its benefits. You may even find that some parts of it work better for you than others. For example, the previewing could be helpful, but if you are a visual learner, recitation may not be as informative. Adapt PQ4R according to your learning style.

Let us take a closer look to see how PQ4R can be used to record and remember what you have gleaned from textbooks, notes, and readings.

P—Preview

QUICK CHECK

Choose a chapter that you want to preview. Next, mark the segments as you complete the previewing process.

Table of Contents   _____

Chapter Summary   _____

Vocabulary Lists   _____

Learning Objectives   _____

Headings   _____

Subheadings   _____

Graphs   _____

Charts   _____

Definitions   _____

Words in Bold   _____

Words in Italic   _____

Previewing is a quick way to give yourself a general idea of what the assignment is about. It paves the way for you to gain a concrete overview of information before listening to lectures or reading more comprehensively. Previewing can help you attack information that may seem overwhelming before you begin. It provides you with the fundamentals upon which you can build more detailed knowledge.

To preview, scan each chapter page by page quickly, extracting the essentials while acquiring an initial familiarity with the information. Skim the table of contents and all headings, charts, graphs, definitions, chapter summaries, vocabulary lists, italic or bold words, and learning objectives. Sometimes it helps to read the summary first, to get a general feeling for the chapter, and then to go back and preview. Reading the first and last sentences of each paragraph can also provide the main ideas under each heading. If you estimate that the reading assignment will take an hour, preview for approximately five minutes. Allow a little more time for material that is especially complex.

As you preview, ask yourself how this new information relates to your education and your career. Look for items with which you are already familiar and then build upon your knowledge. Examine concepts or ideas that interest you or examine new approaches to old ideas.

Q—Question

QUICK CHECK

Record one question you have about this chapter.

....

....

....

While reading, write questions in the margins of the text or on a separate sheet of paper. One way to do this is to turn headings and subheadings into questions. For example, if a heading in a psychology text reads, "Psychoanalysis: Sigmund Freud," you could ask the question: How does Sigmund Freud relate to psychoanalysis? As you read the assignment, answer the question.

Active questioning correlates to active learning. Asking yourself questions as you read forces you to focus on and understand the information you are reading. If you do not ask questions, you may find that your eyes see words your mind never registers. Thoughtful questions indicate that you are reading, digesting, and integrating the written word. Questioning causes you to be more interested and less distracted.

R—Read

QUICK CHECK

Which reading time pattern works best for you?

....

....

....

You have previewed and created questions; now it is time to read. Read actively! One goal in your reading might be to answer all of the questions you have created. Pay attention to the words and associate what you are reading with the concepts you already know. Visualize any ideas, pictures, words, or theory that will help you to recall the material. Change the speed at which you are reading based on the difficulty of the material and your understanding of it. You will need to slow down for more difficult materials and pick up speed when you are familiar with the subject. Pause occasionally during your reading time to ask yourself what you have just read. Some reading assignments, because of their complexity, may dictate that you read the chapter more than once.

Time your reading sessions to your needs. It may work to read for thirty to forty-five minutes and then take a ten-minute break as a reward for your effort. Or you may be more comfortable reading in two- or three-hour sessions. Everyone has different concentration rates, so experiment and find the time pattern that works best for you.

Also, try reading at the time of day you focus best. If you can control your schedule, experiment with early morning, lunch-time, or after-dinner sessions. The times that work best are those you should use routinely.

R—Reflect

Reflection is an integral part of learning and allows you to ponder, contemplate, and rethink what you already know while stretching your mind to integrate new information. After reading a segment of text, put your book down and think about the reading. Allow yourself to be open to any thoughts that come to mind. There can be no time limit or time expectation for reflection because it depends on the simplicity, complexity, or emotional content of the materials that you are reading.

Reflection solidifies new concepts in your memory through reinforcement. It allows you to look at issues with a new perspective, too. Only through reflecting on reading material can you master it.

R—Recite

Have you ever read an entire page and not remembered one word? The technique of recitation can solve this problem. Rehearsing important points out loud allows you to remember them more easily. Reciting keeps data in your short-term memory long enough for it to solidify and enter your long-term memory. Reciting also allows you to use more than one of your senses while studying. Hearing the words through recitation triggers memory, as do sight and touch. That is why writing about your reading, speaking aloud, and following a graph line with your finger as you recite reinforces learning.

How do you use recitation when you study? Read aloud! Read a paragraph, cover the material you have read with your hand, and then recite the main points that you have learned. Another way is to recite out loud terms, concepts, theories, and new information over and over. The experience of hearing your own words is powerful.

Through recitation you will also challenge yourself to know what words say and mean. Hearing the words forces you to stop and examine them for further meaning: What did I just read? What did it mean? This immediate feedback sharpens your focus, increasing understanding and confidence.

Recitation is also practiced in study groups. Teaching the lesson to other group members and asking or answering questions augment your own learning.

R—Review

Cultivate the reviewing habit. Consistent review of recent readings or new notes reinforces learning, especially when done within twenty-four hours. Daily reviewing, even for fifteen minutes per class, eliminates the need for cramming. It is a simple formula: the more you review, the more you remember.

As you conduct your daily review, skip material that you already know; concentrate on concepts that are difficult, confusing, or difficult to remember. If a concept is not clear, look it up, ask your professor or study group members, or review it until it is understandable.

There are many additional tips that will strengthen your study skills. As you read about them, decide which ones you would like to experiment with. But first try out the PQ4R exercise on pages 199 and 200 to reinforce what you have just learned.

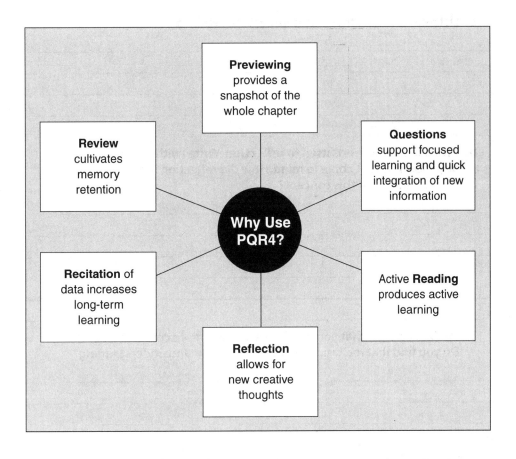

Practice PQ4R

The purpose of this exercise is to practice PQ4R using a current reading assignment.

1. Choose a chapter that has been assigned in one of your classes. Use the PQ4R method as you begin the reading assignment.

   a. **Preview** a chapter. List the main concepts that you just learned.

   _____

   _____

   _____

   _____

   b. Write down **questions** you have from the reading assignment and then answer them. (The answers could come from the text, your instructor, or your study group.)

   _____

   _____

   _____

   _____

c. List new concepts that you learned from **reading**.

_____
_____
_____
_____
_____
_____

d. Pick a topic that lends itself to **reflection**. Write (without censoring) any thoughts that come to mind. How did reflection increase your understanding of this concept?

_____
_____
_____
_____
_____
_____
_____

e. **Recite** concepts that you would like to learn more comprehensively. Do you find that recitation increases retention and understanding?

_____
_____
_____
_____

f. **Review.** Describe reviewing techniques that work best for you. Be specific in your description. ("I like to walk around my room, reciting out loud concepts that confuse me.")

_____
_____
_____
_____
_____

2. Which part of PQ4R worked best for you? Which part is least effective? Provide specific examples to support your answer.

_____
_____
_____
_____
_____

3. Which part of PQ4R best matches your learning style? How can you use the information that you learned from this exercise to help you become a more effective learner?

_____

_____

_____

_____

_____

_____

Study Tips

The following helpful hints can assist you in creating the best possible study environment and study habits. The hints are categorized as follows: Master Basic Study Strategies, Control Your Study Environment, Prepare for the Classroom, Find New Ways to Study Math, Study Science More Effectively, and Use a Computer to Support All Study Techniques.

Master Basic Study Strategies

Search for Meaning.   Information will not be stored in long-term memory unless you believe it is meaningful. Find ways to create meaning in your assignments. Make sure you know what the information means and how it is relevant to you, and your effort will be rewarded by memory.

Create Interest in Your Subjects.   Being interested will enhance your motivation to learn. The more you like what you study, the easier it is to remember. Who wants to remember boring, irrelevant facts? Change your perception and make it interesting.

Learn General Concepts First.   Start with major ideas and concepts. Then break them down into smaller pieces to understand them better.

Manage Your Study Time Wisely.   Make wise decisions about your use of time. Pull out your time management chart, term calendar, or to-do list to keep you on track. Do not procrastinate. Start working on projects and assignments as soon as they are assigned. Thinking "I will do it tomorrow" only creates stress. Set some interim deadlines to keep yourself on schedule.

Schedule Two Hours of Studying Time for Every Class Hour.   This is a formula that you can use to estimate study time weekly. You may find that it works for most classes, or you may find that some classes will take more time and others less. This formula may also change based on the number of tasks that need to be completed and the deadlines attached to each task. Use your priorities as a guide to compute exactly how much time you will need to study each subject.

Study the Hardest Subject First.   Finish the most difficult tasks first. You will have more energy at the start of your study session to tackle tough concepts. Fight the desire to procrastinate. Studying the difficult subject first relieves stress; it also makes the easier subjects seem like a reward for working so hard in the first place.

Overlearn.   You might find yourself studying enough to pass the test. Do you just want to pass the test? Or do you want to learn the information enough to do more than pass the test? You need to permanently remember and understand information in order to do well in advanced classes and learn the skills essential for your career. "Just passing" may not provide you with those skills.

Instead of memorizing information so that you can regurgitate it later on a test, overlearn for permanent memory storage and retrieval. By asking questions, examining, evaluating, reflecting, and repeatedly relearning information, you can retain more details for tests, for later courses, and for your career.

Know When to Ask for Help.   Tutoring is available on your campus; all you have to do is find it. If you feel that you are falling behind in your studies, ask for help now. Most classes build upon the information already presented. Therefore it is important to seek help before you become lost in the material and fear failure.

Create Effective Study Sessions.   Figure out the amount of study time that works for you. You might study best with fifty-minute study sessions and ten-minute breaks. Or you might learn best by studying for two hours with thirty-minute breaks. You probably do not want to study five or six hours without a break, unless you become so focused on the writing of a paper or so interested in a reading assignment that you could not quit if you wanted to. Experiment with different time spans until you find one that works best for you. No matter what the length of your study session, the more often you study and review, the more you will learn.

Narrow Down Information.   It is frustrating to look at a chapter assignment and feel there is no way you could learn everything. The following suggestions will help you narrow down your reading assignments:

▶ Obvious but important: eliminate anything the instructor said should not be studied.

▶ After previewing the chapter, go back and correlate your lecture notes to the text. Place a star or check next to any information that was emphasized in class, prioritizing the mass of information. You now know those are the areas that you should study first. Then go back and sift through other tidbits of information that would be useful to know.

▶ Try to write down all important concepts on one piece of 8" × 11" paper. If you have prioritized accurately, you now can narrow your focus again.

▶ Ask study group members what they feel should be studied and what should be eliminated. Check your assumptions for accuracy, and confirm with your instructor if in doubt.

Be a Kinesthetic Learner (No Head Propping).   Learn by doing! If you passively sit in your chair, propping up your head with your hand, do you think you are really learning? When you study, you need to be energetic and burn calories. That does not usually happen with head propping.

Instead, look for active ways to learn and study. Walk or stand as you read; sing out the words. Throw your note cards on the floor. Stand by each one and see what you can remember about the topic before you pick it up.

Write a term on the front of a Post-it note and a definition on the back: then stick each note to a wall. Walk to the wall, look at the term, and state the definition. Look at the back of the note. Was your answer correct? If you had the right answer, take the note off the wall. If your answer was wrong, leave it on the wall to review later. This process is rewarding because you can immediately see what you have learned and how much is left to master.

> Learn
> to Be
> Comfortable
> with Your Own
> Study Pattern and Style.

Review Your Notes Immediately After Class.   Review your notes while the ideas are still fresh in your mind. It is easier to transcribe words that are difficult to read or fill in fragmented sentences or incomplete thoughts shortly after the lecture. You may not remember this information three or four days from now. Going over your notes after the lecture helps increase memory retention.

Reviewing notes during breaks between classes is an excellent use of time. Find time to review notes again quickly before class begins. This provides continuity as you listen to the new lecture, and it increases retention.

Study When You Are Energetic.   Monitor your energy level. Identify the time of the day when you have the most energy and use it wisely. If you notice that it is easier to concentrate in the morning than at night, you have targeted the best time for you to study. If work schedules or family obligations interfere with your ability to study during your peak times, study as close to the targeted time as possible.

Stay Focused.   Boredom, problems, and daydreaming can all interfere with studying. Find ways to keep yourself focused. Every time your mind wanders, capture your attention and bring it back. Become involved actively in your notes or text instead of focusing passively on your boredom or your personal problems.

If problems divert your attention, write about them. Sometimes jotting down quick notes or reminders on a separate sheet of paper will relieve the anxiety that problems cause, allowing you to quickly refocus on your studies.

If you find that your mind wanders when you start to study, do not despair; it is a common problem. Keep trying; it may take ten or fifteen minutes to get into the study routine.

When you really cannot focus, do study-related tasks. Preview the chapter, rewrite your notes, type key words or definitions on the computer. Actively pursuing related tasks will help you jump into studying quickly.

Visualize Your Lessons.   The more you can create mental pictures of information to be learned, the more memorable the data will be. Draw or visualize the lesson. If you can see it, you are more likely to remember it.

 ## Control Your Study Environment

Always Study in the Same Area.   Studying in the same place all the time improves your concentration. You will not need to adjust constantly to a new study environment, and the inevitable distractions around your study area will be ones that you are used to, so you can deal with them swiftly or even ignore them. If you find that you tire or your attention wanders, walk away from your study area. That way your mind will associate your study area with focused study only.

Experiment with various study locations. Find out whether your desk, the floor, or a library corner works best for you. Avoid studying in bed; falling asleep will not help you in your learning endeavor, and associating active learning with your bed may disrupt your sleeping habits.

Choose Your Study Area Carefully.   Your study environment should be one without distractions. The general rule is no TV, no music, no loud roommates, no ringing phones, and no screaming children. However, the best study environment is a personal choice. You may be able to study only with music on or with your children around you. Experiment. Do not have any qualms, however, about unplugging the phone (or turning on your answering machine), creating mutual study time with your roommates, asking not to be disturbed (hang a sign that says, "Do Not Disturb" or simply say, "I do like you, but I need to study now!"), or creating child-free daily study times.

QUICK CHECK

List three study tips that work best for you that are not listed in this chapter.

1.

2.

3.

The best study environment is a personal choice. You may be able to study only with music on or with your children around you.
© Tony Freeman/PHOTO EDIT.

Choose a Well-Lit Study Area.   When you study in an area that has poor lighting, you may experience eye strain, muscle tension, and irritability. The lack of light may cause you physical discomfort and stress. You want focused concentration when you study, and improper lighting is a distraction and a hazard.

Have Supplies Available Before You Begin.   Do not let your excuse for not studying be that you need a drink, potato chips, pencils, a dictionary, tape, a calculator, disks, or note cards. It is all too easy to waste twenty minutes running back and forth acquiring supplies. Set up your study area before you start studying.

   When you run out of supplies, write them on a shopping list and purchase them ahead of time for your next study session. Do not interrupt your study to shop for supplies at the last minute.

Prepare for the Classroom

Read Before You Enter the Classroom.   Learning starts before the lecture begins. Be sure you have completed the homework and have read the assignment before entering the classroom. Difficult or uninspiring lectures are easier to understand and remember if you know what the instructor is talking about before he or she begins. The assimilation of data takes less effort when you are prepared. Accept responsibility for preparing yourself.

Monitor Your Attention Level.   How attentive are you? Learn to focus on the lecture. Control your daydreams and your attention level. When daydreams or problems pull your focus away, bring yourself back and refocus on classroom activities.

Attend Class.   Do not miss class. Attendance correlates to effective learning and the achievement of high grades. It is hard to know what to study if you are not in class to find out. If you have an emergency and cannot attend, make sure you borrow notes from a reliable friend and record them accurately. If you know ahead of time that you will be absent, ask your instructor what work you will miss and prepare it for next time.

Keep a Positive Attitude.   A positive attitude keeps you open to new ideas and alters old perceptions. Coming into class with the attitude "I will learn something today" correlates directly to the amount of energy you will put into learning and how much you will get out of it.

Listen and Participate in Class. Listening and participating are both integral parts of the learning process in the classroom. It is difficult to gather accurate notes if you are not listening effectively. It is advantageous to participate in class. Active participation makes remembering easier. (Some instructors encourage discussion and debates; others will not tolerate them. Know the instructor's rules.)

Sit in the Front of the Classroom. It is hard to fall asleep in the front row. If you are in the back, there are too many distractions and too much distance between you and the instructor. Choose the front whenever possible.

Make Sure Friends Are a Help, Not a Hindrance. If your friends keep you from being focused on the lecture, let them know that their behavior is not acceptable to you. If they refuse to stop talking in class, sit elsewhere. You are spending a great deal of money and energy to attend school, and you do not want it wasted just because you cannot hear the lecture. Socializing has its own time and place. Good friends will understand and learn quickly not to be distracting.

Expect the Unexpected. Instructors may hurry through the last few minutes of a lecture. Be prepared and stay in your seat until you have recorded everything. Often, tests, projects, or reading assignments are mentioned at the end of class. Ask the instructor not to erase the board until you have recorded everything you need to. If you think you have missed something, ask questions.

Knowing that instructors sometimes ramble, be aware and do not lose interest. The speaker may move quickly back into the lecture, and you might find yourself lost if you have not paid attention. Some professors give pop quizzes; be prepared by keeping up to date with study and review.

Create Questions. Write down questions that relate to the lecture or reading. For the answers, see your instructor, research class materials, or ask your study group members. Even if you think of questions but do not write them down, thinking of questions will keep you involved and focused on learning.

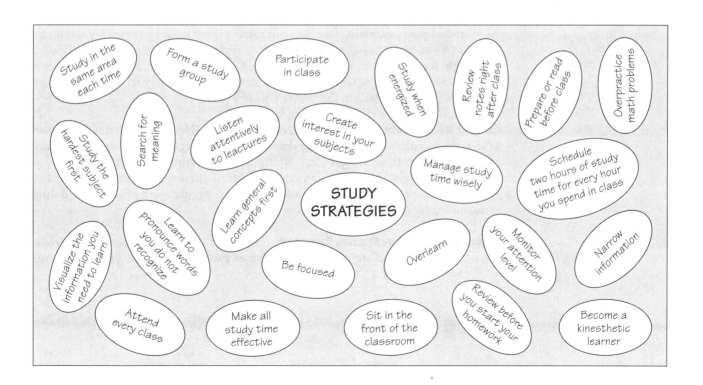

Find New Ways to Study Math*

Math Is an Entirely Different Animal.   In most courses, you are successful because you read the assignments, study, understand the information, and then pass the tests. Math is different because you must prove your knowledge base through application. You not only have to understand the formula, you also must be able to work out *any* problems associated with it.

Math is different because it is linear in format. Each new concept you learn builds on the concepts previously learned. If you skip a class and miss the material presented, you may not be able to understand the next lecture. Once you have fallen behind, catching up becomes difficult.

To be successful at math, you must understand each new mathematical theory before you can proceed to the next one. This understanding comes from doing your homework, working through problems, and striving to understand the basis of each mathematical step. You cannot walk out the door, forget what you have learned, and hope to be successful on the next test you take.

College-level math courses are more difficult than high school math courses. Instructors teach faster and expect you to learn in one semester what it took one year to learn in high school. It is your responsibility to keep up and learn the information as fast as it is being presented. Here are some tips for doing that.

Study with a Partner.   One of the best ways to counter math class difficulties is to find a classmate to study with. Your study partner should be someone you can call when you are stuck on a problem and with whom you can schedule regular weekly meetings. This will economize on your study time and may make working through math problems easier and more enjoyable.

Have the Right Skills Before You Begin.   If you have chosen a math course that requires an extended mathematics background and you do not have the appropriate skills, reconsider. If you are placed in the wrong prerequisite math course and fail it, you may not pass the next math course. It is usually better to pass a lower-level math course with an A or a B than to make a C or a D and risk the possibility of failing the next math course that you take.

Students who have not attended college in ten to fifteen years may find that over time their former math skills, however excellent, have deteriorated. To ensure a good grade on your first math test, you must have the basic skills you had when you finished your last math class. You can refresh these skills by reviewing old math tests or by working through problems in the review sections of similar textbooks. You might want to hire a tutor if you require further assistance. It is imperative not to delay, because waiting will make it harder to catch up. Tutorial support is most effective when begun within the first two weeks of class.

Conquer Math Anxiety.   Math anxiety, or the attitude "No matter what, I will never understand math because I hate it," dooms you to struggle because you are defeating yourself before you even start. Many academic support centers have tutors trained to assist you with math anxiety. In addition, there is software on the market that can create personalized prescriptions for your specific math problems and thus ensure a higher level of success in your courses.

Review the Text Before Starting Homework.   Review all textbook materials that relate to your homework before you begin. This saves you time in the long run. If you are

---

*This section, "Find New Ways to Study Math," is reprinted with permission from *Winning at Math,* by Dr. Paul Nolting, © 1991 Academic Success Press.

not able to work out a problem, you might have a better chance at remembering the location of a similar problem if you have reviewed already.

Also, review all of your lecture notes that relate to your homework before you begin. If you are not able to follow textbook explanations, use your notes for clarification, or call your study partner.

Complete Homework Neatly.   Do your homework as neatly as possible. If you have a question for your instructor, before or after class, he or she will be able to see what your previous attempts at solving the problem were by looking at your work.

Overpractice.   Practice problems repeatedly until you are confident in the procedures needed to do the problem and any versions of the problem correctly. In study groups, time each other and see how accurately you can work problems. Notice how long it takes you to complete the problem. The time constraints simulate the classroom testing situation and help you know prior to a test how much time each problem will take. The more you prepare and practice, the less anxiety you will experience on tests.

Even If You Can Do a Problem in Your Head, Write It Down.   Write down every step of the math problem, even when you can do the problem in your head. This may take more time, but the overlearning process will improve your memory and help you on future tests. Doing every step is an easy way to memorize and understand the material, and it also provides you with a complete model of the problem for future study.

Reworking problems you had wrong allows you to identify where you made the error and is well worth the effort. Use a different-colored pen or pencil for corrections.

If you do not understand how to do a problem, use the following steps:

1. Review the test material that relates to the problem.

2. Review the lecture notes that relate to the problem.

3. Review any similar problems, diagrams, examples, or rules that explain the problem.

4. Refer to another math text, math computer program, or math video to obtain a better understanding of the material.

5. Call your study partner.

6. Skip the problem and contact your tutor or math instructor as soon as possible for help.

Understand Before You Proceed.   Understanding is more important in math than memorization. Do not memorize how to solve problems; instead, know the reason for each step. When similar problems are presented on a test, you will want to know the rules, laws, or properties needed to solve each problem.

Finish with Success.   Do not quit or give up. Always finish your homework by successfully completing as many problems as you can. Even if you get stuck, go back and try to complete the assigned problems before quitting. End your homework experience on a positive note. Feel good about your accomplishments.

Write What You Learn.   After finishing your math homework, take a moment and write down what you have learned. This information will increase your ability to learn new math concepts. Place the writing in your math notebook, and then review it quickly at the beginning of your next math class.

Do Not Commit Academic Suicide.   Do not get behind in class or in your homework. It is academic suicide. If you miss class or do not practice the problems, you will not be able to understand what the instructor is talking about. Getting behind in math is the fastest way to fail the course.

Study Science More Effectively

Many of the math study tips also apply to science. However, studying science may be a different challenge, depending on your interests and academic background. If you have chosen science as your major, you will probably see these courses as fun and challenging. If you are taking science as credit for graduation and feel like you need a little help, then the following tips are for you.

Choose a Science Course That Fits Your Interests, Experience, and Abilities.   Take charge of your education by making smart choices when you plan your semester schedule. Examine course descriptions and prerequisites in the college catalogue before you enroll. Go to the bookstore and evaluate the assigned textbook so that you know what the course will entail before you begin.

Science courses like astronomy, biology, and earth science emphasize learning information. Chemistry and physics emphasize problem solving. Students who have a strong math background may prefer chemistry or physics. By reflecting on the type of science you like, you can choose a course that is compatible with your experience and interests. If you are currently in a class that you know is too difficult, talk to your advisor to discuss alternatives.

Do Not Let Your Attitude Stop You Before You Start.   Choose to have a positive experience in each classroom that you enter. Your image of what science might be is probably different from the reality. When you think of science, do you think of peculiar smells, terms you cannot understand, or professors who look a little different? Let go of your negative perceptions and start fresh. Each time you notice thoughts such as "I do not understand" or "This is confusing," take charge by reading more slowly, rereading, asking questions, seeking tutoring, or setting up more study-group time. As you learn, doubt and frustration will disappear. Remember, you control your learning by managing your attitude and your studying behaviors.

Learn to Pronounce and Understand Science Terminology.   Terms in science may be lengthy, unfamiliar, and difficult to pronounce. They can be daunting when previewing a chapter or even reading one paragraph, yet tests are often based on them. Therefore, it is important to spend extra time slowly reading each paragraph. Break paragraphs into small sections, making sure that you are understanding what you are reading. Science is not a course where you can skim pages and hope to learn information quickly. By correctly pronouncing the terms, correlating terms to definitions, creating note cards, and studying in groups, you can learn science more easily.

Compare and Contrast Graphs, Illustrations, and Appendixes to Your Reading.   Reading alone may not be enough. Use graphs and illustrations to complement your reading. Be sure to spend extra time understanding graphs and illustrations because they often make concepts clearer than words. The idea that a picture is worth a thousand words is especially true for science. Graphs and illustrations may be easier to recall than specific terms.

Appendixes in your text support lectures and readings. They often provide chapter summaries, answers for end-of-chapter quizzes, classifications and tables, or additional graphs or techniques that support your current learning strategies.

Make the Most of Science Labs.   The classroom and reading assignments provide theoretical scientific knowledge. The labs allow you to practice what you have learned from lectures or readings. Always try to understand the relationship between lectures, readings, and lab assignments.

Resist the urge to skip lab and do it later. The time you miss from labs can be difficult to make up and may cause you to lag behind in handing in homework or understanding the application of theory.

Ask questions before you start the lab. Make sure you know what the purpose of the experiment is and what procedures you should follow before you begin.

Write an outline of your lab reports in an organized, neat format before you leave the room. If you wait until you go home, you might forget important, specific points that should be included. If your notes are messy or difficult to read, you may not be able to interpret them. Always proofread and reread lab assignments before handing them in.

Use a Computer to Support All Study Techniques

Your computer can increase your organizational ability and improve your capacity to learn. You can store information, create your own study guides, type study questions, compose an analysis of information you have already learned, and use CD-ROM study aids to enhance and support your current study strategies.

Store Data.   By storing significant information on files in your computer, you will save time and be more organized. With the dates for significant projects or exams recorded on your computer-generated calendar, you will have easy access without having to remember where you put your daily calendar. You can even scan handouts from instructors to keep in easily accessible files for retrieval. Use your computer to store any information relevant to your study sessions.

Create Study Guides.   After reading an assignment or listening to a lecture, you can create your own study guide of terms, definitions, and formulas that will support your study efforts.

QUICK CHECK

List three Internet addresses that correlate with the courses you are taking now.

1.

2.

3.

Create Practice Tests.   Practice tests are a good way to study, whether alone or in a study group. After reading your assignment or studying your notes, create a computer-generated test. Include questions and problems in different formats (e.g., true-false and fill-in-the-blanks) and be sure your test covers all of the material for which you are responsible. By using computer graphics, different fonts, italic, and bold, your review process becomes easier and more fun.

Type to Learn.   After studying, sit at your computer, pick a topic, and type anything about it that comes to mind. Through free-writing, you can assess how much you know and how much you still need to learn while simultaneously reviewing each topic.

Use Educational CDs.   Educational games are available that will reinforce concepts and offer an opportunity for fun. You can work at your own pace and choose your level of learning.

Surf the Internet.   When you are stuck and cannot find the answer to a question, access the Internet, where there are hundreds of thousands of accessible resources. Surfing the web is an enjoyable way to enhance and reinforce your studies. Be aware, however, that some web sites are more credible than others. When reading information from the Internet, do not forget to use your critical thinking and problem-solving skills to assess its accuracy. If you choose a site from a nationally known organization or publishing company, you can be more confident of the accuracy of the information. When in doubt, ask your instructor.

EXERCISE

Practice Study Strategies

The purpose of this exercise is to integrate and practice various study strategies.

1. What study strategies do you use currently that are not mentioned in this appendix? Why do these strategies work for you?

    a. _____

    _____

    _____

    b. _____

    _____

    _____

    c. _____

    _____

    _____

2. List three new study strategies discussed in this appendix that you will use. Try them for three consecutive study sessions and then write about their strengths and weaknesses.

    a. _____

    _____

    _____

    _____

    b _____

    _____

    _____

    _____

    _____

    c _____

    _____

    _____

    _____

Note Taking

Linda Stevens Hjorth

OBJECTIVES	STUDY STRATEGIES CHECKLIST

By the end of this appendix, you will be able to ...

1. Diagnose your note-taking style, learn how to improve it where needed, and implement techniques that work for you.

2. Understand how listening enhances note-taking from lectures.

3. Identify your instructor's teaching style and know how it affects your notes.

4. Learn note-taking techniques for texts and lectures—such as the outline format, the Cornell format, the diagram format, and the note card format—and understand which one works best for you.

5. Take notes in labs effectively.

The purpose of the following checklist is to help you evaluate the effectiveness of your study strategies.

Check the appropriate answer:

1. Are your notes still understandable when you reread them?   YES _____ NO _____

2. Do your notes include memory triggers for test preparation?   YES _____ NO _____

3. Do your notes prepare you adequately for tests?   YES _____ NO _____

4. Do your notes help you understand concepts?   YES _____ NO _____

5. Do your notes indicate what material is important to know?   YES _____ NO _____

6. Do your notes organize the material for you?   YES _____ NO _____

7. Does taking notes keep you more focused during lectures?   YES _____ NO _____

8. Do your notes reflect good listening skills?   YES _____ NO _____

9. Do your notes state specific facts (dates, names, quantities, dimensions observed in lab)?   YES _____ NO _____

10. Does your note-taking style change based on the complexity or simplicity of the information presented or the instructor's style?   YES _____ NO _____

If you are a successful note-taker, your answer to most of these questions will be yes. If you said yes to most or all of them, write the reasons for your success.

_____

_____

Write about the questions to which you answered no by recording specifically what you need to learn from this appendix to improve your note-taking. Remember that your note-taking strategies are good or you would not have gotten this far in your educational career. Answering no to some questions means that there are areas in which you need to practice or try new note-taking strategies.

_____

_____

Notes help you retain information and organize thoughts and ideas. Whether you are in a lecture hall, a science lab, or the library doing research for a paper, effective note-taking is very important.

Note-taking means writing down what you want to remember in a format you can follow later. Important concepts can be difficult to retain in your memory, no matter how interested you are or how hard you try. Notes are crucial not just to test-taking but also to learning and to understanding lectures and texts. Good note-taking skills are important on the job as well.

Notes are not just written words. They can be drawings, colored diagrams, flow-charts, sentences, paragraphs, or outlines. Good note-taking is not a haphazard process. Writing notes is purposeful. It helps you learn and retain a wealth of information, increases your focus and attention, and keeps you involved actively in reading a textbook or listening to a lecture. Notes can help you work effectively in study groups. You can correlate your own notes with those of other study group members, to check their accuracy and to fill in the gaps.

This appendix presents several note-taking formats with which you can experiment. It will help you learn the most effective and workable techniques for taking notes in lectures and labs and while reading. Notes are effective if they work for you.

First, let us analyze your current note-taking style—what works and what does not—and adjust it wherever necessary.

Examining Your Current Note-Taking Style

It should be obvious that to take good notes you must pay attention to the lecture and record what you hear. What is more difficult is deciding what to record and which format to record it in. If your notes suffer from any of the following common flaws—confusion, incompleteness, lack of test relevance, and ineffectiveness—read on.

What if My Notes Are Confusing?

Whether you use an outline, sentence fragments, or key words, the important question is, When your notes are a few hours or days old, will you still be able to understand what you wrote as well as its significance? If you do not understand your own notes, what is the purpose of writing them down in the first place?

You can make your notes more understandable by doing the following:

Effective Notes Are Created Through a Purposeful, Organized, Focused Effort.

▶ Write at the top of the notebook page the date and the page or number of the chapter you are covering.

▶ Write numbers on all notebook pages in case they become separated from each other.

▶ Number theories or concepts as you record them. Use subtitles or an outline format where appropriate to help clarify the presentation of a mass of information.

▶ Type your notes, either during class or afterward. The typing process will provide you with notes that are easier to study because they are easier to read. Some students use laptop computers during lectures to ensure accuracy and to increase their speed in note-taking. (Some instructors may not allow this; know the rules for each class.)

▶ Leave blank lines to add details and clarification later. Go back and fill in the lines with additional information that you remember or want to correlate with the reading assignment.

▶ Review the notes shortly after taking them.

How Do I Know if My Notes Are Comprehensive Enough?

Did you provide yourself with enough information in your notes to

▶ Remember and understand what the lecturer meant?

▶ Retain important information about concepts, definitions, problems, formulas, or theories?

▶ Reflect the essence of what you have been reading and studying?

If not, you can improve the situation by focusing on facts. Perhaps you need to write down more than you are doing now by seeking out actively what you may be missing: during a lecture, ask questions; when reading an assignment, reread; before a lab, prepare a list of what you need to record and then fill in the details.

What if My Notes Do Not Prepare Me for Tests?

QUICK CHECK

Use three adjectives to describe your note-taking style. How can you improve your notes?

Do you study your notes faithfully only to find that you are still not prepared for tests? If so, you can increase your note-taking skills as follows:

▶ Study the last test and compare the questions you missed to the notes that you took on that specific topic to see where the gaps were and how you can improve your note-taking.

▶ Ask the instructor questions to clarify any confusing areas in your notes.

▶ Ask the instructor to look at a couple of pages of your notes to make sure that you have recorded the correct information.

▶ Correlate the words in your notes to commonly used words in the text or the lecture, thus enhancing your understanding of concepts instead of mechanically memorizing terms or definitions.

▶ Write and study your notes for application in real life. For example, in a business course you might ask, "How does this theory apply to a business in which I am the manager?"

▶ Take notes that are focused on the specific content presented by the instructor. Do not allow yourself to get lost in generalities.

When you feel that your notes are not preparing you effectively for tests, do not give up. By using the preceding techniques (changing your note-taking style; paying more attention to detail; and asking for help from classmates, tutors, or instructors), you will become more successful in note-taking and test-taking.

What if My Note-Taking Style Seems Ineffective?

One reason for ineffective note-taking is that your note-taking style may need to change for different courses. The notes you take in algebra will be different from the ones needed for anatomy. For example, algebra notes are detailed, step-by-step notes, whereas in anatomy a sketch with labels may be enough. Notes in a literature class could be more free form than those in a physics course.

Note-taking style often changes with the amount of information you already know. If you are familiar with lecture materials, note-taking is less laborious. If the material being presented is new, complex, or confusing, your notes may need extensive detail. This chapter presents various note-taking formats that you can use. You may find that the diagram or note card format is appropriate in some situations and that the Cornell or outline format is appropriate in others. You may need to find one note-taking format that you can adjust or use different formats for different situations. As you read about various note-taking styles in this chapter, decide which ones will suit note-taking for specific classes.

Recording Notes from Lectures

Listen Attentively

The first step in taking good notes from lectures is to listen attentively. That means paying explicit attention to all communication cues: body language, voice, language, and eye contact. Here are some suggestions for increasing the amount of useful information you can gain through attentive listening.

Focus on Words and Their Meaning.   Words have symbolic meanings that can be different for different people. When you listen to a lecture, what meaning do the instructor's words have for you? Is your interpretation correct? Distorting the meaning of the instructor's words can contribute to the learning of wrong information. Your judgments and opinions can impair your ability to understand the instructor's viewpoint. Suspend them. Focus on the here and now—listen first, take notes on what you hear, and only later evaluate what has been said. As you listen, quietly ponder, challenge, think critically, and question what is being said in order to understand the meaning of the words. When unsure, ask questions or look up the concept in the text for clarification.

Be sure to pay special attention and record notes when the instructor says, "Please remember," "Please note," "Pay attention to," "The six steps are," "Facts you need to know," and "Do not forget." Use a star or check to signify an especially important point. Later, when you review your material, you will know the areas on which to spend the most time and energy.

Ask Questions to Clarify Meaning.   The best communication goes two ways: back and forth between communicators. Most instructors want to explain concepts so that you will understand them and will not leave the classroom confused. Therefore, ask questions to understand and learn. This is called feedback. It is likely that several other people in the classroom have the same question, so do not feel embarrassed to ask. When your questions have been answered, record the specific explanation in your notes.

How do you keep yourself focused when taking notes?
© Susie Fitzhugh.

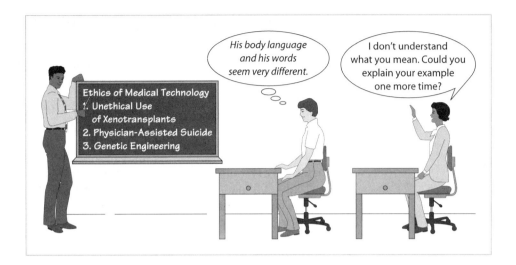

Be Aware of the Instructor's Nonverbal Messages.   Messages without words can be a very strong mode of communication. Watch body language: an instructor's excitement about teaching certain topics may be communicated nonverbally. His or her animation can be a clue to the relative importance of the point being made and help you answer the question, Will this be on the test?

Keep Eye Contact with the Instructor.   The more you watch the instructor, the easier it will be to listen carefully to what is said. It should also prevent you from falling asleep! One thing is certain: you cannot take good notes if you do not listen. Another important factor in good note-taking is understanding how the instructor's teaching style affects your ability to record comprehensive notes.

Adjust Note-Taking to Your Instructor's Lecture Style

QUICK CHECK

Which teaching style works best for you?

Style refers to the instructor's energy level, body language, eye contact with the audience, and use of props like boards, computers, and overheads. Style can also describe the relationship that the instructor builds with you and the other students in your class. One instructor might rush into a room and move swiftly from podium to board, projecting high energy. Another instructor may use every bit of energy just to speak loud enough for you to hear. This type of instructor may never stray far from the podium and may show little or no enthusiasm. A third may be somewhere in between.

Some instructors place emphasis on factors that will help you learn the materials more effectively. These instructors will often provide an outline of the lecture, grant extra time for note-writing, emphasize and reiterate main ideas, use examples, write important dates on the board, and explain the goals of the lecture. Other instructors impart great quantities of information without doing any of these.

The instructor's style can affect the way you take notes. The high-energy instructor might be easier to take notes from because you are kept awake, unless he or she speaks so fast that you cannot keep up. The low-energy instructor might not be able to keep you motivated. Understanding that the teaching styles of instructors affect the way you take notes can help you consciously change your note-taking style.

Experiment with notes to identify when you should use short telegraphic notes rather than long, detailed notes. Listen, understand, and then write in the briefest format possible. Make sure, however, that your telegraphic style does not lose the meaning because you shortened the information too much. Full-length sentences are appropriate when the concepts are confusing or important. You might use telegraphic writing

---

Create your own symbols for commonly used words. Here are some examples:

4	for	R	are	C	see
ok	okay	B+	before	Y	why
EZ	easy	U	you	—	negative

Use a wavy line (~) to indicate "ing."

work~   be~   hear~   help~   shovel~

---

when the psychology professor says, "The stimulation of the lateral hypothalamus will cause the start-eating center to be destroyed, creating an aphagic or very skinny organism, because it does not know when to start eating." A telegraphic format would be "destroy lateral hypothalamus = skinny rat = aphagic = does not eat."

Use symbols in ways that have meaning for you. Be aware that similar symbols mean different things in different courses. Take "O," for example: in biology, O means female; in flowcharts, O means connector; in math, O means circle; in stamp collecting, O means used; and in weather classes, O means clear (Grolier, Encyclopedia of Knowledge, 1995).

The nature of the lecture or the personality of the lecturer often guides you in this note-taking style selection. A fast-speaking instructor presenting complex information will require explicit attentiveness and telegraphic notes. An instructor who has a less intense teaching style might allow you to become more relaxed in your note-taking style.

Alter your note-taking style to adjust to the instructor's teaching style by using the following suggestions:

▶ When your instructor does not start the lecture with a list or explanation of goals for the lecture, try to create your own based on what you have read about the topic and on previous lecture content, and incorporate it into your notes.

▶ When you cannot hear the instructor, or if the instructor speaks too fast or does not allow adequate time to record notes, ask the instructor to speak louder and slow down. Sit in the front of the class to hear better. Do not let your notes suffer because you are afraid to make changes or ask the instructor to repeat information.

▶ When you are not sure what the instructor means, do not record confusing notes. Instead, ask the instructor for a more detailed explanation during or after class.

▶ Experiment to identify when you should use telegraphic notes versus long, detailed notes.

Students in large classrooms can prevent distraction and increase learning by focusing, listening, and then using appropriate note-taking formats.
© Andrea Burns.

Adjust Note-Taking to Your Learning Style

How does your current note-taking format correlate with your learning style?

....

....

....

....

....

There are many different note-taking techniques. It is up to you to choose the one that works best for you. If you learn best by hearing, know that listening is your key to note-taking success and write down only those concepts that you know you will not remember through hearing alone. If you learn best through visual cues, then you may need to pay more attention to overheads or board notes. If you learn best through hands-on experience, then you probably look forward to lab classes or study groups where you can put theory into action. You may want to experiment with the following popular and successful note-taking formats until you find one or two that match your learning style.

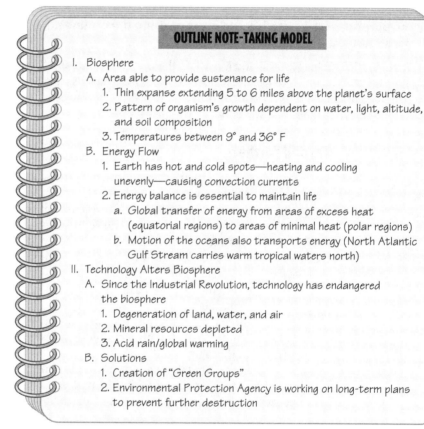

OUTLINE NOTE-TAKING MODEL

I. Biosphere
   A. Area able to provide sustenance for life
      1. Thin expanse extending 5 to 6 miles above the planet's surface
      2. Pattern of organism's growth dependent on water, light, altitude, and soil composition
      3. Temperatures between 9° and 36° F
   B. Energy Flow
      1. Earth has hot and cold spots—heating and cooling unevenly—causing convection currents
      2. Energy balance is essential to maintain life
         a. Global transfer of energy from areas of excess heat (equatorial regions) to areas of minimal heat (polar regions)
         b. Motion of the oceans also transports energy (North Atlantic Gulf Stream carries warm tropical waters north)
II. Technology Alters Biosphere
   A. Since the Industrial Revolution, technology has endangered the biosphere
      1. Degeneration of land, water, and air
      2. Mineral resources depleted
      3. Acid rain/global warming
   B. Solutions
      1. Creation of "Green Groups"
      2. Environmental Protection Agency is working on long-term plans to prevent further destruction

Source: Adapted from *Grolier Encyclopedia of Knowledge.* Copyright © 1995 by the Grolier Educational Corporation.

Note-Taking Formats

Outline Format

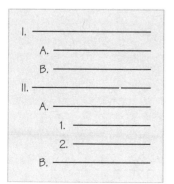

Outlines list main ideas and follow them with minor ideas, enabling you to differentiate the two quickly when reviewing. Usually, an outline includes the main idea, then a supporting minor idea, and then details, which can be followed by even more specific details.

The outline format is efficient if your learning style is focused on details, numbers, and organization. Outlining lets you place your notes in an organized format when you are in class, saving the extra time it would take to reorganize them later. Because you are using numbers and sentence fragments, you can record essentials quickly. This format allows you to focus more on the lecture and less on the note-taking process.

Even if you do not write an outline in your notes, you can create an outline later using your computer. If you use software that has an outline feature, you will be able to scroll through the text and code every heading in your notes to create an outline. This process allows you to organize your notes while reviewing them.

Another way to review from an outline is to look at the major concepts, cover the minor ideas with a piece of paper, and see what you can remember without peeking. Continue to work through all of your notes until you feel comfortable in your knowledge of the material. If you have never used this format, it may be awkward at first. But with practice, you will become more comfortable.

<table>
<tr><td colspan="2" align="center">**EXERCISE**</td></tr>
</table>

Outline Note-Taking Format

The purpose of this exercise is to practice using the outline note-taking format.

Examine the Outline Note-Taking Model on the previous page, and then choose a class in which to use the model to take notes. Always state the main idea first to reinforce the focus of your notes as you write. Be sure to include specific details that will enhance your learning.

Cornell Format

Psychology	A science that studies behavior and mental processes.
Models of Treatment for Abnormal Psychology	1. Physiological 2. Psychodynamic 3. Cognitive 4. Sociocultural 5. Behavioral

The Cornell format allows you to create a review sheet while taking notes. Draw a vertical line from the top to the bottom of a page of notebook paper. Leave two or three inches to the left of the line. This space is for terms and questions. The right column is for definitions, summaries, and answers correlating to data on the left.

The Cornell note-taking format works best if you need structure as you take notes. The line helps you focus on the content and correlates content with the terms, theories, or formulas that you must learn. If you have a less focused learning style, you will find this method helpful when preparing for a test. You can fold the edge of your paper to create a study guide. With the answers hidden, test yourself on the more detailed facts written on the right-hand side.

When you are taking a test, try to visualize the words on the right and left side of your notes. Your note-taking format can serve as a visual memory trigger that helps you choose the correct answer on the test.

<table>
<tr><td colspan="2" align="center">**EXERCISE**</td></tr>
</table>

Cornell Note-Taking Format

The purpose of this exercise is to practice the Cornell method of note-taking.

Examine the Cornell Note-Taking Model on the next page, and then choose a class in which to use the model to take notes. The first step is to draw a vertical line on the page. Then list terms or questions on the left side and the corresponding theory or answers on the right side. Remember that you can use these notes as a review sheet when studying for tests.

CORNELL NOTE-TAKING MODEL	
(MAIN IDEA) Abraham Maslow's Hierarchy of Needs	
Five levels (from lower level to higher level)	1. Physiological needs 2. Safety and security needs 3. Love and belonging (social needs) 4. Esteem needs 5. Self-actualization
Physiological needs	Survival needs: air, food, water, appropriate body temperature, avoidance of pain
Safety needs	After meeting physiological needs, people look for security in their lives. This could include living in a safe environment, job security, medical insurance, or anything that would protect their physiological needs.
Love and belonging (social needs)	After meeting their safety needs, individuals look to meet their social needs through love, friendship, and belonging to social groups.
Esteem needs	After meeting social needs, interest moves to the need to be recognized, and to feelings of self-confidence, self-respect, status, and prestige.
Self-actualization	After meeting all of the previous needs, individuals work to reach their own potential, including the ability to be creative, reach self-generated goals, and feel competent in life.

Source: Adapted from B. Reece and R. Brandt, *Effective Human Relations in Organizations.* © 1996 Houghton Mifflin Company.

Diagram Format

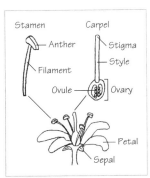

If you find it difficult to stay focused on a lecture, draw pictures or diagrams that illustrate the instructor's ideas. It may not be the most conventional method, but if it works for you, use it.

Drawing diagrams is most effective in classes where you find writing words to be difficult or confusing, classes in which pictures are more effective than words, or classes that are just plain boring. Of course, you can combine written words with your pictures to emphasize and clarify ideas.

Even if you take your lecture notes in the Cornell or the outline format, you may want to draw diagrams as well. Use colored pencils or markers later to highlight the diagrams you created in class for better retention and retrieval of test data. A visual image will trigger your long-term memory.

The diagram format is an advantage if you learn best by doing and seeing. If you are a visual learner, you may find in test situations that the diagram will be easier to recall than the written format. The act of drawing the concept may make it easier for you to learn. Remember: looking at a diagram is different from drawing it yourself. The more you practice drawing diagrams, the easier it becomes.

Listening for signal words helps you listen for ideas. For example, if an English instructor says, "You can use seven different patterns to organize details in a paragraph," then you should number from one to seven on your paper, skipping lines between, and listen for the seven patterns and the instructor's explanations. If you get to the fifth pattern and realize that you don't have anything written down for the fourth one, then you know you have missed something in the lecture. At this point, you should ask a question.

Figure 1	Signal Words and Phrases

1. To indicate that another main idea or example follows:

also	furthermore	another
in addition	moreover	

2. To add emphasis:

most important	above all	of primary concern
remember that	a key idea	most significant
pay attention to	the main idea	

3. To indicate that an example follows:

for example	to illustrate	such as
for instance	specifically	

4. To indicate that a conclusion follows:

therefore	in conclusion	finally
consequently	to conclude	so

5. To indicate an exception to a stated fact:

however	although	but
nevertheless	though	except

6. To indicate cause or effects:

because	due to	consequently
since	reason	result
for	cause	effect

7. To indicate that categories or divisions will be named or explained:

types	parts	groups
kinds	characteristics	categories

8. To indicate a sequence:

steps	numbers (1, 2, 3, …)
stages	first, second, etc.

9. To indicate that items are being compared:

similar	different	equally
like	in contrast	on the other hand
advantages	disadvantages	contrary to

EXERCISE 1

APPLY WHAT YOU HAVE LEARNED about signal words by doing this exercise with group members. Follow the guidelines for successful collaboration that appear on the inside back cover. Read the following paragraph. Next, identify as many signal words as you can and discuss their meaning in the sentences in which they appear, using Figure 1 as a reference. Then discuss and answer the questions. When you arrive at consensus, record your answers and evaluate your work.

Most of us assume that listening is an innate skill. Aren't most people born with the ability to sleep, breathe, see, and hear? But is hearing the same act as listening? Although most of us can hear perfectly well, we are not all good listeners. What, you might ask, are the characteristics of a good listener? First, a good listener makes a commitment to listen. Second, a good listener focuses attention on the speaker. For example, a good listener is not reading the newspaper or watching television while listening to a friend explain a problem. Most important, a good listener is genuinely interested in the speaker and in what he or she says. In conclusion, listening is not something you should assume that you do well. It is a lifelong skill that can be improved with earnest practice and hard work.

1. **What signal words indicate that an example is to follow? What example does the writer give?**

_____

2. **Write the signal word that indicates that categories or divisions will be explained.**

_____

3. **Write the signal words that indicate sequence.**

_____

4. **What does the writer believe is the most important characteristic of a good listener?**

_____

5. **What is the writer's concluding idea about listening?**

_____

Group Evaluation:
Evaluate your discussion. Did everyone contribute? Did you accomplish your task successfully? What additional questions do you have about signal words? How will you find answers to your questions?

_____

_____

Develop a Personal Note-Taking System

The third strategy for classroom success is good note taking. There is no best way to take notes. The suggestions offered in this appendix have worked for many students. Experiment with them, and then adapt them to find the style of note taking that consistently gives you good results. Complete the Awareness Check on the next page before you begin reading this section.

EXERCISE 2

FORM A GROUP WITH FOUR or five students. Using traits, prepare a short demonstration on listening behavior. Let one person in the group be the lecturer. Let other group members demonstrate passive or active listening habits. The group member acting as the lecturer should be able to explain to the class which group members were good listeners and which were not. Practice your demonstration. Your instructor may call on one or more of the groups to present in class.

Guidelines for Note Taking

▶ Keep track of your notes by heading your paper with the *date, name of course,* and *lecture topic.* Number consecutive pages. Later, when you study, you'll be able to match up class notes and textbook notes or assignments on the same topic.

▶ Use standard sized paper—8½" by 11"—that will fit into most notebooks or folders. Small sheets of paper won't hold enough writing and may get lost or out of order.

Awareness Check

HOW EFFECTIVE ARE YOUR NOTE-TAKING SKILLS?

To see where you need improvement, evaluate your lecture notes from a recent class. Read them over and answer yes or no to the following questions.

Yes	No	
☐	☐	1. Did you date your notes and number the pages?
☐	☐	2. Did you write the course name or number on your notes?
☐	☐	3. Did you write down the topic of the lecture?
☐	☐	4. Did you use 8½" by 11" paper to keep in a loose-leaf binder?
☐	☐	5. Did you take notes with a ballpoint pen?
☐	☐	6. Are your notes easy to read?
☐	☐	7. Is this set of notes in the same notebook as all your other notes for this class?
☐	☐	8. Are your notes organized into an informal outline or other logical format?
☐	☐	9. Are you able to distinguish the speaker's main ideas from the examples that illustrate them?
☐	☐	10. As you read your notes, are you able to reconstruct in your mind what the lecture was about?

If you answered no to any of these questions—particularly the last two—then your note-taking skills may need improvement. Try the guidelines that follow for improving your note taking.

▶ Keep the notes for one class separated from the notes for other classes. Use separate notebooks for each class or use dividers to distinguish different sections in one notebook. Some students like to use spiral notebooks. Others prefer to use a loose-leaf binder so that lecture notes, textbook notes, and the instructor's handouts may be taken out of it and reorganized for study purposes.

▶ Use a ballpoint pen for taking notes. Ink from felt-tip pens blurs and soaks through the paper, spotting the sheets underneath. Pencil smears and fades over time. Many students prefer to use blue or black ink because other colors, such as red or green, are hard on the eyes.

▶ If you know your handwriting is poor, print for clarity. Illegible or decorative handwriting makes notes hard to read.

▶ To speed up your note taking, use standard abbreviations and make up some of your own for words or phrases that you use often. Make a key for your abbreviations so you won't forget what they mean. See Figure 2 for a list of some common abbreviations. For even greater speed while taking notes, omit the periods from abbreviations.

▶ Copy into your notes anything that is written on the board or projected on a screen. Test questions often come from material that is presented in these ways.

▶ Take organized notes. Use a system such as one of those suggested later in this chapter or devise your own. Make main ideas stand out from the examples that support them. Do not write lecturers' words verbatim. Summarize ideas in your own words so that they will be easier for you to remember.

▶ As soon as possible after class, review your notes to fill in gaps while the information is still fresh in your mind. The purpose of taking notes is to help you remember information. If you take notes but don't look at them until you are ready to study for a test, you will have to relearn the information. To retain information in your long-term memory, review it frequently.

▶ To fill in gaps, compare notes with a classmate or see the instructor.

Figure 2	**Commonly Used Abbreviations and Symbols**
1. equal: =	11. introduction: intro.
2. with: w/	12. information: info.
3. without: w/o	13. department: dept.
4. number: #	14. advantage: adv.
5. therefore: \	15. organization: org.
6. and: +	16. maximum: max.
7. and so forth: etc.	17. individual: ind.
8. for example: e.g.	18. compare: cf.
9. against: vs.	19. association: assoc.
10. government: gov't.	20. politics: pol.

The Informal Outline/Key Words System

Ideas that are organized in a logical pattern are easier to remember than isolated facts and examples that don't seem to relate to one another. Try this simple, two-part system to improve your note taking.

Draw a line down your paper so that you have a 2½" column on the right and a 6" column on the left. Take notes in the 6" column, using an informal outline. Make main ideas stand out by indenting and numbering the details and examples listed under them. Skip lines between main ideas so that you can fill in examples later or add an example if the lecturer returns to one of these ideas later on. After the lecture, write key words in the right margin that will help you recall information from your notes.

Figure 3 shows a student's lecture notes on the topic "Studying on the Right Side of the Brain." The student has used the informal outline/key words system. On the left side of the page, the student has outlined the lecture given in class. Later, on the right side of the page, in the margin, the student has written key words or abbreviations that show at a glance what the lecture covered.

When you use this system, wait to write in the key words until you are reviewing your notes.

The Cornell Method*

Developed by Dr. Walter Pauk of Cornell University, the Cornell method is a note-taking system that has worked for many students. One version of the system involves six steps: *recording, questioning, reciting, reflecting, reviewing,* and *recapitulating.*

Begin by dividing an 8½" by 11" sheet of notebook paper into three sections, as shown in Figure 4, page 226. Then follow these steps for taking notes from a lecture:

1. **Record** facts and ideas in the wide column. After the lecture, fill in any gaps and neaten up your handwriting, if necessary, so that you will be able to read your notes when you review them later.

2. **Question** facts and ideas presented in lectures. Write questions about what you don't understand or what you think an instructor might ask on a test. Write your questions in the left margin beside the fact or idea in the wide column. Writing questions helps you strengthen your memory, improve your understanding, and anticipate test questions.

3. **Recite** the facts or ideas aloud from memory and in your own words. If you summarized them in your notes in your own words, then this will be easy to do. If you are an auditory learner, reciting will improve your retention because you will be using listening, your preferred mode. To see how much you remember, cover up the wide column of your notes and recite from the key words or questions in the left margin. Recite the key word or question first; then try to recall and recite the whole fact or idea. To check yourself, uncover the wide column and read your notes.

4. **Reflect** on what you have learned from the lecture by applying the facts and ideas to real-life situations. Determine why the facts are significant, how you can use them, and how they expand or modify your prior knowledge.

---

*Walter Pauk, *How to Study in College*, Seventh Edition. Copyright ©2001 by Houghton Mifflin Company. Used with permission.

Figure 3   The Informal Outline/Key Words System

Study Skills 1620   Sept. 18

Studying on the Right Side of the Brain	
Visual thinking	
1. Use graphic techniques like diagrams, maps, etc. to organize information into a meaningful pattern.	def.
2. Visual learners need to make verbal information "visual" or they will have a hard time remembering it.	reason for using "visuals"
Fantasy	
1. The ability to create and use mental images is another kind of visual thinking.	def.
2. To understand the stages in an organism's life cycle, imagine you are the organism going through the stages.	ex. of fantasy
Hands-on experience	
1. Get involved in a direct experience of what you are learning.	def.
2. Do lab experiments, take field trips, role play, look at or touch objects as they are described. Go through the steps of a process.	hands-on activities
Music	
1. Common belief: music distracts while studying.	
2. Music can accelerate learning.	effect of music on learning
3. Studies show retention improved when students read to music.	
4. Instrumentals that match the feeling or mood of the information to be remembered are the best type of music.	

Figure 4   **The Cornell Method: Setting Up the Paper**

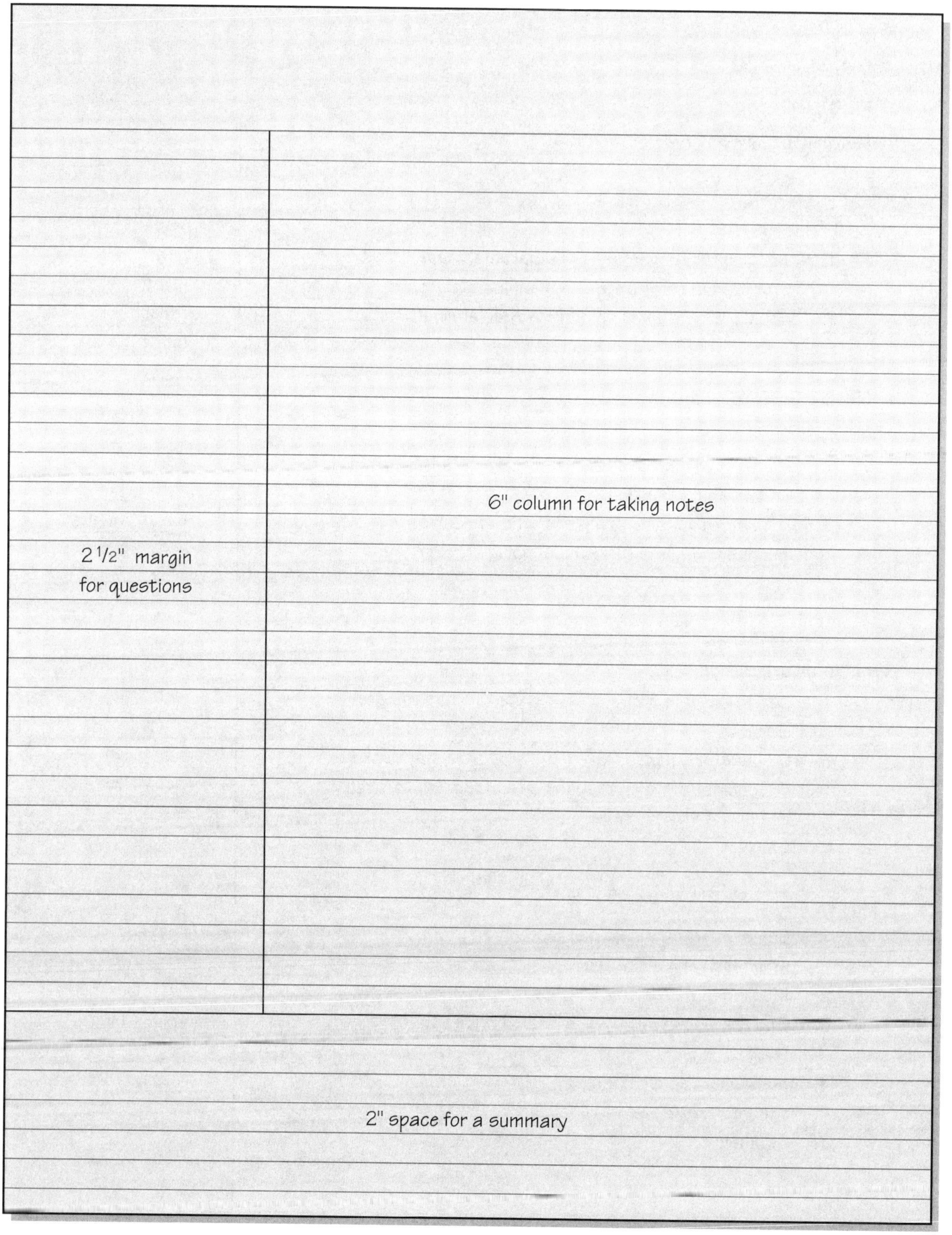

6" column for taking notes

2 1/2" margin
for questions

2" space for a summary

5. **Review** and recite your notes every day. A good way to begin a study session, especially if you have trouble getting started, is to review your notes. Reviewing reminds you of what you have learned and sets the scene for new information to be gained from the next assignment.

6. **Recapitulate** by writing a summary of your notes in the space at the bottom of your paper. You can summarize what you have written on each page of notes, or you can summarize the whole lecture at the end of the last page. Doing both a page summary and a whole-lecture summary is even better.

Now, clarify these steps in your mind by examining the student's lecture notes shown in Figure 5, page 228.

Matching Note-Taking Style and Learning Style

What if you are not a linear thinker? What if a 1, 2, 3 order of information does not appeal to you because you don't think that way, and instructors don't always stick to their lecture outlines? You may prefer a more visual style of note taking. Try *clustering*. Start a few inches from the top of the page and write the speaker's first main idea in a circle near the middle of the page. If the speaker gives an example, draw an arrow to another circle in which you write the example. If the speaker presents another main idea, start a new cluster. Figure 6, page 229, shows an example of the cluster note-taking technique. This student's notes will help her visualize the information she wants to remember. An advantage of clustering is that if the speaker leaves one idea and returns to it later, it is easy to draw another arrow from the circle and add the example. Clustering is a nontraditional note-taking procedure, but if it works for you and if it makes note taking easy and pleasant, then don't hesitate to use it.

Figure 5   **The Cornell Method: One Student's Notes**

Intro. to Literature 2010   Sept. 18

	The Five Elements of Fiction
	1. Plot
How does the	a. Events and setting
plot of the	b. Plot development
story develop?	* conflict
	* complications
	* climax
	* resolution
	2. Character
What is the	a. Dynamic
difference between	* well rounded
a dynamic and a	* motives
static character?	b. Static
	* flat
	* stereotype
	3. Point of view
What are the	a. First person
four points	b. Omniscient
of view?	c. Limited omniscient
	d. Dramatic
How is the	4. Theme
theme of the	a. Meaning or significance
story revealed?	b. Revealed through interaction of five elements
What makes one	5. Style/Tone
writer's style	a. Mood or feeling
distinctive?	b. Choice of words, use of language

The writer uses five elements of fiction—plot, character, point of view, theme, and style/tone—to develop the story. Through the interaction of these elements, the meaning of the story is revealed and the reader can understand its significance.

Figure 6   Clustering: A Visual Form of Note Taking

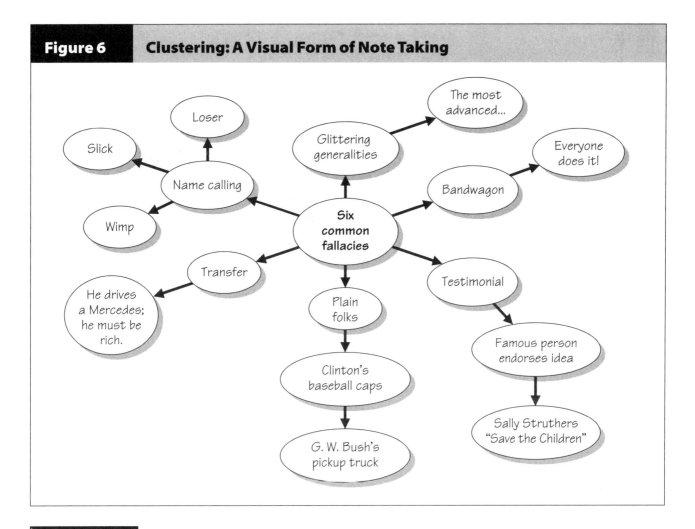

EXERCISE 3

EXERCISE 3

IN THIS APPENDIX YOU HAVE learned three effective ways to organize your notes: (1) the informal outline/key words system, (2) the Cornell method, and (3) clustering. Reread the sections of this chapter that describe these three techniques and then use the following diagram to try clustering. Fill in each circle. Then add arrows and circles to the cluster to complete your notes about the three techniques.

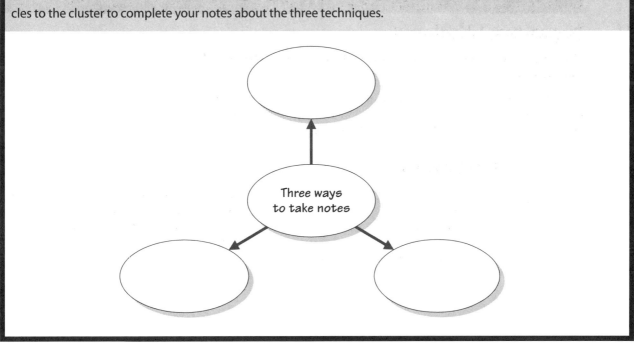

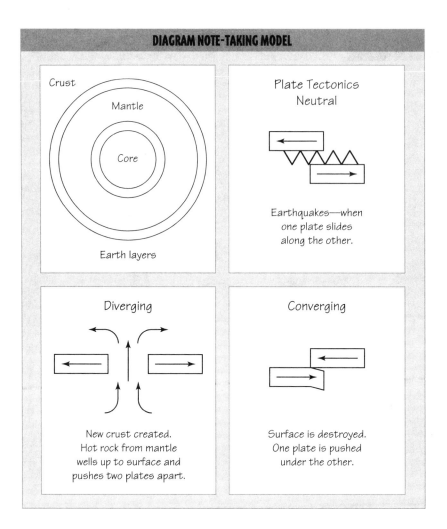

Source: From *1001 Things Everyone Should Know About Science* by James Trefil. Copyright © 1992 by James Trefil. Used by permission of Doubleday, a division of Random House, Inc.

EXERCISE

Diagram Note-Taking Format

The purpose of this exercise is to practice the diagram method of note-taking.

Examine the Diagram Note-Taking Model above, and then choose a class in which to use the model to take notes. Use as many diagrams as you feel necessary. Make sure that they are detailed and understandable.

Note Card Format

(Front)   (Back)

No matter what your learning style, note cards or index cards can be useful for refining your notes. Writing notes in class, copying them to note cards, and then reviewing them as often as possible will increase your memory retention. Record, rewrite, review, review, review, and review. It is difficult to forget information after going through this process.

Source: From *1001 Things Everyone Should Know About Science* by James Trefil. Copyright © 1992 by James Trefil. Used by permission of Doubleday, a division of Random House, Inc.

QUICK CHECK

List two ways that you like to study with note cards.

1. ....
   ....
   ....

2. ....
   ....
   ....

Note cards are wonderful: they fit into pockets, briefcases, and purses. There are many ways to use note cards—be creative!

▶ Use different cards for different concepts.

▶ Write a term, formula, or name on the front of the card and a related definition, problem, or theory on the back.

▶ Pull out the cards and study wherever you are and whenever you want—for example, while waiting at the doctor's office or standing in line at the bank.

▶ Color code your cards, using a different color for each subject to separate your materials visually.

▶ Use thin-tip markers to write formulas, charts, terms, or concepts in different colors.

▶ When studying, write any question for the instructor on a note card. Ask questions from the cards before or at the start of class.

▶ Place a note card with hard-to-remember terms on the refrigerator or mirror. Seeing the posted concept constantly will help you remember it.

▶ Use completed note cards in study groups as a guide for quizzing each other.

▶ Do not let note cards interfere with your social life. Remember to put them away once in a while to talk to friends and family.

▶ Remember: put a rubber band around each set of cards in case you drop them!

Note Card Note-Taking Format

The purpose of this exercise is to practice taking notes with note cards.

Examine the Note Card Note-Taking Model on the previous page, and then choose a class in which to use the model to take notes. Use 3″ × 5″ cards to complete this assignment.

Tape Recorders in the Classroom

If you are unable to take notes for any reason, then a tape recorder is a great solution. Shut the tape recorder off when unrelated material is being presented. As soon after class as possible, listen to and edit the tape. Delete information that is not needed, and enhance areas that are weak. This process is similar to editing your notes after you write them.

It may also be appropriate to use a tape recorder when you have an instructor who talks very fast. The recorder can pick up any information that you may have missed. Another study technique that you can use with tape recorders is to record information that you want to remember (terms, definitions, formulas) and then, when you are doing other tasks around the house or perhaps while working on your car, listen to your prerecorded tape until you are sure that you have learned the taped information.

Keep in mind one disadvantage of using the tape recorder in class to take notes: some students report that they do not listen as carefully because they assume they can depend on their tape later on. Listening is an important requirement for learning, and only by listening can you ask intelligent questions when you need to. Also remember that you always run a risk of mechanical failure. Check your tape, plug, and batteries often.

Proper Classroom Etiquette Demands That You Ask Your Instructor for Permission to Use a Tape Recorder in Class.

Recording Lab Notes

You have probably had several years' experience listening to lectures and recording notes. However, you might find that the traditional format used in lectures will not work in a lab. When you are taking notes in biology, chemistry, computer engineering, electronics, language, or medical labs, for example, you may need to

▶ Use more abbreviations.

▶ Write shorter sentences.

▶ Use diagrams.

▶ Record what you see instead of writing down what you are told.

▶ Write more details.

▶ Record cause and effect.

The two most important words to remember when creating lab notes are *what* and *why.* These words will be helpful to you as you narrow down the subjects presented in labs and incorporate them into your notes. Always record the date, class name, and topic with the correlated chapter number in the textbook. This will save you hours when you try to correlate lecture, chapter, and lab notes later.

LAB NOTES MODEL

Date _____

Class   (Biology, chemistry, physics, computer engineering, etc.) _____

Topic and Chapter No. _____

WHAT? (Create a title for each new subtopic you study in lab.)

- What did you learn both generally and specifically in lab today?

- What is most important to remember about this topic? (Be specific.)

- What is the objective of this lab?

- In what ways does the lab correlate with the lecture?

- What will you need to remember from this lab?

- What did you observe, hear, or learn that will help you integrate concepts learned in class?

- What can be done differently to change the final results of the lab?

- In what ways does that change relate to your lecture notes? Tie this change into your notes for easy recall of lecture information.

WHY?

- Why are you conducting this lab experiment?

- Why did you use this particular format, material, or reactants?

- Why is this experiment important?

- Why did you observe your specific result?

ADDITIONAL NOTES: (Add any information that is not included in the above questions.)

EXERCISE

Practice Taking Notes in Lab

The purpose of this exercise is to practice taking organized, efficient notes in a lab.

Examine the Lab Notes Model on page 121. Then select a lab and use this format to take notes. Remember to include more abbreviations, shorter sentences, more diagrams, and more specific details than you would in a lecture class.

Date _____

Class _____

Topic and Chapter No. _____

WHAT? (Subtopic) _____

_____

_____

_____

_____

_____

_____

_____

_____

WHY? _____

_____

_____

_____

_____

_____

_____

_____

ADDITIONAL NOTES: _____

_____

_____

_____

_____

Group Presentation Skills

Teresa Hayes

When working as a team to present some information, it is important that the final product is as professional and interesting as possible. Use the following guidelines any time you are asked to deliver a presentation as a group.

Before the Presentation

Practice the entire presentation from start to finish at least once with all team members before delivering the speech in front of your actual audience. If you can, get someone from outside the group to watch your speech and give feedback. Also, try to simulate the exact conditions of the physical environment where you will actually give the speech. So, try to get in the classroom or room where the presentation will take place. This will help decrease some anxiety because when you go up in front of the room to deliver your presentation it will be at least a little familiar and therefore less intimidating.

Practice the presentation from start to finish *with* your visual aid. This ensures that you will have everything you need ahead of time (avoiding the "I went to Kinko's to pick it up but it wasn't ready!" syndrome) and you can figure out the who, how, and when aspects: who will carry the visual and/or get it set up, how it will fit in with the overall presentation, and when and how often you should refer to the visual. (See the Powerpoint section for more details on using technology in your presentation.)

If time constraints are a problem, minimally the team should get together and have the person who is giving the introduction practice the entire introduction including a transition to the first speaker. Next, have the second speaker give the first sentence or two of his or her presentation and read the transition to the next speaker, and so on until the last person practices the conclusion in its entirety. We'll talk more about what transitions are and how we use them in a group speech when we discuss the body of the speech.

During the Presentation

Just like an individual presentation, a group speech should have a format that is logical, well-organized, and easy for the audience to follow. That means it should have an introduction, a body, and a conclusion. Since there is more than one speaker, a group speech should include transitions between speakers. Also, if there is a Question and Answer session, there are some special considerations to be made when conducting a Q-and-A as a team.

Before we get to the introduction, we should pause and address enthusiasm. A big part of getting your audience interested and enthused about your speech/topic is to show a lot of enthusiasm yourself. A frequent reminder that my students hear is "enthusiasm starts from your seat!" If there is no particular order to the presentations, volunteer to go first! All team members should show enthusiasm, as a display of lack of enthusiasm by even one member can bring down the attitude of the group, and thereby lower expectations from your audience: If *you* don't care about your speech and/or want to deliver it, why would the audience want to hear it? Another frequent reminder to my students: *act* enthusiastic and you'll *be* enthusiastic. Nervous? That's normal, and so is everyone else! Underprepared? Avoid letting your audience know by saying things like "I've had to work overtime all week so I didn't get a chance to practice." Not feeling your best? Fake it. Go for a walk up and down some stairs to get the adrenaline flowing, pump yourself up, talk to your team members to get psyched up. Remember: if you are enthusiastic about your speech, that enthusiasm will be contagious and your audience will be enthusiastic as well.

The Introduction

For a team presentation, introductions should include the following: introductions of team members, a brief statement about what each team member will cover, and a transition to the body of the speech.

Choose one person to do the introduction but it is best if all team members help to write it. When making the introduction, the speaker should be sure to have correct pronunciation of each team member's *real* name (Jaroslaw should only be introduced as Jerry if that is how he prefers to be addressed, not because the speaker can't pronounce his name!) First names are usually sufficient for a team speech.

Briefly give your audience an idea of what each team member should discuss. That means finding out ahead of time what each team member will be covering; we don't want any questions about who's doing what in what order when we are in front of our audience.

Lastly, have a transition written out so that when you complete your introduction you can hand the floor over to the next speaker. The transition should include who will be speaking next as well as what the topic is that person will discuss: For example: "Now that you know who we all are and an idea of what our presentation will include, I would like to introduce Tasha, who will start with the causes of global warming."

The Body

The body of a group speech should run smoothly, and the best way to accomplish this is through the use of transitions and practice. We should use transitions between speakers, and individual speakers should feel free to use as many transitions as possible. For example: "Now that you know what global warming is I would like to discuss three possible causes of global warming."

Each speaker should have her or his transition to the next speaker written out completely, and it should include the speaker's name and what he or she will discuss. Do not rely on memory for your transition. You may have been working side-by-side with Muhammad for a month and have heard his part of the speech several times, but once you're in front of your audience with some adrenaline flowing, it is possible you may draw a complete blank. So have your transition written out and at the ready.

Each speaker should use the extemporaneous speaking style to deliver his or her speech. The extemporaneous speaking style means that you have carefully prepared your speech ahead of time and have thoroughly practiced your speech so that all you need to have with you to deliver your speech is an outline with some key points that you plan to address. It is always best not to read word-for-word off of a sheet of paper or note cards. It is better to refer to your notes to jog your memory about what it is you are going to talk about, and then look at your audience and speak conversationally about that point or idea. Use your most polished professional conversation style, no slang and not too casual. ("Good evening" is better than "hey, how's it going . . .")

As each person is delivering his or her part of the speech, other team members should be quiet and respectful, looking at the speaker and not talking to each other or perusing their own notes. By the time the team is in front of the audience, the audience's *perception* should be that the team is well-prepared and well-organized. Any last-minute issues or plans that need to be addressed or made should be worked out by the time the group is in front of its audience.

The Conclusion

The conclusion, similar to the introduction, should include a re-introduction of team members (first names) and a very brief summary of what each person discussed. Have one person deliver the conclusion and make sure it is written and practiced ahead of time. Finish with a clincher—something that clearly lets your audience know your presentation is over—and/or thanking the audience for their time. Avoid the urge to finish with "that's it!" Write and practice a strong finish.

Question and Answer Session

Find out ahead of time if your presentation is expected to include a Q-and-A session. If so, have the person who delivers the conclusion open up the floor for questions.

Most importantly for a group presentation, questions should be shared by the team, meaning the group leader—official or unofficial—should not field all the questions. Most questions will fall naturally into someone's "field of expertise," and some fields may get more questions than others. But if it is possible for each team member to address a question, it gives the appearance of good solid teamwork and collaboration.

Take questions seriously, answer respectfully and, if you know the questioner's name, use it. Try to approach questions in a positive way. In an atmosphere of higher learning people are generally not asking questions to put you on the spot or to try to make you look bad; generally questions will result from an interest in your topic and a desire to learn more. Try to view questions as a challenge to your critical thinking skills—good practice for job interviewing and board meeting situations.

Using Powerpoint

It is absolutely crucial when using Powerpoint—crucial!—that there are no typos to be seen. Have every person in the group, and anyone else you can get for that matter, read over the presentation checking for spelling and grammar errors; there is nothing worse than having a mistake blown up on a big screen for everyone in the world to see.

Keep in mind the purpose of a visual aid is usually to enhance and support the information in the presentation; it is generally not a presentation in and of itself. So spend time thinking about and choosing colors, fonts, point size, sound effects, visuals, and animation so that it enhances the presentation without distracting the audience. While it may be tempting to put on an impressive slide show, it is more important that the audience is listening to the speakers, and the messages they are trying to convey, than to be impressed with your technological brilliance.

Make sure you practice the entire presentation with the Powerpoint from start to finish. You might have one person in charge of working the Powerpoint until it is his or her time to speak, or you may switch off, but this should all be worked out—and practiced—ahead of time. Speakers should be able to give a simple nod to advance a slide, and the audience should see a synchronized display of collaboration among team members.

Finally, it is extremely important that the team is prepared for technical difficulties! Bring copies of the Powerpoint demonstration, overheads, or some sort of back-up plan for the inevitable occurrence of technological difficulties. And if you do find yourself in this situation, try to avoid bringing attention to it, i.e. "Well, I did have a chart to show you, but . . ." Your audience will appreciate your preparedness and professionalism if you can adapt to the situation and successfully present your material relying on your knowledge and flexibility as well as that of your colleagues.

Assessments

Isa N. Engleberg

Assessment

Group Attraction Survey

Directions   Think of an effective group in which you currently work or have worked in the past. Try to keep the group you select in mind as you complete this assessment instrument. The following 15 statements describe possible reasons why you joined or are attracted to your group. Indicate the degree to which each statement applies to you by marking whether you (5) strongly agree, (4) agree, (3) are undecided, (2) disagree, or (1) strongly disagree. Work quickly and record your first impression.

_____   1. I like having authority and high status in the group.
_____   2. I want the other group members to act friendly toward me.
_____   3. Group members help each other solve personal problems.
_____   4. I am proud when the group achieves a goal or an objective.
_____   5. I try to be an active participant in group activities.
_____   6. Some group members are close friends.
_____   7. I become upset if group members waste time and effort.
_____   8. I like to do things with group members outside the group.
_____   9. Group members are excellent decision makers and problem solvers.
_____   10. Group members like me.
_____   11. I work hard to be a valuable group member.
_____   12. I try to influence the opinions and actions of group members.
_____   13. I like it when group members invite me to join their activities.
_____   14. I enjoy talking to members, even when the conversation is unrelated to the group's goal.
_____   15. I try to get group members to do things the way I want them done.

Scoring

Seek Task Achievement
   Add your responses to items 4, 7, and 9: _____

Seek Social Goals
   Add your responses to items 3, 8, and 14: _____

Seek Inclusion
   Add your responses to items 5, 11, and 13: _____

Seek Control
   Add your responses to items 1, 12, and 15: _____

Seek Affection
   Add your responses to items 2, 6, and 10: _____

A score of 12 or above in any category indicates that this source of attraction is an important reason why you joined and stay in this group. A score of 6 or below indicates that this source of attraction was not an important factor in why you joined and not a major reason why you stay in this group. Examining your attraction to other groups in which you work may result in different scores.

Notes

1. Napier, R. W., & Gershenfeld, M. K. (1999). *Groups: Theory and experience* (6th ed.). Boston: Houghton Mifflin, p. 74.
2. Maslow, A. H. (1954). *Motivation and personality.* New York: Harper & Row.
3. Schutz, W. (1994). *The human element: Productivity, self-esteem, and the bottom line.* San Francisco: Jossey-Bass.
4. In his more recent works, Schutz refers to this need as *openness*. However, we find that students understand this concept better when we use Schutz's original term—*affection.*
5. Ellis, D. G., & Fisher, B. A. (1994). *Small group decision making: Communication and the group process* (4th ed.). New York: McGraw-Hill, p. 51.
6. Robbins, H., & Finley, M. (1995). *Why teams don't work: What went wrong and how to make it right.* Princeton, NJ: Peterson's/Pacesetter Books, p. 26.
7. Tuckman, B. W. (1965). Developmental sequence in small groups. *Psychological Bulletin, 63,* pp. 384–399.
8. Robbins & Finley, p. 191.
9. Dianna Wynn is a trial consultant for *Courtroom Intelligence,* a consulting firm specializing in communication in the courtroom.
10. Fisher, B. A. (1970). "Decision emergence: Phases in group decision making." *Speech Monographs, 37,* pp. 53–66.
11. Duarte, D. L., & Snyder, N. T. (2001). *Mastering virtual teams* (2nd ed.). San Francisco: Jossey-Bass, pp. 116–117.
12. Duarte & Snyder, p. 183.
13. Poole, M. S., & Roth, J. (1989). Decision development in small groups, V: Test of a contingency model. *Human Communication Research, 15,* pp. 549–589.
14. Andrews, P. H. (1996). Group conformity. In R. S. Cathcart, L. A. Samovar, & L. D. Henman (Eds.), *Small group communication: Theory and practice* (7th ed.). Madison, WI: Brown & Benchmark, p. 185.
15. Pavitt, C., & Curtis, E. (1994). *Small group discussion: A theoretical approach* (2nd ed.). Scottsdale, AZ: Gorsuch, Scarisbrick, p. 178.
16. Napier & Gershenfeld, pp. 143–146.
17. Barbato, C. A. (1997, November). *An integrated model of group decision-making.* Paper presented at the meeting of the National Communication Association, Chicago, IL, p. 19.
18. Moreland, R., & Levine, J. (1987). Group dynamics over time: Development and socialization in small groups. In J. McGrath (Ed.), *The social psychology of time.* Beverly Hills, CA: Sage, p. 156.
19. Napier & Gershenfeld, pp. 152–153.

Assessment

Auditing Team Talk

Directions   Circle the term that best describes the extent to which the members of your group engage in productive team talk.

When your group communicates...			
Do members use plural pronouns rather than singular ones?	Very Often	Sometimes	Rarely
Do members use language that acknowledges shared needs?	Very Often	Sometimes	Rarely
Do members solicit opinions and express the need for cooperation?	Very Often	Sometimes	Rarely
Do members talk to one another on equal terms?	Very Often	Sometimes	Rarely
Do members use casual language, nicknames, slang?	Very Often	Sometimes	Rarely
Do members express empathy and liking?	Very Often	Sometimes	Rarely
Do members express interest in solving problems?	Very Often	Sometimes	Rarely
Do members use a nonthreatening tone and nonjudgmental language?	Very Often	Sometimes	Rarely
Do members paraphrase each other?	Very Often	Sometimes	Rarely
Do members ask "what if" questions?	Very Often	Sometimes	Rarely
Do members propose objective criteria for solutions?	Very Often	Sometimes	Rarely
Do members summarize areas of agreement?	Very Often	Sometimes	Rarely

Scoring   Analyze your group's team talk by looking at the number of times you circled *Very Often, Sometimes,* and *Rarely.* The more times you circled *Very Often,* the more likely it is that your group engages in productive team talk. The more times you circled *Rarely,* the more likely it is that team talk inhibits group progress and success. To get a more accurate assessment of team talk for your entire group, everyone should complete the questionnaire and share their responses. Is there a consistent response to each question? If there are significant disagreements on several questions, the members of your group may benefit from a discussion about the nature of their team talk.

Assessment

Personal Report of Communication Apprehension (PRCA-24)

Directions   This instrument is composed of twenty-four statements concerning feelings about communication with other people. Please indicate the degree to which each statement applies to you by marking whether you (1) strongly agree, (2) agree, (3) are undecided, (4) disagree, or (5) strongly disagree. Work quickly; record your first impression.

   _____   1. I dislike participating in group discussions.
   _____   2. Generally, I am comfortable while participating in group discussions.
   _____   3. I am tense and nervous while participating in group discussions.
   _____   4. I like to get involved in group discussions.
   _____   5. Engaging in a group discussion with new people makes me tense and nervous.
   _____   6. I am calm and relaxed while participating in a group discussion.
   _____   7. Generally, I am nervous when I have to participate in a meeting.
   _____   8. Usually I am calm and relaxed while participating in a meeting.
   _____   9. I am very calm and relaxed when I am called upon to express an opinion at a meeting.
   _____   10. I am afraid to express myself at meetings.
   _____   11. Communicating at meetings usually makes me feel uncomfortable.
   _____   12. I am very relaxed when answering questions at a meeting.
   _____   13. While participating in a conversation with a new acquaintance, I feel very nervous.
   _____   14. I have no fear of speaking up in conversations.
   _____   15. Ordinarily I am very tense and nervous in conversations.
   _____   16. Ordinarily I am very calm and relaxed in conversations.
   _____   17. While conversing with a new acquaintance, I feel very relaxed.
   _____   18. I'm afraid to speak up in conversations.
   _____   19. I have no fear of giving a speech.
   _____   20. Certain parts of my body feel very tense and rigid while I am giving a speech.
   _____   21. I feel relaxed while giving a speech.
   _____   22. My thoughts become confused and jumbled when I am giving a speech.
   _____   23. I face the prospect of giving a speech with confidence.
   _____   24. While giving a speech, I get so nervous I forget facts I really know.

Scoring   The PRCA permits computation of one total score and four subscores. The subscores are related to communication apprehension in each of four common communication contexts: group discussions, meetings, interpersonal conversations, and public speaking. To compute your scores, merely add or subtract your scores for each item as indicated below.

Subscores	Scoring Formula
Group Discussion	18 + scores for items 2, 4, and 6; − scores for items 1, 3, and 5.
Meetings	18 + scores for items 8, 9, and 12; − scores for items 7, 10, and 11.
Interpersonal Conversations	18 + scores for items 14, 16, and 17; − scores for items 13, 15, and 18.
Public Speaking	18 + scores for items 19, 21, and 23; − scores for items 20, 22, and 24.

To obtain your total score for the PRCA, simply add your four subscores together. Your score should range between 24 and 120. If your score is below 24 or above 120, you have made a mistake in computing the score. Scores on the four contexts (groups, meetings, interpersonal conversations, and public speaking) can range from a low of 6 to a high of 30. Any score above 18 indicates some degree of apprehension. If your score is above 18 for the public speaking context, you are like the overwhelming majority of Americans.

Norms for PRCA-24:

	Mean	Standard Deviation
Total Score	65.5	15.3
Group	15.4	4.8
Meetings	16.4	4.8
Interpersonal	14.5	4.2
Public Speaking	19.3	5.1

Source: *PRCA-24* reprinted with permission from the author. See James C. McCroskey (1993). *An Introduction to Rhetorical Communication,* 6th ed. Englewood Cliffs, NJ: Prentice Hall, Inc. p. 37.

Assessment

Team Motivation Inventory

Directions   This instrument can be used to measure the motivation level of a group in which you are currently a member or have worked in the past. Complete the instrument on your own. Use the following scale to assign a number to each statement:

(5) strongly agree

(4) agree

(3) neutral

(2) disagree

(1) strongly disagree

_____ 1. I work very hard in my group.
_____ 2. I work harder in this group than I do in most other groups.
_____ 3. Other members work very hard in this group.
_____ 4. I am willing to spend extra time on group projects.
_____ 5. I try to attend all group meetings.
_____ 6. Other members regularly attend group meetings.
_____ 7. I often lose track of time when I'm working in the group.
_____ 8. Group members don't seem to mind working long hours on our project.
_____ 9. When I am working with the group, I am focused on our work.
_____10. I look forward to working with the members of my group.
_____ 11. I enjoy working with group members.

_____ 12. Group members enjoy working with each other.

_____ 13. I am doing an excellent job in my group.

_____ 14. I am doing better work in this group than I have done in other groups.

_____ 15. The other members are making excellent contributions to the group.

_____ 16. I am willing to do whatever the group needs in order to achieve our goal.

_____ 17. I trust the members of my group.

_____ 18. The other group members are willing to take on extra work.

_____ 19. I am proud of the work my group is doing.

_____ 20. I understand the importance of our group's work.

_____ 21. Everyone is committed to successfully achieving our goal.

_____ 22. I am proud of the contributions I have made to the group.

_____ 23. The group appreciates my work.

_____ 24. I am proud to be a member of this group.

_____ 25. This group really works well together.

Scoring and Interpretation

Add your ratings for all of the statements. A score below 75 indicates a low level of group motivation. Scores between 76 and 99 represent a moderate level of motivation. Any score above 100 suggests the group is highly motivated. Compare your score to those of other members in your group. You may discover that you share similar feelings about your group and its tasks.

If the group is highly motivated, the group can proceed and expect positive results. Otherwise, the group should discuss why some members are more motivated than others. Is there disagreement about the goals or the group, the way the task is structured, or the expectations of members? Are some members doing most of the interesting work while others are relegated to routine assignments? Do some members feel left out or ignored?

If most group members lack motivation, the group may need to discuss its reason for being. Has the group been assigned a task but not given clear directions or a justification for doing the assignment? Is the task too difficult or too complex for the group to handle? Are the expectations unclear or unreasonable? Are some members making it difficult for others to participate?

Source: The Team Motivation Inventory acknowledges the contributions of other inventories, including the JML Inventory in Alexander Hiam's *Motivating and Rewarding Employees* (Holbrook, MA: Adams Media, 1999) and The Encouragement Index in James M. Kouzes and Barry Z. Posner's *Encouraging the Heart: A Leader's Guide to Rewarding and Recognizing Others* (San Francisco: Jossey-Bass, 1999).

Notes

1. See Rotter, J. B. (1996). Generalized expectancies for internal versus external control of reinforcement. *Psychological Monographs, 80,* pp. 1–28; Petri, I. L. (1996). *Motivation: Theory, research, and applications* (4th ed.). Pacific Grove, CA: Brooks/Cole, pp. 245–254.

2. Nelson, B. (1997). *1000 ways to energize employees.* New York: Workman, p. 83.

3. Bowen, R. B. (2000). *Recognizing and rewarding employees.* New York: McGraw-Hill, p. 30.

4. Larson, C. E., & LaFasto, F. M. J. (1989). *TeamWork: What must go right/What can go wrong.* Newbury Park, CA: Sage, p. 73.

5. Bormann, E. G. (1996). *Small group communication: Theory and practice.* Edina, MN: Burgess International Group, p. 86.

6. Bernstein, D. A., et al. (2001). *Psychology* (5th ed.). Boston: Houghton Mifflin, p. 378.

7. Bernstein et al., p. 380; Petri, pp. 257–259.

8. Bormann, p. 90.
9. Kotter, J. P. (1999). *John P. Kotter on what leaders really do.* Boston: Harvard Business School, p. 60.

Assessment

Ross-DeWine Conflict Management Message Style Instrument

Directions   Below you will find messages which have been delivered by persons in conflict situations. Consider each message separately and decide how closely this message resembles the ones that you have used in conflict settings. The language may not be exactly the same as yours, but consider the messages in terms of similarity to your messages in conflict. There are no right or wrong answers, nor are these messages designed to trick you. Answer in terms of responses you make, not what you think you should say. Give each message a 1–5 rating on the answer sheet provided according to the following scale. Mark one answer only.

In conflict situations, I

1	2	3	4	5
never say things like this	rarely say things like this	sometimes say things like this	often say things like this	usually say things like this

_____ 1. "Can't you see how foolish you're being with that thinking?"

_____ 2. "How can I make you feel happy again?"

_____ 3. "I'm really bothered by some things that are happening here; can we talk about these?"

_____ 4. "I really don't have any more to say on this . . . (silence)."

_____ 5. "What possible solutions can we come up with?"

_____ 6. "I'm really sorry that your feelings are hurt—maybe you're right."

_____ 7. "Let's talk this thing out and see how we can deal with this hassle."

_____ 8. "Shut up! You are wrong! I don't want to hear any more of what you have to say."

_____ 9. "It is your fault if I fail at this, and don't you ever expect any help from me when you're on the spot."

_____ 10. "You can't do (say) that to me—it's either my way or forget it."

_____ 11. "Let's try finding an answer that will give us both some of what we want."

_____ 12. "This is something we have to work out; we're always arguing about it."

_____ 13. "Whatever makes you feel happiest is OK by me."

_____ 14. "Let's just leave well enough alone."

_____ 15. "That's OK . . . it wasn't important anyway. . . . You feeling OK now?"

_____ 16. "If you're not going to cooperate, I'll just go to someone who will."

_____ 17. "I think we need to try to understand the problem."

_____ 18. "You might as well accept my decision; you can't do anything about it anyway."

Scoring Instructions

By each item, list the rating (from 1 to 5) you gave that item. When you have entered all ratings, add total ratings for each column and divide by 6. Enter the resulting score in the space provided.

SELF Items	ISSUE Items	OTHER Items
1. _____	3. _____	2. _____
8. _____	5. _____	4. _____
9. _____	7. _____	6. _____
10. _____	11. _____	13. _____
16. _____	12. _____	14. _____
18. _____	17. _____	15. _____

	SELF Items	ISSUE Items	OTHER Items
Your Total Score	_____	_____	_____
Average Score	(13.17)	(24.26)	(21.00)

All of us may use one of the following styles in different settings and under different circumstances. People do tend to have a predominant style which is evidenced by the kinds of messages sent during conflict situations.

The SELF items deal with one's personal interests in the conflict situation. These messanges suggest that one's primary concern is in resolving the conflict so that a person's personal view of the conflict is accepted by the other. This is a "win" approach to conflict resolution.

The ISSUE items deal with an emphasis on both parties dealing with the problem. These message statements suggest an overriding concern with the content of the conflict rather than the personal relationship.

The OTHER items deal with neither the conflict issues nor personal interests, but emphasize maintaining the relationship at a cost of resolving the conflict. These statements suggest that one would rather ignore the problem to maintain a good relationship with the other person.

The averages are an indication of scores one might expect to receive. Scores that are higher or lower than these means indicate a higher or lower use of this message style than would normally be expected.

Source: DeWine, S. (1994). *The consultant's craft: Improving organizational communication.* New York: St. Martin's, pp. 268–272; Ross, R. G., & DeWine, S. (1988). Communication messages in conflict: A message-focused instrument to assess conflict management styles. *Management Communication Quarterly, 1,* pp. 389–413.

Assessment

Shafir's Self-Listening Test

Self-knowledge is the first step toward self-improvement. This test looks at how you listen in a variety of situations and settings. Carefully consider each question and indicate whether or not you consistently demonstrate each behavior.

Do you

1. Think about what *you* are going to say while the speaker is talking?

   ☐ Yes, consistently   ☐ No, almost never   ☐ Sometimes

2. Tune out people who say things you don't agree with or don't want to hear?

   ☐ Yes, consistently   ☐ No, almost never   ☐ Sometimes

3. Learn something from each person you meet, even if it is ever so slight?
   ☐ Yes, consistently   ☐ No, almost never   ☐ Sometimes

4. Keep eye contact with the person who is speaking?
   ☐ Yes, consistently   ☐ No, almost never   ☐ Sometimes

5. Become self-conscious in one-to-one or small group conversations?
   ☐ Yes, consistently   ☐ No, almost never   ☐ Sometimes

6. Often interrupt the speaker?
   ☐ Yes, consistently   ☐ No, almost never   ☐ Sometimes

7. Fall asleep or daydream during meetings or presentations?
   ☐ Yes, consistently   ☐ No, almost never   ☐ Sometimes

8. Restate instructions or messages to be sure you understood correctly?
   ☐ Yes, consistently   ☐ No, almost never   ☐ Sometimes

9. Allow the speaker to vent negative feelings toward you without becoming defensive or physically tense?
   ☐ Yes, consistently   ☐ No, almost never   ☐ Sometimes

10. Listen for the meaning behind a speaker's words through gestures and facial expressions?
    ☐ Yes, consistently   ☐ No, almost never   ☐ Sometimes

11. Feel frustrated or impatient when communicating with persons from other cultures?
    ☐ Yes, consistently   ☐ No, almost never   ☐ Sometimes

12. Inquire about the meaning of unfamiliar words or jargon?
    ☐ Yes, consistently   ☐ No, almost never   ☐ Sometimes

13. Give the appearance of listening when you are not?
    ☐ Yes, consistently   ☐ No, almost never   ☐ Sometimes

14. Listen to the speaker without judging or criticizing?
    ☐ Yes, consistently   ☐ No, almost never   ☐ Sometimes

15. Start giving advice before you are asked?
    ☐ Yes, consistently   ☐ No, almost never   ☐ Sometimes

16. Ramble on before getting to the point?
    ☐ Yes, consistently   ☐ No, almost never   ☐ Sometimes

17. Take notes when necessary to help you remember?
    ☐ Yes, consistently   ☐ No, almost never   ☐ Sometimes

18. Consider the state of the person you are talking to (nervous, rushed, hearing impaired, etc.)?
    ☐ Yes, consistently   ☐ No, almost never   ☐ Sometimes

19. Let a speaker's physical appearance or mannerisms detract you from listening?
    ☐ Yes, consistently   ☐ No, almost never   ☐ Sometimes

20. Remember a person's name after you have been introduced?
    ☐ Yes, consistently   ☐ No, almost never   ☐ Sometimes

21. Assume you know what the speaker is going to say and stop listening?
    ☐ Yes, consistently   ☐ No, almost never   ☐ Sometimes

22. Feel uncomfortable allowing silence between you and your conversation partner?
    ☐ Yes, consistently   ☐ No, almost never   ☐ Sometimes

23. Ask for feedback to make sure you are getting across to the other person?
    ☐ Yes, consistently   ☐ No, almost never   ☐ Sometimes

24. Preface your statements with unflattering remarks about yourself?
    ☐ Yes, consistently   ☐ No, almost never   ☐ Sometimes

25. Think more about building warm working relationships with team members and customers than about bringing in revenue?
    ☐ Yes, consistently   ☐ No, almost never   ☐ Sometimes

Scoring   Compare your answers to those on the following chart. For every answer that matches the key, give yourself one point. If you answered "Sometimes" to any of the questions, score half a point. Total the number of points.

1. N	6. N	11. N	16. N	21. N
2. N	7. N	12. Y	17. Y	22. N
3. Y	8. Y	13. N	18. Y	23. Y
4. Y	9. Y	14. Y	19. N	24. N
5. N	10. Y	15. N	20. Y	25. Y

Total points: _____

Interpretation of Results

21+ points: You are an excellent listener in most settings and circumstances. Note which areas could use further improvement.

16–20 points: You usually absorb most of the main ideas but often miss a good portion of the rest of the message due to difficulties with sustained attention. You may feel detached from the speaker and start thinking about other things or about what you are going to say next.

10–15 points: You may be focusing more on your own agenda than the speaker's needs. You easily become distracted and perceive listening as a task. Personal biases may get in the way of fully understanding a speaker.

9 points or less: Most of the time you experience listening as a boring activity. You might complain that your memory is poor and feel great frustration when trying to retain information and succeed in a classroom situation.

Note: If you answered "Sometimes" to many of the questions, then obviously you are a sometimes listener. Chances are your ability to concentrate may be at fault and/or you are a highly critical individual and quick to judge whether a listening opportunity is worthwhile. However, there have been times when you have experienced the satisfaction of being fully absorbed in what someone has to say.

Source: "Self-Listening Test" from *The Zen of Listening: Mindful Communication in the Age of Distraction* (pp. 28–33) by Rebecca Z. Shafir. Copyright ©2000. Reprinted by permission of Quest Books/The Theosophical Publishing House, Wheaton, IL.

INFORMATION LITERACY AND LIBRARY RESOURCES

Susan M.S. Chang

The need to access information is a universal one, and this need will be with you long after you finish school. Many people think that using information and library resources relates only to doing a research paper or finding the information required in an assignment. In truth, people need information in all aspects of their lives, whether it be a personal or family issue (What car should I buy? Where's the best place to build our dream house? How do I design a Web page?) or work-related (How do I find the right job? Where can I get those statistics my boss wants? How can we expand our business into new markets?). The Internet has vastly improved our access to information, and the wealth of information available to us all is exciting and challenging. It seems like we have the world at our fingertips, just a touch of the keyboard away. But the very magnitude of the amount of information available to us is what sometimes makes finding the answer to our questions more difficult, rather than less. The Internet is not very well organized, and efficient use of this wonderful resource involves more than simply typing a keyword into your favorite search engine and clicking <search>! And, believe it or not, traditional resources such as books and periodicals are often a more efficient source of information than random Web surfing. Many of these traditional resources are now delivered electronically, which should satisfy the "high tech" tastes of even the greatest bibliophobe.

The trick to efficient information retrieval is to know what resource to use when. At times, a quick keyword search using a search engine will provide the answer you need. Other times, using the more traditional resources such as books and periodicals will fill your information needs more quickly and completely. Electronic databases are often just what you need. All these resources are valuable, and once you have a sense of which resource to use for different information needs, you will have made a good start. Of course, you must also know how to evaluate these resources and to use them properly, avoiding plagiarism. Therefore, this appendix will discuss:

▶ Structuring your research

▶ Choosing the proper resource(s)

▶ Efficiently using the appropriate tools to access these resource(s)

▶ Using and evaluating these resource(s)

▶ Citing and documenting your research

STRUCTURING YOUR RESEARCH AND DEFINING THE TOPIC

Often when students begin to research a topic, they do so with a less-than-clear idea of exactly what that topic is. It is very important that you carefully define your topic so that you can approach the research in an efficient and appropriate way. To assist with this, it is often very helpful to consult reference materials from your library. Reference materials include encyclopedias (both general and subject-specific), dictionaries and handbooks, and are frequently offered in both print and electronic format. By reading through these general discussions of your topic, you should be able to:

▶ Define your topic

▶ Determine exactly what it is you wish to learn

▶ Clarify the question(s) that need answers

▶ Fill in the gaps in your understanding of the topic

Another advantage to beginning your research in the reference collection is that you will be able to narrow or broaden your topic as need be. Often people choose topics that are too broad to handle within the scope of the assignment or task. For example, if the assignment is to write a five page paper on a business topic, you would be hard pressed to cover a large topic such as "e-commerce" in the space allowed. By familiarizing yourself with the topic, you should be able to identify a smaller topic to focus on, such as "marketing forces behind the growth of e-commerce".

Conversely, you may find while exploring the reference collection that your topic is too narrow, and there may not be enough information to support your paper. You may need to broaden your topic instead. In either case, good reference materials such as an encyclopedia will help define your topic appropriately.

In addition to consulting reference resources, it is important to ask yourself questions, the answers to which will help you determine the resources to consult next. Ask yourself:

▶ How familiar am I already with the topic?

▶ Do I need in-depth, comprehensive information or just a few details?

▶ Is the topic very time-sensitive; is it very current and still changing?

▶ Is the topic public knowledge? Well documented or obscure?

▶ What are my time constraints in obtaining the information I need?

(Don't procrastinate!)

Now is a good time to start defining appropriate search terms, keywords and subject headings. In particular, start thinking of synonyms for your subject—many topics are referred to by several different names (e.g., "death penalty" and "capital punishment; "assisted suicide" and "euthanasia"). This will impact search results, particularly when you are doing a keyword search (see "Keyword vs. Field Searching" below). Try to think of both narrower and broader terms as well, so that you will be prepared to search indexes and tables of contents.

Example

Research Topic: Marketing forces behind the growth of e-commerce

Primary Search Terms:

(1)   E-Commerce

             Synonyms or related terms: Electronic Commerce

                                              Internet Commerce

                                              Internet Business

                                              Business to Business Commerce

             Narrower terms: Online Sales

                                              Online Advertising

(2)   Marketing

             Synonyms or related terms: Public Relations

                                              Demographics

             Narrower terms: Advertising

                                              Merchandising

Remember, you can combine the various search terms in different ways. Hint: On Proquest Direct, and many other databases, you can find suggestions for related or narrower terms by clicking on <Subject List>.

Exercise

For a topic of your choosing, try to find at least two related search terms and two narrower search terms to assist you in your database and index searching. Is there also a broader term which might be helpful?

Research Topic: _____

             Synonyms or related terms: _____

                                           _____

             Narrower term: _____

                                           _____

                                           _____

Broader term: _____

CHOOSING THE APPROPRIATE RESOURCES:

As mentioned above, the Internet is not your *only* resource—while very valuable indeed, other resources may in fact be more appropriate for particular information needs. The difficulty is in deciding which resource to use, and to use all resources appropriately.

PRIMARY SOURCES

Primary sources are first-hand accounts of events or time periods, and can be found in many different formats. First-hand accounts can be derived from interviews, diaries, pictures, letters, etc., and can be very valuable sources for "color" as well as facts. You may find that interviewing an expert in the field you are researching is a valuable way to get direct information as well as opinions. Likewise, an "eye-witness" account of an event, or an era, may give you an excellent sense of time, place and impact. You can find these eye-witness accounts in many different resources, such as newspapers, autobiographies, and manuscripts as well as through face-to-face contact.

REFERENCE MATERIALS

Reference materials include encyclopedias, handbooks, dictionaries, directories, and almanacs, both general and subject-specific. They are a very good source of facts, dates, timelines, etc., and may be the quickest way to locate answers to specific, objective questions. However, their usefulness is not limited to this purpose. As mentioned in section (1), reference sources are often an excellent place to begin your research on a topic. They can give you a good, solid overview of the topic you will be studying, fill in gaps in your understanding of the topic, help you determine the additional resources you will need, and finally, help you narrow or broaden your topic if need be. A good reference source can "ground" you in your topic and help you structure your research. And today, many reference sources are available in both print and electronic format!

MONOGRAPHS

Monographs are detailed, comprehensive books which provide in-depth coverage of a single topic. In most libraries, monographs make up the circulating portion of the book collection. They are useful when you need complete, truly in-depth information about your subject, and can add greatly to your knowledge and understanding of your topic. You can also retrieve information selectively through careful use of the index and/or table of contents of monographs. The positive side to monographs is their comprehensiveness; the negative is that they are usually not good sources for very current, up-to-date information. The good news for those who prefer using electronic resources whenever possible is that many monographs are now available as electronic, or "e" books. Check your library's web page for links to e-books.

AUDIOVISUALS

Video- and audiocassettes have become standard materials in academic libraries, and can be very useful learning tools as they add extra dimension to the printed word in books. They can be excellent primary sources, and the visual or audio stimuli can truly make your subject come alive.

PERIODICALS

"Periodical" is a term used to describe a publication that comes out "periodically", such as magazines, journals and newspapers. Issues of periodicals may come out daily, weekly, monthly or quarterly, and thus they are an excellent source of the current, up-to-date information lacking in books. Bear in mind, however, that a three page magazine article will by necessity cover a fairly specific, narrow topic and will not have the depth of a 250-page book.

Magazines are "general audience" publications covering popular topics. They are excellent resources for learning about current events, social issues and issues of general interest. In contrast, journals are research-oriented, academic, scholarly publications and are "peer-reviewed". Before an article appears in a journal, a panel of the author's peers will review it, and will verify that it represents quality research and truthful information. Therefore, journals are usually more reliable and credible than many magazines. Their scholarly approach and focus may require some sophistication, however.

Periodicals are now published in both print and electronic format. Electronic delivery over the Internet has greatly increased most library patrons' access to full-text periodicals. It is important to stress that while the periodical may be "delivered" over the Internet, it is not just an Internet site, but a "real" magazine or journal article equivalent to the print version.

ON-LINE AND CD-ROM DATABASES

Many on-line and CD-ROM databases consist of materials which were once available only in print format, usually as reference books, monographs or proprietary reports. These information databases are very useful for in-depth information in specific subject areas, and in addition to containing a great deal of information are easily searchable due to the electronic format.

INTERNET SITES

Last, but by no means least, Internet sites have become extraordinarily valuable sources of information from educational, governmental, business and organizational entities. The Internet is responsible for a veritable explosion of information, much of which was previously unavailable or difficult to find and obtain. In particular, the Internet is very useful for obtaining government publications. Used appropriately, the Internet is an incredible resource!

Hopefully, this discussion has helped you see that a number of different resources are available to you and that all may be valuable and useful in different situations. Particularly when writing a research paper, it is important to use many different resources to ensure that you have gotten the best, well-rounded and documented information.

EXERCISE

For the following information needs, indicate which resource(s) would be best to use:

1. You need to find out the capital of Botswana and its current population _____

2. You want to know more about the most recent school shooting _____
_____

3. You've heard much about the charismatic speeches given by a well-known public figure and want to have more than the transcript of the speeches _____

4. You want to learn more about starting your own business, from start to finish _____

5. You would like to have a better understanding of some of the newer telecommunications technologies _____

6. You want to learn more about an organization devoted to animal rights _____

7. You have been hearing about research currently being conducted to explore new treatments for bipolar disorder _____

8. You would like to know what it was like to immigrate to the United States from a war-torn country _____

Sometimes, several different resources can augment and supplement each other.

ACCESSING THE RESOURCES

Now that you know which resources you want to use, how do you access them? You know how to find the Internet, of course, and can access on-line databases from the Library's computers and Web page. This section will focus on finding books, audio-visuals and periodicals using the online catalog and periodical indexes. Later sections will address the "nuts and bolts" of electronic database searching and using the Internet.

BOOKS AND AUDIOVISUALS

The tool used to find books and audiovisuals in your college library is the online catalog. Nearly all college campuses have left behind the old card catalogs and now provide their catalog in an electronic version, often Internet based. While catalog databases differ from college campus to campus, most have similar features and allow for keyword as well as title, author and subject searches. You will find help using the online catalog in the library and/or on the library web page.

You should be able to find the following information from a record on the online catalog:

▶ **Location:** Books and audiovisuals can be shelved in a number of locations in the library. "Main Stacks" and "Circulation" are common terms for materials such as monographs, which circulate for the maximum time period—often two or three weeks. "Reference" houses the reference collection discussed earlier. Usually the reference collection is separate from the circulating collection, and most often these materials are for in-library use only. "Periodicals" is where you will find magazines and journals, of course, and often the "Audiovisuals" are shelved in a separate location as well. The location for electronic books is often an Internet link. Many libraries have special locations for archival or otherwise specialized collections. Finally, most libraries have "Reserve" collections, which are materials that circulate for shorter loan periods, are often specifically meant for a particular class, and are shelved behind the circulation desk.

▶ **Status:** Most online catalogs will indicate whether an item is already checked out to another patron and when it is due back to the library. Many online catalogs allow patrons to put a hold on books such as these, so that when the book is returned they will be able to check it out first. Other status entries include "Lost" or "Overdue".

▶ **Call Number:** While most public and school libraries shelve books according to the Dewey Decimal System, you will find that most academic, college and university libraries use the Library of Congress System instead. This may seem a bit confusing at first, but you will soon grow accustomed to it. Library of Congress call numbers all begin with at least one letter, usually two, and occasionally three. Thus the collection is organized alphabetically by call number. Each letter of the alphabet represents a general area of study (see general outline); for instance, you will find technology books in the "T's" and the social sciences in the "H's". The second letter further narrows the topic, such that telecommunications books are shelved under "TK" and business books under "HF". The number that follows the letter should be considered a whole number up to the decimal point, and anything after the decimal point is a decimal number. If you need assistance at first in locating items, don't hesitate to ask the library staff for help. Soon you will become familiar with the area(s) of the collection that house those items of most interest to you, and you will be able to browse the collection as well as use the online catalog to find materials you need.

GENERAL OUTLINE
LIBRARY OF CONGRESS CLASSIFICATION

A —GENERAL WORKS
B —PHILOSOPHY. PSYCHOLOGY. RELIGION
C —AUXILIARY SCIENCES OF HISTORY
D —HISTORY: GENERAL AND OLD WORLD
E —HISTORY: AMERICA
F —HISTORY: AMERICA
G —GEOGRAPHY. ANTHROPOLOGY. RECREATION
H —SOCIAL SCIENCES
   HF—BUSINESS AND ACCOUNTING
J —POLITICAL SCIENCE
K —LAW
L —EDUCATION
M—MUSIC AND BOOKS ON MUSIC
N —FINE ARTS
P —LANGUAGE AND LITERATURE
Q—SCIENCE
   QA—COMPUTER SCIENCE
R —MEDICINE
S —AGRICULTURE
T —TECHNOLOGY
   TK—TELECOMMUNICATIONS
U —MILITARY SCIENCE
V —NAVAL SCIENCE
Z —LIBRARY SCIENCE

PERIODICALS

Indexes are used to access periodicals. Up until the last decade or so, most indexes were only available in paper format—and they were tedious to use. You needed to look up your subject heading, then write down the citations to articles found there, find the magazine or request it through interlibrary loan, and photocopy the article(s) you needed. Today, electronic indexes, whether Internet or CD-ROM based, have completely revolutionized access not just to the citations to magazine and journal articles but also to the full text of these articles themselves. This means that you have access not simply to the print periodicals physically found in the library, but often to thousands of additional publications.

Libraries subscribe to many different electronic full text periodical indexes, but the examples illustrated in the section below demonstrate search strategies that apply to most of them. Remember to always use the "Help" screens when using a database for the first time or when switching between databases.

ELECTRONIC DATABASE SEARCHING

Electronic databases, without a doubt, have placed enormous amounts of information at our fingertips. The Internet, "E" books, subject databases, catalogs and full-text indexes make finding information much easier. However, there are a number of ways that you can refine your electronic search techniques to make searching even more efficient. This section will discuss a few of these techniques, using examples from an electronic periodical index called Proquest Direct. While the examples are specific for Proquest Direct, the strategies and techniques should be applicable to most other databases with some adaptation.

KEYWORD vs. SUBJECT SEARCHING

Keyword searching and subject searching are entirely different approaches to locating information. It is very important to understand the difference between them and the times when each is appropriate.

Keyword searching is a "blind" approach. The computer has no idea what you are looking for. You simply type in words that you think would appear in the articles you want to see, and the computer looks for those words, without knowing their meaning. For example, if you do a keyword search using the word <windows>, the results will include articles on Windows NT as well as those on storm windows and the window of opportunity. Keyword searching is appropriate when you are unsure of the proper subject heading for your topic and/or when you want to combine two different topics.

Subject searching is, for the computer, a "smart" search, in that the computer "knows" what you are looking for and is not just searching for a random juxtaposition of letters. You tell the computer the topic you want to research and it looks for materials that were catalogued or indexed under those subject headings. In other words, the search is only conducted in the appropriate field of the record, which in this case is the subject heading field. Subject searching is more precise but somewhat less flexible.

To do a subject search, you must know the exact subject heading that is used by the cataloguer or indexer. For instance, which term will produce hits: euthanasia, mercy killing or assisted suicide? If you choose the wrong term, you may get zero hits. For this reason, it is often useful to begin with a keyword search. You will get some irrelevant articles, and will miss some relevant ones, but if you find an article that is exactly right, you can look at the citation and find the subject headings listed there. You can then do a subject search using the exact subject heading and in that way get all the relevant materials.

The following is a basic keyword search on "workplace violence":

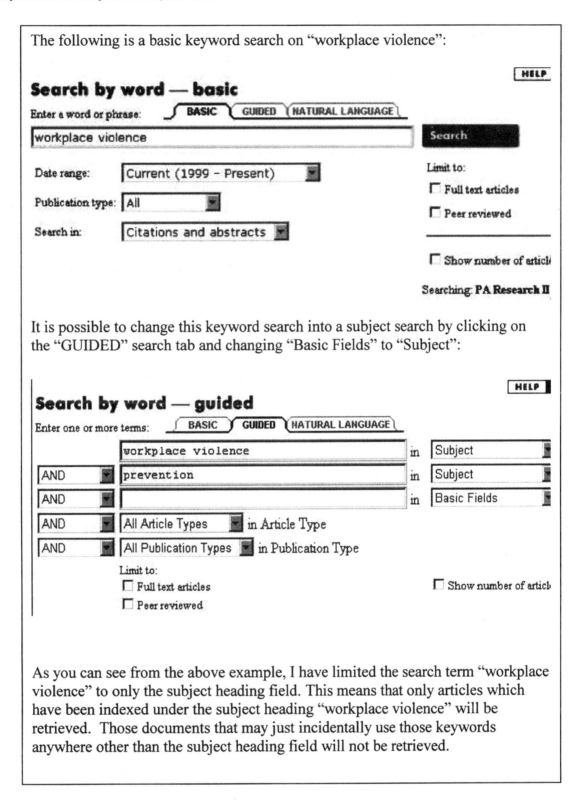

It is possible to change this keyword search into a subject search by clicking on the "GUIDED" search tab and changing "Basic Fields" to "Subject":

As you can see from the above example, I have limited the search term "workplace violence" to only the subject heading field. This means that only articles which have been indexed under the subject heading "workplace violence" will be retrieved. Those documents that may just incidentally use those keywords anywhere other than the subject heading field will not be retrieved.

As seen in the example, the subject heading field can be useful for streamlining your search to make the results more accurate and efficient. It is also very useful in other ways, particularly in suggesting additional search terms or search terms that might narrow your subject down. Therefore, pay close attention to the subject headings which are listed in the articles you retrieve—they may be very useful in refining your search.

NARROWING YOUR SUBJECT

You may have noticed in the example that a second subject heading has been added to the search screen (that is, "prevention"). Including additional search terms is one approach to making your topic more manageable. When your initial search yields an unreasonable number of "hits", you know that your topic is too broad. Proquest, for instance, will only retrieve 50 "hits", since that is probably far more than most students are looking for. Try to find an aspect of the broader subject that interests you. For example, "workplace violence" is too broadly documented. By scanning some of the articles, and in particular looking at the other subject headings used, you can find a more manageable subject to research—in this case, what is being and can be done to prevent workplace violence. These additional search terms can be added to the search screen using Boolean operators.

BOOLEAN OPERATORS AND OTHER 'TRICKS OF THE TRADE'

Boolean operators are words used to combine more than one word or phrase to further refine your search or to get more comprehensive results. The most common Boolean operators are "and", "or", and "not".

And: The connecting "and" is used to narrow your search down. You are adding to the requirements that must be fulfilled for an article to qualify for your search results. For instance, if you type "workplace violence **AND** prevention", only articles which specifically refer to both these terms will be retrieved.

Or: he connecting "or", conversely, broadens your search. It is useful when a subject is referred to in various ways. For instance, if you type "capital punishment **OR** death penalty", you will retrieve articles regardless of which synonym the author uses.

Not: Sometimes this will be written "and not". This connector eliminates specific aspects of your topic which you do not want to see. For instance, if you type "antitrust legislation **AND NOT** Microsoft", you will retrieve articles which discuss antitrust legislation but make no mention of Microsoft. Likewise, if your search term has 2 distinct meanings, you can eliminate articles which have no relevance to your search - for example, "greyhound **AND NOT** bus" if you are interested in articles about the dog, not the transportation system.

ADDITIONAL SYMBOLS

+ or ?: These symbols are used for what is termed truncation, to find a root word with different endings. For example, "depart+" will yield articles with the key words of depart, departed, department, departs, etc. Some databases will retrieve plural forms of the word automatically, while others will require truncation symbols.

( ): Many databases use parentheses to indicate phrases or to combine three different terms and more than one Boolean operator to combine subsets of words. For instance, typing "telecommunications and (education or research)" will retrieve records which contain 'telecommunications' and either the term 'education' or the term 'research'.

N or N + a number: The 'n' stands for 'near', meaning the two words or phrases should be separated by no more than a given number of other words, but can be in either order. When no number is specified, the number of terms between words is standard on that database.

W or W + a number: The 'w' stands for 'with' and is more restrictive than 'n' in that the two words or phrases must be in the same order as entered.

Remember that all databases are different! Some will use "+" and others will use "?" for truncation, for instance. Databases vary greatly over the way phrases should be used in search terms. Some databases allow for "natural language" searches, but many don't. So be sure to check the "help" screen when using a database for the first time or switching between databases.

SEARCH LIMITS

Many databases allow you to limit your search in other ways. For instance, Proquest Direct allows you to limit how many months and/or years of articles you want to search; e.g., you can choose to search only the most recent six months for a rapidly changing topic. Proquest Direct also allows you to limit your search to just "peer reviewed" journals (see section 3), or only those articles available full text (just in case you procrastinated and don't have time to wait for Interlibrary Loan!). Remember, the more you can tailor your search to your specific needs, the more precise and efficient the results will be.

In summation, electronic databases have replaced and augmented many traditional resources over the past decade. They include subject-specific databases, electronic books, and full text electronic journals, and many are delivered over the Internet. While they have simplified the research process in many ways, they are not always used as efficiently as their features allow. Learning to do field-specific (e.g. subject) searches and using Boolean operators, limits and truncation will streamline your research and information retrieval steps. Use the electronic databases appropriately and efficiently, and you will be pleased with the results!

USING THE INTERNET

The Internet is a remarkable resource, providing access to more information for more people than could have been imagined just a decade ago. Used appropriately and in conjunction with other resources, the Internet will be a valuable source for most of your information needs. However, two important facts must be remembered when using the Internet:

▶ No one is in charge of the Internet. This means that it is essentially unorganized.

▶ Anyone can put anything (legal, at least) on the Internet. This means that the page you just accessed could be a pack of lies.

Appropriate, careful and evaluative use of the Internet is essential, and this section will discuss ways to address these two facts. First, you need to know ways to access the information the Internet provides, even though it is unorganized. Second, you need to know how to evaluate the information you access to ensure you have retrieved true, reliable and unbiased information.

ACCESSING INTERNET SITES

Most people access the Internet using the search engine with which they have become most comfortable. They enter a keyword, hit search, sigh and begin sifting through the links they have retrieved. In many cases, this is satisfactory enough. But recent studies have shown that search engines, no matter how large, only have access to a fraction of what is present on the Web, and what's left is termed "the Invisible Web". How can you retrieve information from the sites the well-known search engines can't "see"? It is essential that you are aware of the different types of search engines and directories available to you to assist you in getting comprehensive results. Single, multiple, specialized search engines as well as subject directories will all be useful.

Single Search Engines: There are a number of single search engines on the Web, including Yahoo, AltaVista, HotBot, Excite, Google, and Northern Light to name just a few. Some are true search engines, while others combine search engine capabilities with human-compiled directories. An excellent site, which compares search engine features and capabilities, is SearchEngineWatch (http://www.searchengine watch.com), reviewing the various features of the search engines to help you choose the best one for your present needs. Many single search engines can perform fairly sophisticated searches, using Boolean terms, field searching and limits, as well as sort results. However, keep in mind that none of the single search engines even comes near to accessing all of the sites on the Web.

Multiple Search Engines: Multiple search engines, also called "metasearch" or "megasearch" engines, take your search term(s) and run simultaneous, parallel searches of selected single search engines. Some of the more well known multiple search engines are MetaCrawler, Dogpile and Ixquick. On the positive side, since the search is being conducted in more than one search engine, the chances are good that what one single search engine might miss, another will find. However, since most multiple search engines only retrieve a fixed number of sites from each single search engine, the results will not be comprehensive. Also, each single search engine may allow for different Boolean terms, limits, etc., and the advanced search features they allow when searched individually may not be available when doing a multiple search engine search. A good discussion of single searching versus multiple searching can be found in the aforementioned site (6).

Specialized Search Engines: Many subject-specific search engines are available, and more are being developed constantly. Since these search engines focus narrowly on the sites related to a particular subject, they are often more precise and may in fact have much more comprehensive and less superfluous results. You can find directories of such specialty search engines at the aforementioned site (compiled by Danny Sullivan, editor of SearchEngineWatch), and at http://www.completeplanet.com, (compiled by the search-technology company BrightPlanet).

Subject Directories: Subject directories are collections of links to Internet sites arranged under specific subject headings. While many subject directories include a search engine, the advantage to a well-designed subject directory is that you may not need to do a "search" at all! Links are provided to what are considered by the sponsor of the site to be the best sites for researching a particular topic. Often the site is described and evaluated, and this may help in determining the quality of a site. Yahoo is perhaps the most widely known subject directory, although in truth most people use Yahoo for its search engine. Many subject directories have been designed by librarians, and do an excellent job of providing a collection of subject-specific, quality Web sites. Some good subject directories include About.com (http://www.about.com), Librarians' Index to the Internet (http://www.lii.org), Argus Clearinghouse (http://clearinghouse.net) and Digital Librarian (http://www.digital-librarian.com). The librarians on your campus most likely have compiled a subject directory on the library Web page as well, and this will be an excellent source closely aligned to your curriculum.

Successful Web searchers use a combination of the above approaches to accessing information on the Internet. Try using single engine search engines when you need to use advanced search techniques, multiple search engines when you need to "spread a wide net", specialized search engines for technical database needs, and subject directories for general information-gathering on a topic. All these tools bring organization to the Internet and will help the efficiency of your search.

EVALUATING WEBSITES

Remember, anyone can put anything on the Internet, just as long as it's legal. So there is nothing to stop someone from putting false information on his or her site. While traditional resources may have errors, and even false information, before these resources are added to the library collection, the librarians evaluated them for quality. With Internet resources, you're on your own! It is very important that you scrutinize each Web page you use for your research, or your own work will be suspect.

Think in terms of the standard newspaper interview questions:

WHO:
- Who is responsible for the content of the page? (Note that this is not necessarily the webmaster). Can you tell? You should be able to.

- What are the qualifications of the person(s) responsible for the content? Are they experts in their field? Are their titles and affiliations spelled out?

WHAT:
- Is the material presented documented? If not, can it be? Is it biased? Is it fact or opinion? Is it broad in scope?

WHERE:
- How does this address look? What is the domain address? While the distinctions have become somewhat blurred, ".com" is a commercial site (they're probably trying to sell you something!), ".org" is an organization site (watch for bias), etc.

- Is the site easy to navigate?

- Are their links to other sites? Are they accurate and up-to-date?

- Is there advertising on the page?

- Has the site won awards, or been reviewed elsewhere?

WHEN:
- On what date was the page created?

- When was it last updated?

- Does it seem like it will be around for a while, or is it just a temporary site?

WHY:
- Why does this site exist? What are the motives of the creators of the site for putting this information on the Web? To inform? To share information? Or to promote or sell something?

You must be a critical evaluator of Internet sites. Your research will only be as good as the sources you use.

EXERCISE

Using a subject directory such as Librarians' Index to the Internet (http://www.lii.org"), choose a site related to your major and answer the evaluation questions outlined above:

Site: _____

WHO: _____
_____
_____

WHAT: _____
_____
_____

WHERE: _____
_____
_____

WHEN: _____
_____
_____

WHY: _____
_____
_____

Now, use a multiple search engine such as Dogpile (http://www.dogpile.com) to search a keyword from your field. Answer the questions for the first "hit" your search finds:

WHO: _____
_____
_____

WHAT: _____
_____
_____

WHERE: _____
_____
_____

WHEN: _____
_____
_____

WHY: _____
_____
_____

Was the site you found using the search engine of equal quality to the one from the subject directory? Explain. _____

CITATION AND DOCUMENTATION

Proper documentation is essential to the research process, now more than ever. Because the Internet makes "cut and paste" so easy, plagiarism is on the rise on college campuses. You will need to provide verifiable citations with your research. You will also need to understand what plagiarism is and how to avoid it.

Often students are not aware that paraphrasing without citing the source is plagiarism. They believe that as long as they change the order of the words around, they do not have to cite the source. This is a less obvious form of plagiarism than the "cut and paste" variety, but nonetheless is still plagiarism. *Merriam-Webster's Collegiate Dictionary,* 10th edition, defines the verb "plagiarize" as follows: "to steal and pass off (the ideas or words of another) as one's own : use (a created production) without crediting the source". Any information you use in your research that is not considered "common knowledge" must be credited to the source. But how do you define "common knowledge"? When unsure, it's always best to err on the side of caution. Always credit the source when using other people's theories or ideas.

Precise documentation is also very important. There are several styles of documentation that dictate the format of a citation for various types of sources, including books, periodicals, on-line sources, primary sources and the Internet. The most commonly used are the MLA (Modern Language Association) and APA (American Psychological Association) styles. The manuals for these can be found in your library; always verify the style preferred by your professor.

CONCLUSION

Throughout your life, you will need information—this is undisputable fact. Accessing that information in a world of rapidly changing information delivery can be a challenge, but with the proper approach you will learn to gather the information you need efficiently and appropriately. Find out what you need to know by:

▶ Structuring your research

▶ Choosing the proper resource(s)

▶ Efficiently using the appropriate tools to access these resource(s)

▶ Using and evaluating these resource(s)

▶ Citing and documenting your research correctly

One last very important point: your librarian may be your best resource. Academic librarians will not find the information for you, because the skills you will learn in finding the information for yourself are necessary to lifelong learning. However, librarians are there to teach you those skills and help you find the information you need. Don't hesitate to ask for help from the experts!

BIBLIOGRAPHY AND WORKS CITED:

(1) *About the Human Internet.* 21 Apr. 2001 <http://www.about.com>.

(2) Anderson, Margaret Vail. *The Digital Librarian: a Librarian's Choice of the Best of the Web.* 21 Apr. 2001 <http://www.digital-librarian.com>.

(3) Argus Associates Inc. *The Argus Clearinghouse.* 21 Apr. 2001 <http://www.clearinghouse.net>.

(4) BrightPlanet. *CompletePlanet.* 21 Apr. 2001 <http://www.complete planet.com>.

(5) Grassian, Esther. *Thinking Critically About World Wide Web Resources.* UCLA College Library. 21 Apr. 2001 <http://www.library.ucla.edu/libraries/college/help/critical/index.htm>.

(6) Sullivan, Danny. *Search Engine Watch.* 21 Apr. 2001 <http://www.searchenginewatch.com<.

Acknowledgements

Page 5: From *Becoming a Critical Thinker*, Fourth Edition by Vincent Ryan Ruggiero. Copyright © 2002. Reprinted by permission of Houghton Mifflin Company.

Page 9: From *Becoming a Critical Thinker*, Fourth Edition by Vincent Ryan Ruggiero. Copyright © 2002. Reprinted by permission of Houghton Mifflin Company.

Page 19: "On the Assassination of Malcolm X", from *The New York Times*, February 22, 1965. Copyright © 1965 by The New York Times. Reprinted by permission.

Page 20: Excerpt from "Assassination of Malcolm X," March 5, 1965. From *LIFE Magazine*. © Time Inc. Reprinted by permission.

Page 20: Excerpted from *The New York Post*, February 22, 1965.

Page 20: Excerpted from the *Associated Press*, February 22, 1965.

Page 21: From *The Amsterdam News*, February 27, 1965. Reprinted by permission of N.Y. AMSTERDAM NEWS.

Page 23: Excerpts from *Rational Problem Solving* by Louis W. Ascione & Lynn McCutcheon. Copyright © 2003 by Lynn McCutcheon. Reprinted by permission of Houghton Mifflin Company.

Page 46. From *Business Ethics*, Sixth Edition by O.C. Ferrell, John Fraedrich & Linda Ferrell. Copyright © 2005 by Houghton Mifflin Company. Reprinted by permission of Houghton Mifflin Company.

Page 51: Excerpts from *Thinking Critically, A Concise Guide* by John Chaffee. Copyright © 2004 by Houghton Mifflin Company. Reprinted by permission of Houghton Mifflin Company.

Page 73: From *"Critical Thinking and Obedience to Authority"*, by John Sabini and Maury Silver. , Reprinted with permission from National Forum: The Phi Kappa Phi Journal, Winter 1985, pp 13-17.

Page 81: Excerpts from *Thinking Critically, A Concise Guide* by John Chaffee. Copyright © 2004 by Houghton Mifflin Company. Reprinted by permission of Houghton Mifflin Company.

Page 103: "Young Hate," by David Shenk, *CV Magazine*. Reprinted by permission of the author.

Page 109: As reprinted in Instructor's Resource Manual to accompany *Organizational Behavior in Action: Cases & Exercises*, Sixth Edition by Steven B. Wolff & S. Wohlberg © 2001 by Houghton Mifflin Company. Case notes written by Steven B. Wolff and Maida Williams. Used with permission.

Page 117: Excerpts from *Rational Problem Solving: Integrating Procedure and Logic* by Louis W. Ascione & Lynn McCutcheon. Copyright © 2003 by Louis W. Ascione. Reprinted by permission of Houghton Mifflin Company.

Page 127: As reprinted in *Business Ethics*, Sixth Edition by O.C. Ferrell, John Fraedrich & Linda Ferrell, copyright © 2005, pp 300-306. Case prepared by Leyla Baykal and Debbie Thorne McAlister for classroom discussion. Reprinted by permission of Debbie Thorne McAlister.

Page 133: From *Rational Problem Solving: Integrating Procedure and Logic* by Louis W. Ascione & Lynn McCutcheon. Copyright © 2003 by Louis W. Ascione. Reprinted by permission of Houghton Mifflin Company.

Page 147: From *Business Ethics*, Sixth Edition by O.C. Ferrell, John Fraedrich & Linda Ferrell. Copyright © 2005 by Houghton Mifflin Company. Reprinted by permission of Houghton Mifflin Company